On Drugs

On Drugs

DAVID
LENSON

 University of Minnesota Press
Minneapolis
London

Published by the University of Minnesota Press
111 Third Avenue South, Suite 290, Minneapolis, MN 55401-2520
Designed by Will Powers and set in Galliard and Rotis types
by Stanton Publication Services, Inc.
Printed in the United States of America on acid-free paper

LIBRARY OF CONGRESS CATALOGING-IN-PUBLICATION DATA

ISBN 0–8166–2710-x (hc)

A catalog record for this publication is available from the Library of Congress.

The University of Minnesota is an
equal-opportunity educator and employer.

For Pam Glaven

CONTENTS

Writing about Drugs

There is always money for, there are
always doctorates in, the learned foolery of
research into what, for scholars, is the all-important
problem: Who influenced whom to say what when?
ALDOUS HUXLEY   The Doors of Perception

What we have here is a work of pharmacography, a writing about drugs. That's a chewy name for a very problematical undertaking. Almost everybody who writes about drugs today does so with some kind of authority—academic, governmental, legal, religious, techno-logical, medical, or cultural—and the lines of discussion are usually traced by the methods and traditions of the institutional priesthoods. But the investigation of drugs is no dispassionate inquiry. Even the most arid statistician believes that his or her "results" have the power to change public policy and perhaps even human behavior. There is a sinking suspicion that scholars and investigators tend to fashion their studies to confirm a preexisting political bias toward criminalization, medicalization, or deregulation. It is more than twenty years since President Richard Nixon formally declared the War on Drugs, and the writers who have been working in the field during this weary time are very much wartime intellectuals. Like the social theorists of the 1930s or the political scientists of the Cold War, their work has been created, judged, and pigeonholed by its relationship to ideol-ogy and global events. The luxury of disengagement has been denied them. And so the rivalry among authorities has led only to the pres-ent stalemate.

Then too, it is a rare occasion when the disciplines actually do consider one another's findings. In a wartime setting, it is a struggle for power and influence as each professional authority tries to bring drugs, suppliers, users, and enforcers into its exclusive jurisdiction. Beneath the smoke of technical discourse, what's really at stake is control of vast resources: research grants, funding for interdiction and "treatment," and potential profit from redrawing the line be-

tween prescription and street drugs. Beyond these immediate materi-
alities, there are scrambles for less tangible forms of intellectual control: redefinitions of mind, soul and body, sickness and health, madness and sanity, individual and community, freedom and restriction.
At least partly because of drugs and the war against them, consciousness itself has become a battlefield.

During the "Just Say No" (that is, "Just Say Nothing") phase of
the war, the only permissible discourse in any discipline was antidrug
polemic. Although the Clinton administration did nothing to
change the Reagan-Bush policies or reduce expenditures for combating drug use, it did change the accompanying rhetoric to the point
where there now seems to be an opportunity to speak about the unspeakable. Since history teaches us that the next silencing of drug talk
is never far away, it would be a pity if this opportunity were squan-
dered on the old academic squabbles. But the war has taken its toll.
Writing about drugs without the proper credentials is still hardly
more defensible than taking them.

I have undertaken this project precisely because I am unqualified
to do so. Although I could brandish academic degrees (like those
mysterious Ph.D.s who used to write apologetic prefaces to pornographic novels), nothing in my professional background qualifies me
for what I want to do. Of course my literary training has its own
biases. I tend to consider the activities of the professions engaged in
power plays over drugs as verbal constructions first and foremost,
and the following survey of the kinds of writing about drugs tends to
treat them primarily as exercises in language. Although the interdis-
ciplinary traditions of comparative literature may come in handy for
this enterprise, they need to be fortified with a stronger *anti*disciplinary attitude. I say this because most drug writing still falls into
generic categories, the default options. And nothing new can come
from any one of them alone.

There are roughly seven of these genres. Taken in no special order,
they are, first, the universe of clinical studies conducted by physicians, biologists, and psychologists who investigate the biochemical
and behavioral effects of psychoactive substances on living organ-
isms; second, pharmacology, a specialized wing of biochemistry that
records the physical composition of drugs and their impact on
human and animal brains; third, work by historians, social scientists,
and legal scholars on the relationship of drugs to the body politic
and the body of law, including histories of the use and prohibition of

particular substances, and studies of users as deviant subgroups; fourth, literary and popular memoirs or confessional narratives by users, ex-users, and narcotics agents; fifth, works of drama, fiction, and poetry that depict drug use of various kinds; sixth, the so-called literature of recovery (practical and inspirational texts designed to aid the reader in giving up a drug or drugs); and seventh, writing located at the crossroads of anthropology, psychology, and mysticism, and containing metaphysical and religious speculations prompted by the effects of psychedelic drugs.

Each of these genres has its own conventions. Clinical literature follows the empirical method common to all the natural sciences, seeking objectivity through controlled experimentation and analysis of the results. Because it is always looking for "facts," it can deal with subjective factors like feeling only circuitously—by deciding that certain behaviors correlate to certain sensations (pacing to nervousness, for example), and then by statistically reobjectifying those behaviors. To enhance its objectivism, it depersonalizes the author, who is usually pluralized anyway, behind a deadpan narrative whose tone implies that the data has been gathered and interpreted *correctly*. The authors plan and stage the events they narrate, a procedure not altogether different from a travel writer booking and taking the trip he or she intends to write about. The upshot in either case is a self-generating, self-referential discourse, with an additional criterion: that the experiment or voyage must be capable of duplication, so that the reader can supposedly repeat the procedure with identical results. Although this appears to tie the clinical report to an objective and external reality, in fact it insulates the findings within the boundaries of the rules that created them in the first place.

Clinical literature suffers from the same logical defect that plagues all empirical science—that is, it can form its conclusions only from the evidence it has itself collected. To recall a parable from sophomore philosophy class: an empiricist can ask how many legs a cow has, hypothesize that it has four, go out and interview five hundred cows, count the legs and divide by five hundred, and, having gotten the answer four, conclude with the purportedly factual proposition that "A cow has four legs." But it is always possible that the five hundred and first cow interviewed would have had three legs. The empirical procedure can never predict the future, even though it pretends that it can, and even though it claims that predictability is a criterion for the validity of its theories. Although it can learn new things from the data it collects, the notion that another sample will yield the same conclusions is an article of faith and nothing more. Applying measures of statistical validity for its body of evidence, it abandons any claim to understanding the individual datum. In the area of drug research, this results in an implicit assertion of drugs as causes of fixed effects, as if the effects were inherent in the drugs instead of in the relationship of drug and user. This commits the empiricist to a crudely materialistic approach. Twenty years ago Andrew Weil speculated that there is a relationship between this kind of science and the causal assumptions of people who misuse drugs: "I am . . . struck by a curious symmetry between people who abuse drugs and people who study them. The person who is convinced that highs come in drugs, if he is negatively oriented toward society, becomes a drug abuser; if he is positively oriented toward society, he becomes a drug researcher."[1]

Pharmacology—the second genre—gives extraordinarily precise molecular descriptions of drugs, and of their physical effects on the brain. This knowledge, realized in nuts-and-bolts technical skills, has led to syntheses of many new drugs by both corporate and underground biochemists. It has also led to a more precise understanding of brain chemistry, so that the assessment of physiological drug effects has become to some degree independent of behavioral inference. Of course most of this literature is inaccessible to lay readers, expressed as it is in a runic gabble of Cs and Os and Hs arranged in geometric patterns. Lately it has fallen to psychiatrists like Solomon H. Snyder and Peter D. Kramer to explicate pharmacology in the English language, since their branch of medicine straddles the hard and therapeutic sciences. Pharmacologists are not writers so much as engineers. They can tell us that a certain substance is a seratonin reuptake inhibitor, but they do not presume to say what it feels like to have seratonin lingering in one's synapses. Since psychotherapy has declined to interest itself in drugs, psychiatrists in possession of pharmacological information have taken up the ticklish task of discussing the impact of drugs on individual users. Balancing molecules and case histories, they mediate between new products and the idiosyncrasies of their patients. The impression one gets from studying this literature is that the days of humanistic psychology are really over. What the future seems to hold is an array of synthetic drugs that will alter brain function with digital exactitude. If the pharmacologist is in charge of designing the product, the therapist (or drug dealer, for that matter) will in turn become an engineer who adapts the new technology to the needs and desires of an individual patient or customer. Since clinical literature seems doomed only to chronicle stereotypy in amphetamine-challenged rats until the grant runs out, pharmacology and its psychiatric translations will probably merge as a literature of increasing excitement and importance, analogous to particle physics and the new genetics, and will eventually interact with them.

Legal, sociological, and historical studies also operate within a tight set of rules, that is, the laws, customs, and practices that surround the use and/or interdiction of drugs in a given time and place. Often the author begins with a predetermined opinion: that more or less tolerance of drugs would be preferable, or that the laws ought to be upheld or altered. Evidence drawn from surveys, from historical records, or from statute is then arranged in a pattern that the author hopes will lead the reader to the same conclusions. Since these texts are concerned with society, their aims are social. This time the *reader* is in effect pluralized—less an individual than a part of the polity that the discourse is about. The author hopes to "contribute to the public debate." This means that this kind of writing is also self-referential, since the text adds to the selfsame body of discourse it is analyzing. Many studies of this sort are explicitly ideological in design. For example, Thomas Szasz's *Our Right to Drugs* advocates the repeal of drug prohibition from a libertarian viewpoint. His argument requires the reader to accept the axiom that the free market by itself can solve the problem of drugs (along with every other problem in the world). Liberal arguments for "medicalization" conversely require the acceptance of an axiom that legitimates the state's interest in the blood-streams of its citizens. If clinical literature is motivated by facts, social literature is driven by factions. This factionalism has become especially strident as agitation for a relaxation of the cannabis interdiction appears to be gaining ground, and as several judges and mayors of large cities have called for an end to the war and one of its principal artilleries, federal mandatory minimum prison sentences.

Among historians, the current factional struggle is centered on the interpretation of the 1960s and the counterculture. Prohibitionists and conservatives point to that era as a time of social unrest and disintegration caused in part by the widening use of drugs. Medicalizers and liberals tend to see drug use as symptomatic of social diseases of various kinds, or as a specific response to the Vietnam War.

The former construe the moment as an irrational heresy against Consumerism, the latter as an indictment of the totalization of commercial values over all others. The battle spills over from the library to the classroom, as college curriculum committees are asked to consider all sorts of cultural studies courses (film studies, rock and roll) that may require approaches to drug use different from the outright condemnation demanded by wartime conditions. For some time now historians have been the only humanist scholars willing to undertake problems involving drugs, although courses on the 1960s are becoming more common in literature departments. It is surprising that philosophers (apart from Jacques Derrida and Dan Brock) have shown so little interest.

The genre of drug confession is well demarcated. It includes literary efforts like Thomas De Quincey's *Confessions of an English Opium-Eater*, Fitz Hugh Ludlow's *The Hasheesh Eater*, Aleister Crowley's more fictional *The Diary of a Drug Fiend*, Jean Cocteau's *Opium*, and Henri Michaux's *Miserable Miracle*, as well as popular gut-spillers like Gelsey Kirkland's *Dancing on My Grave* or Richard Smart's *The Snow Papers: A Memoir of Illusion, Power-Lust, and Cocaine*. There are also belletristic works with confessional elements, such as Charles Baudelaire's *Artificial Paradises*. Because De Quincey's status as originator is universally acknowledged, the genre tends toward revelation tinged with self-service and penitent sermonizing. Its strength lies in recording the subjective elements of drug consciousness, which is precisely what clinical and social-science narratives cannot do. But this strong subjectivity is prone to slide into impressionism at a moment's notice. Most narrators spend substantial time reporting what the effects of a certain pharmaceutical were on a certain night. If they are trying to be accurate (and not just making the stuff up, which is always possible), what is our relation to their experience supposed to be? A contact high? A chastening testimony? Why do we want to read their splashings? Doesn't pure subjectivity lead either to solipsism (no readers) or to an occasion for voyeurism (best-seller)? These texts raise many of the same problems that autobiography and confessional poetry do. They demand that the reader recapitulate the writer's experience, either through his or her own or by empathy. And so a confession can be understood only insofar as it entails an indeterminate number of other, similar discourses.

Even more problematic is the confession's separation of the author into two beings, one a character whose exploits are recorded, and the other a narrator who is recounting and usually judging them. It is a mime in a mirror. The confessing voice, as Michel Foucault has pointed out, is caught in a duplicity that depends upon concealment as a precondition for revelation.[2] Half of the author—the character— is at risk because exposure is the paramount danger of drug experience. For this reason the other half often tries to palm itself off as a dispassionate philosopher, or at least a moralist. Since the reader under these circumstances could be either a fellow user or a stand-in for the police, many confessions, like De Quincey's, go to great if apologetic lengths to make the reader an accomplice. This leads to a pervasive ambivalence, which (especially in later texts like Michaux's) can make an irritated reader wonder why the narrator would ever have taken the drug in question a second time, if suffering and repugnance are the inevitable results. The moral turning point, where ecstasy transmutes into revulsion and horror, becomes a fixation, and an unfortunate convention of the genre.

After the facts, factions, and fixations, we come to the fictions. There are many novels concerned with drugs, such as M. Ageyev's *Novel with Cocaine,* Aldous Huxley's *Brave New World* and *Island,* all of William Burroughs's work, Philip K. Dick's *A Scanner Darkly* and many of his others, Carlos Castaneda's Don Juan series (fantasy masquerading as anthropology), William Gibson's cyberspace trilogy, Robert Stone's *Children of Light,* and Jay McInerney's *Bright Lights, Big City.* Novels featuring alcohol use are simply too numerous to mention. There are also dramatic works, such as *Long Day's Journey into Night* and *The Connection,* and poetry from Coleridge to Baudelaire to the Beats and their countercultural successors. It is impossible to generalize about literature's portrayal of drugs, just as it is to generalize about its portrayal of anything else. But one striking aspect of imaginative drug writing, and of the confession too, is the overrepresentation of male authors in the pharmacopantheon. Women writers like Anaïs Nin and Marge Piercy, who do portray drug use, tend to be more interested in these behaviors as they reflect on other aspects of experience, such as madness and sexuality. But this is another issue, and one not limited to drug writing. Peruse the bibliography of any scholarly work on drugs and you'll find that citations of male authors outnumber those of women by better than ten to one. Perhaps this gives support to Terence McKenna's thesis that all drugs generally available in the West, with the exception of some of the psychedelics, are products of a male dominator culture. Maybe this explains why almost all of the male imaginative writers on the subject, including all of those just listed, are really writing about domination and submission when they write about drugs. It is no accident that one of Castaneda's volumes is entitled *Tales of Power*. This is nowhere more explicit than in Burroughs's *Naked Lunch* with its savage and parodic equation of the authority of doctors and dealers, and the submission of patients and junkies. In Stone's works as well, heroin and cocaine cause the internalization of male vulnerability, so that it is prone to reassert itself in the form of violence. Like the drug confession, drug fiction is shot through with cryptic, worldly moralizing of the sort men enjoy during the calm after gunplay.

From fiction, then, to fixing. The literature of recovery depends upon the translation of drug experience into a self-contradictory matrix of denial and confession. Memory is invoked in lurid detail, and then erased. Anonymity effaces the user's full name, so that the self is no longer discernible as the sum of its actions and beliefs. Then that transposition of self into otherness is given the name of God. These narratives ritualize an amnesia in which the ex-user (ex-cused) barters guilt for passivity and determinism. No matter which "addiction" is in question—alcoholism, someone else's alcoholism, or the love of cake or cocaine—the user is exonerated from free will, and in so doing demeans her or his history of being high. Perhaps the most telling condemnation of drug use is that it drives so many former takers into recovery. Worshiping causality, these texts recoil the user into the Modernist past, into an obsessive metanarrative that only reinforces the supremacy of the drug itself, as opposed to the user's experience of it.

The seventh genre originates in the traditions of Eastern and Western mysticism, but also in William James's *The Varieties of Religious Experience*. Its first practitioner is Aldous Huxley, in *The Doors of Perception*, *Heaven and Hell*, and his last novel, *Island*. Huxley's family background in the natural sciences provides a tension between biology, chemistry, and metaphysics on the one hand, and Buddhism and humanism on the other. This legacy is played out in the work of Timothy Leary and Richard Alpert, who come to it from experimental psychology, and that of natural scientists like Albert Hofmann and Humphrey Osmond. Although its popular tracts tend to interpret the effects of psychedelics in a facile Buddhist vocabulary, the East-West problem is in fact one of Huxley's and Leary's central issues. Both believe that peyote, psilocybin, mescaline, and LSD have the capacity to propel humanity to the next evolutionary leap. But in order to describe that imminent change, they are caught between the incompatible vocabularies of rationalism and the occult. After being drummed out of the Harvard psychology department, Leary refurbished himself as a demotic philosopher. But acid metaphysics also gave birth to works in other genres: the fiction of Jack Kerouac and Ken Kesey, and the poetry of Allen Ginsberg. The tradition has been carried on in the 1980s and 1990s by Terence McKenna. This kind of drug writing, while failing all the tests of philosophers and theologians, still raises questions about spirituality, perception, ethics, and reason, and as such is the closest in many ways to the present study.

What I hope will distinguish this book is not only that it wants to belong to none of these categories, but that it tries to find that forbidden focus, the *user's point of view*. I am not a physician, a group leader, a lawyer, or a priest, and I do not wish to confess. I want to know what different drugs do to different minds under different circumstances. I'm curious about the implications of drug consciousness for philosophy and psychology, for religion and literature. I believe that these problems have to be remapped as the generation that smoked pot and ate LSD and snorted cocaine comes to its seniority. But this book doesn't need to straiten itself in a single demographics, either. Drugs are allegories of human nature. By exaggerating certain aspects of our species-character, they dramatize the anomalies and dilemmas of consciousness. If we are really gods in monkey bodies, what are we made of but self-contradiction? To get at this, we have to climb out of the categories that have shaped the discussion of drugs so far. But this is not easy.

Aware of the failure of the humanities to address the question of drugs, I first planned a piece of would-be philosophy, a Phenomenology of Drugs and Consciousness. I thought that the rhetoric and vocabulary of philosophical discourse could bring impartiality to a subject prone to impressionism and hysteria. I was imagining a language without emotion and a text without anecdotes that could develop outside the daily politics of drug use—another master argument obeying "logical laws," as if it were possible to make universal statements about all drugs at all times in all situations for all people. But there is no longer any such language. Satisfying though it might be to write about drugs from a unified analytical perspective, the effect would be only to reprofessionalize the investigation. The urgency of the subject demands a discussion that cannot risk being roiled or marginalized by any hermetic lingo.

And so, with considerable regret, I abandoned this plan. Never have I wished so ardently for the impersonal armor of systematic thought as now, when the very fact of taking up this subject is so discrediting. Never has "the death of the author" been more desirable—and more advisable. The "Just Say No" campaign of the Reagan years was designed to preclude exactly this kind of talk. Drugs are the Unspeakable, and yet this is what I have to speak about. A properly dead author could endow this project with respectable necrography, and uphold what Allen S. Weiss calls the "prohibition against the use of the word 'I' in the critical or theoretical text."[3] By at least playing possum, if not actually dying, I could create an "invisible image" of myself as a disinterested and disembodied philosopher taking up an unpleasant matter against my will, doing a dirty job that someone has to do, my self-effacement necessitated by an ongoing social crisis that must enlist everyone, even reluctant metaphysicians. I could have focused an objective eye, while still trying to avoid through some sort of phenomenological method the inadequacy of hard science for examining the subjective.[4] Phenomenology, for all its soupiness, was at least willing to talk about emotions like pleasure and anxiety.

Self-concealment would also serve as protection from another pitfall of pharmacography: the suspicion that it is itself an aspect or aftereffect of drug consciousness. Talking and writing about drugs affect a user's experiences (or the memory of them) just as certainly as drugs affect writing and speech. There is an inevitable reciprocity. Discussion about which drugs to do and where to get them always precedes an actual administration. It is a discourse of anticipation, and is part of the high as certainly as the ringing bell became part of dinner for Pavlov's dog. Drug talk, along with the physical setting of an administration, establishes the conditions under which the intoxication takes place. But even when no administration ensues, this discourse is still part of drug consciousness. It is driven by desire, and the purity of desire is best maintained when talk is *not* followed by action. Because there is no more eroticized kind of speech, it too easily triggers the confessional's simultaneous impulse to conceal and reveal. And if preliminary drug speech is driven by desire, retrospectively it is a language of gloating, loss, and/or regret. It is the closure

of a trajectory that begins in desire, and therefore leads either to the
rekindling or renunciation of desire. The depths of misery and the
heights of ecstasy are defined by this exercise in circular reasoning.

The spectral metaphysician would be making a different sacrifice
from the one he intended. In his terror to avoid confession he would
run straight into one of the booby traps of empiricism: that the individual fact is at the same time necessary and insufficient. Sure, some
authorial depersonalization (if not the ultimate depersonalization of
death) is needed if the discussion is to have more breadth than a psy-
choanalytical case history. But what then? Pluralize the author in the
clinical manner? A multiplication of egos would do nothing against
this empirical deficiency, since the ego would have to be multiplied
to infinity in order to make a "valid" statement. To avoid both of
these avoidances (confession and anesthesia), the metaphysician
would be in danger of pointing his scope to the center of the problem while avoiding its extremes. But drugs, after all, are precisely
about extremes, extremists, extremities, and extremisms. And so we
have to ask: What position is there between the clinical and the confessional? And if there is one, what use is it?

Let's say that I wanted to generate an author who is neither dead,
identical with myself, nor (like the phenomenologist) merely an
anthropomorphized method. Where would such a creature get its
authority? From what sources would it gather materials, draw illustrations, and make generalizations? I have neither the desire nor the
training to write a biochemical survey of the various drugs, nor to
make a taxonomy. These undertakings are best left to pharmacologists, who have already done them amply enough. Nor do I want to
review the spurious taxonomies of the law, or the social-psychological
literature. The currently fashionable response to such an impasse is to
transmute oneself into a Freudian, since that terminology does at least
designate a dynamic between civilization and desire, a fault line that
runs straight through the heart of the drug question. But here too
there is a fatal difficulty. There is a psychoanalytic commonplace that
all users of a given drug have in effect the same personality, so that
neither therapy nor analysis can be conducted until the patient has
stopped getting high. In short, drugs are of no intrinsic interest to
most psychoanalysts. This may be sound policy for a practitioner, but
for the author of a book on drugs it would mean working as a
Freudian in one of that method's deliberate blind spots. I am not so
interested in the pre- and postdrug psyche of the user as in the user's

consciousness as it is specifically determined by the drug experience—
before, during, and after. To interrupt an appraisal of active drug
awareness on historical or prospective grounds would be counter-
productive. Also, even though I am just as fascinated by ideology as
by any other human construction, I prefer the toolshed metaphor:
why limit myself to a rake when there are holes to be dug, and the
outbuilding contains shovels, pitchforks, and hoes?

As to the question of how I know what I know, I will neither suppress this knowledge nor engage in confession. In assuming that literally outlawed voice—the user's—I can only assure readers that I am
not an "intellectual carpetbagger."[5]

I want to thank my colleagues in comparative literature at the
University of Massachusetts for covering for me during the yearlong
sabbatical it took to complete this project. Professor Don Eric Levine
suggested the title; Michael Degener, Michael Turits, Raymond Hor-
vath, and Melinda Nutting, graduate students in the department,
were willing to talk about the unspeakable; Professor Peter Fenves of
Northwestern University helped me think out the narrative puzzle;
and Professor Sut Jhally of the UMass Department of Communication had some practical advice I haven't heeded ("Who cares about
method?"). Only Don Levine actually saw the manuscript, however;
the others are at worst accessories before the fact.

There are those who believe that if
a text on this subject does not expend
most of its breath condemning use and users, it
must be promoting drugs. The author is aware of the
problems inherent in getting high in contemporary America,
and a careful reader will see that this study tries to address these
problems rather than dismissing them with slogans.

Perhaps the text should pay more attention to the special case of very young people using psychotropic drugs. This is a specific set of problems relating to education and learning in general, and to the eternal crisis that is puberty. It would probably be better if very young people did not use drugs. But they do. It might be better if people in general did not use drugs. But they do.

Except in a passage treating the history of drug prohibition, I do not directly undertake the question of race and drug use. There is no doubt that the War on Drugs has been a pretense for the oppression and imprisonment of African-Americans and Americans of Latin extraction. But the vast majority of users in this country are Caucasian. Since this study is concerned with consciousness on the one hand and Consumerism on the other, I have written as if Americans of all colors are human and live under the same ruling metaphysic.

I have not explicitly treated the War on Drugs as an extension of class warfare, though it certainly is. Poor defendants receive longer sentences than those with the means to pay for well-connected lawyers. But it is also true that a user wanting drugs will find the means to purchase them, whether by cashing in a certificate of deposit or robbing a package store. My concern here is what happens when the user has procured the drugs.

I treat users as sentient beings exercising choice, concentrating on what they have in common rather than the various differences that divide them. I acknowledge the limitations imposed by this decision.

PART I

*Drugs, Sobriety,
and the
Metaphysics of
Consumerism*

The Very Short
History of Sobriety

Westerners have a long history of
thinking in opposites, and when we think
about intoxication we tend to construct it in
opposition to another condition called sobriety. Sobriety is supposed to be the primary or "natural" condition, the
thesis, and intoxication is assumed to be secondary, unnatural, and
antithetical. We think: at the moment I am straight, or I am high.
"Straight" is the default option; we need to do nothing to achieve it.
"High" requires a deliberate intervention, a conscious and active
negation of "straight."

Or so it seems. But what would sobriety mean if there were no
such thing as intoxication? If it is nothing more than a state of consciousness free of the influence of inebriating drugs, having no inherent content of its own, it then atomizes according to the influences
of specific drugs. Even if I sniff a half gram of cocaine I may still be
sober as far as heroin or alcohol is concerned. The attempt to keep
"sobriety" from fragmenting into "pot sobriety," "caffeine sobriety,"
"psilocybin sobriety," and a long string of other sobrieties depends
upon the conflation of all intoxicating substances into a single category called "drugs." The purpose of this crude simplification is clear
enough. It is intended to provide rhetorical cover for the War on
(generalized) Drugs and the plethora of social controls that have
been implemented in its name.

If sobriety denotes the absence of the influence of drugs,[1] it cannot be investigated until we have some idea what we mean by a drug.
From Erich Goode in 1972 to Andrew Weil and Winifred Rosen in
1993, pharmacographs have recognized that a definition of "drug" is
hard to come by.[2]

> A common definition of the word *drug* is any substance
> that in small amounts produces significant changes in
> the body, mind, or both. This definition does not clearly
> distinguish drugs from some foods. The difference

between a drug and a poison is also unclear. All drugs
become poisons in high enough doses, and many
poisons are useful drugs in low enough doses. Is alcohol
a food, a drug, or a poison?[3]

Perhaps it was more than bureaucratic expediency that caused the
United States government to create the *Food and Drug* Administration. In the gray area between nutrition and intoxication stand sugar,
salt, and spices. Even the ordinary usage of the term "drug" is utterly
ambiguous. While the War on Drugs rages on, you can still drive past
a mall and see a seven-foot neon sign reading DRUGS on the facade
of a chain pharmacy. We assume that this is possible because there is a
clear distinction between drugs taken for medical purposes and those
taken for recreation, but this boundary too is far from rigid. In my
lifetime amphetamines have crossed over from prescription to street
drugs, and marijuana may soon cross back into prescribability as a
treatment for glaucoma, the side effects of chemotherapy, and some
AIDS-related illnesses. And with the advent of molecular engineering
the distinction has blurred even more. The difference between Prozac
and Ecstasy is mostly a matter of marketing.

The unavoidable fact of the matter is that a substance becomes a
drug in the pejorative sense when and only when a law interdicts it—
only when somebody decrees that it is a drug, that it is another
antithesis to sobriety. It becomes an official medicament when its
availability is restricted by prescription. Other substances with psychoactive powers, such as sugar and many herbal remedies, are for
some reason unregulated, or classified as vitamins, minerals, or
foods. This dubious taxonomy was not accomplished in a single
instant. It was the product of many discrete legislative actions over a
long period of time. As one substance after another was interdicted
or restricted, the operant definition of sobriety also changed. And for
each of these changes, it is not difficult to find an ulterior motive.

In its long history of drug prohibition, American law has generally distinguished among alcohol, marijuana, cocaine, opiates, and
prescription drugs as different classes of substances, and their illegal
possession and distribution have fallen into corresponding classes of
misdemeanors and felonies. Federal legislation outlawed (or inter-
dictively taxed or restricted) different groups of drugs at different
times. The prescription system had its origins in the Food and Drugs
Act of 1906. Smoking opium was banned in 1909. The Harrison

Narcotic Act of 1914 outlawed the sale of cocaine and opiates. The Eighteenth Amendment prohibiting "the manufacture, sale, or transportation of" alcohol was ratified in 1919. Heroin was proscribed in 1924, and the Marijuana Tax Act was signed into law as late as 1937. All of these landmark federal laws were, however, only broad consolidations of baffling tangles of state legislation that made (and still make) all sorts of arbitrary and minuscule distinctions among psychoactive substances. The acts that made these plants and chemicals illegal were neither rational nor scientific, but, like all legislation, were products of political partisanship and compromise that buried the real issues altogether. This chaotic and adjustable legal taxonomy has never resembled any of the pharmacological and biochemical systems of classification, which have always tended to make very fine distinctions, down to intimate molecular diagrams. These charts plainly show that no two drugs are the same, but they do show similarities between related drugs, like cocaine and the amphetamines.

With the Comprehensive Drug Abuse Prevention and Control Act of 1970, the United States established

> five schedules for drugs, depending on the potential for
> abuse and dependency and the accepted medical use of
> each drug. Schedule One is reserved for drugs that
> are not permitted to be used in medical practice, such
> as heroin and LSD; Schedule Two contains the most
> dangerous prescribable drugs, such as morphine and
> cocaine; Schedule Three is for those less dangerous,
> including most barbiturates; Schedule Four, for chloral
> hydrate and meprobamate; and Schedule Five, for
> mixtures of low levels of narcotics such as codeine in a
> cough syrup.[4]

This catalogue has nothing to do with the chemistry or character of the drugs in question, but is based on a ratio of utility to danger, with that proportion rising in each successive class. Utility consists of prescribable application, whereas danger is located in the drugs' "potential for abuse and dependency" (in other words, in their potential for getting users high). This streamlining of classifications seems, in retrospect, to be an important step toward the dismantling of all taxonomy during the antidrug crusades of the 1980s. The "Zero Tolerance" and "Just Say No" campaigns, and then the ambitious revival of Richard Nixon's 1973 "War on Drugs," abrogated even the simplified distinctions of the 1970 law and consolidated all recreational stuffs into a single class called "drugs." The ensuing polemics for sobriety were based on largely unarticulated models of society and consciousness defined only as "freedom from intoxicants." The term "drugs" has since become a shorthand for any number of pharmacological deviations from these models, whatever they may be; that is, the particular deviation now matters less than the raw fact of deviation itself. The previous drug-specific laws each established a new category of sobriety: freedom from morphine, freedom from cannabis, freedom from alcohol. But the recent abolition of taxonomy is clearly part of an attempt to construct sobriety as an absolute condition.

But deviations from what? By what standard of sobriety are all the deviations caused by myriad drugs recognized and then conflated into one? I won't be coy about this. I believe that words like "sober" and "drug-free" are meaningless, and that "sobriety" is a cultural construction created for the furtherance of a political and economic agenda. The fact that the legal history shows a cumulative and piecemeal process strongly suggests that the present-day notion of sobriety, far from being "natural" or intuitive, is the result of nearly a century of social engineering. Perhaps it simply takes that long to implant another dubious dialectic into public and popular discourse. The great irony is that Plato, usually credited with establishing the Western hegemony of dialectical reasoning, shows Socrates exercising logical clarity while drinking large quantities of red wine with his acolytes. There are many other ways to think about drugs, but until we can machete our way past the concept of sobriety-as-an-absolute we will have no chance at them.

Pharmaka
1 *and*
Pharmakos

*Since the issues are about values, it is
difficult to talk about them without falling
into a partisan camp. Words like "drugs" and "drug
culture" are negatively loaded. They make automatic, invidi-
ous distinctions which connote "evil," "strange," and "illegal," and
they invoke a distance that suggests "not me" rather than "like me."*
NATHAN ADLER

The use of drugs for pleasure has been characteristic of human life
and society from the beginning of recorded history. If this assertion,
supported by every discipline that has studied the past of the species,
were simply accepted as a statement about our nature, there would
be no War on Drugs with its three hundred thousand prisoners, or
its multibillion-dollar budgets for soldiers and matériel. And there
would certainly be no need for this book. But the practice of getting
high, among all the other unflattering things that could be ascribed
to humans, offends us particularly.

The War on Drugs has been with us for as long as we have
despised the part of ourselves that wants to get high. Odysseus had
to drag three of his crew back from the clutches of drug fiends:

> So off they went and soon enough
> they mingled among the natives, Lotus-eaters—Lotus-eaters
> who had no notion of killing my companions, not at all,
> they simply gave them the lotus to taste instead . . .
> Any crewman who ate the lotus, the honey-sweet fruit,
> lost all desire to send a message back, much less return,
> their only wish to linger there with the Lotus-eaters
> grazing on lotus, all memory of the journey home
> dissolved forever. But *I* brought them back, back
> to the hollow ships, streaming tears—I forced them,
> dragged them under the rowing benches, lashed them fast
> and shouted out commands to my other, steady shipmates,

"Quick, no time to lose—embark in the racing ships!"—
so none could eat the Lotus, forget the voyage home.[1]

Not only were these sailors prepared to desert, they would not even
"send a message back" about their experience. Already the high is
unspeakable, and already the official response is arrest and restraint,
along with the admonition to the rest of the crew to "Just Say No."
Then as now, the high is excluded from the circle of language and the
"voyage home," and its disciples are reduced from speech to inarticu-
late tears of withdrawal. And in all these centuries, very few languaged reports have come back from behind the lines.

The encounter with the Lotus-Eaters takes only a half inch of the
vast canvas of *The Odyssey*. This is because it is just a minor skirmish
in the larger war that began in *The Iliad* and whose ramifications are
still being confronted as Odysseus tries to find his way home. Similarly, our own War on Drugs cannot be understood in isolation. Its
declaration by President Richard Nixon in 1973 came just as American forces were returning from Vietnam, and just as the countercultural revolution was disintegrating at home. Then it grew, during the
1980s, in inverse proportion to the waning of the Cold War. The
same generation that fought in Vietnam or against that conflict in
the streets of America became the drug war's early armies—on both
sides. And now, in the absence of other *Iliads,* it is *the* war, a civil
strife that makes battlefields of our home cities. The 1960s slogan
"Bring the War Home!" has been enacted. Odysseus, too, had to face
slaughter in his own house when he finally returned to Ithaca.

The War on Drugs is about competing myths of home. For a culture
determined by war, home exists primarily as something to defend.
But defend against whom? The common public purpose of World
War II had to be preserved by the identification of a new enemy, the
antithesis of the new suburban life among diminutive yards and the
lazy bubbling of V-8 engines coming home. Communism—the *other*
bad Modernism—was perfect for this purpose. At first glance, it was
totally Other, and could be fought as an endless and nostalgic reprise
of the old war's Asian and European theaters. But the most dangerous Other is always the one least distinguishable from oneself, the
one that might really *be* oneself. It is a peculiar feature of history that
peoples with strong historical, physical, and cultural affinities tend to
detest each other with the most venom. This may be seen in the ani-

mosity of Greeks and Turks (which began in the *Iliad* and continues today); of Jews and Arabs, with their common Semitic origins; of Irish Protestants and Catholics; or of Sunni and Shiite Muslims. To sustain hatred in the face of resemblance, the demonized Other must be portrayed as a spurious version of the "real" people. The Russians were useful in the imaging of this enemy, not only because they were our traitorous former allies, but because they looked like, but were not, us.

But a threat located in distant Eastern worlds could not be immediate enough to maintain a nation at peace on a garrison footing. The most useful sort of enemy must be capable not only of resembling but actually *being* one of the "real" people. Then the constant danger of impersonation can be stressed: the enemy imitating a real American, or the Other infiltrating the homeland unnoticed. Communism, as an internationalism, could be anywhere, right down the street or in the next room. As Senator Joseph McCarthy tried to show, it could even be lurking in the federal government, or—worst of nightmares—in the so recently victorious U.S. Army. Alger Hisses or Julius and Ethel Rosenbergs had to be locally and indigenously available for scapegoating because of their deep and allegedly long-standing—though quite invisible—foreignness. And so the strictest conformity of all—conformity of consciousness—was exacted as the price of Elysium, and became the hallmark of the Cold War. This principle would survive as a foundation of the War on Drugs.

Another Cold War principle that would later be applied to the War on Drugs is that occasionally a limited hot war needs to be fought in order to reinforce the difference between "us" and the enemy. The Korean War served that purpose well for the Cold War, since it was a conflict old-fashioned and contained enough to generate a map in the daily newspapers, a battle line that could be watched moving up and down, a clear diagram of us against them. But less than a year before the Korean War ended, the first hydrogen bomb was detonated at Eniwetok atoll on November 12, 1952. By the time intercontinental ballistic missiles were deployed in the mid-1950s, and the strategic policy known as Mutually Assured Destruction (MAD) was instituted, an ambiguity arose that roiled the distinction between us and Other even more than the notion of impostership. Now the defeat of the Communist Other was nuclearly inseparable from our own.[2] This new and inescapable conflation of Self and Other accounts for the schismatic domestic reaction to the Vietnam

War. Vietnam, like Korea, was intended to provide a limited theater for the enactment of the Cold War drama, but because of Vietcong activity in the south it yielded no clear map of a moving front. Us and Other were geographically, and then ideologically, interpenetrated. Domestic political opposition to the war rippled out into broader cultural insurgency, and the counterculture was born.

At its heart the counterculture was a conservative movement, a reaction back into the old individualist idealism of the American nineteenthth century. As such it was a Romantic revival, and arguably the last gasp of a dying Modernism. It shared Edenic visions with the previous generation but could not accept their exclusivity and miniaturization, reaching instead for transcendental profundities descended from those of Emerson and Thoreau. It is no coincidence that the era's poet laureate, Allen Ginsberg, modeled his career and public persona so closely on Walt Whitman's. The counterculture was a reassertion of the notion that every individual is a self-contained cosmos, and that the accidental contains the key to the universal. It believed in the progressive synthesis of historical dialectics, and in antique metanarratives like Love, World Peace, and Community. It rejected not only the memories, art, ethics, and politics of the previous generation, but its very consciousness, whatever it was that made hatred of the Other worth the price of extinction.

Because it was a revolution of consciousness, it is not surprising that it chose marijuana and LSD as both its symbols and its instruments. The use of these drugs was not limited to the stateside resistance. It spread just as quickly to the troops in Vietnam, many of whom came home converted to countercultural values and ways of life. Because the war was going badly, a scapegoat was needed. The counterculture and allied political dissent from the war effort were conflated under the rubric of drugs. When the policy called Vietnamization was instituted, leading to the withdrawal of the last American combat troops on August 11, 1972, it was only a matter of time until the fall of Saigon in April of 1975, formalizing the end of the first lost war in America's history. The declaration of the War on Drugs in 1973 represented a relocation of the enemy from a country half a world away to our own cities and towns. It was—and to some extent still is—a war of revenge against U.S. citizens held responsible for the defeat in Vietnam. As such it was perfectly compatible with the continuation of the Cold War as well. After Nixon's resignation in 1974, the intent to prosecute the War on Drugs was emblematized by President Gerald Ford's appointment of Nelson Rockefeller as vice president, since Rockefeller, as governor of New York, had implemented the most draconian drug laws in the nation's history.

Of course the counterculture failed, as utopianism by definition has to, and sooner or later most of the aging hippies gave up and accepted the consumerist principle that all value must be expressed in monetary terms. But the War on Drugs continued, ebbing and flowing according to the needs of temporal politics. With the waning of the Cold War, military/corporate America's search for new adversaries also led to terrorism and its putative centers in Iran, Libya, and Lebanon. But despite the official martyrization of their regional victims and international hostages, terrorists could never adequately replace Communists and drug users as America's antithesis, principally because they were depicted and perceived as *too* completely Other. Their threat remained inalterably foreign, despite (for one example) President Ronald Reagan's effort to convince the press that Libyan hit squads had entered the country to assassinate him. Terrorists by their very nature remained outside the American body politic. Their imaging was simply too heterogeneous, whereas Russians and other Eastern Europeans physically resemble Westerners closely enough to allow them to be depicted as negative images of the same civilization.[3] Any American could be a Russian spy, whereas a terrorist (at least as depicted in the media) infiltrating the States would stand out like a wooden nickel and be detected instantly.

And so, as the 1980s went by, another solution had to be found, one that encompassed both the fear of a foreign adversary and the distinct possibility that this enemy had already gained a foothold on domestic soil, and had in some way already infected the polity. This Other was once again identified by the expediently nonspecific name of "drugs." Drugs seemed to have an alien origin, but could still be present in the most intimate corners of domestic life: in our bathrooms, our cars, our offices, and among our families—just like Communism. The scapegoat could then be both totally Other (Colombian, Peruvian, Panamanian, Bolivian) and at the same time as close as one's own bloodstream. And so the Cold War was replaced by the War on Drugs. Eventually a hot war—the December 1989 invasion of Panama—was conducted in its name (and partly because of the drug war's ongoing prosecution, the 1991 Persian Gulf War was fought without permitting American troops the use of alcohol). But all along the enemy was the ensuing generation, and its ancient opposition to the Vietnam War. The War on Drugs was, on one level, nothing more than a final battle conducted by the generation of World War II against their own children, who would usurp them so soon. And the elders were correct to choose heterogeneity of consciousness as the point of vulnerability. Inserted here, the knife would keep them in power at least a little longer.

In *Ceremonial Chemistry,* Thomas Szasz has a chapter entitled "The Scapegoat as Drug and the Drug as Scapegoat" in which he develops the etymological connection between the ancient Greek word for scapegoat *(pharmakos)* and the word for drug *(pharmakon).* Although Szasz has a different version of it,[4] the basis of this connection is as follows: While the Greeks used the word *pharmakon* to designate both healing and toxic drugs, at its origin it appears to have referred primarily to purgative medications. This is discernible because of the survival of the related word *pharmakos,* which means "scapegoat," or the one who must *be purged* in order to make the social body healthy. Northrop Frye, in *The Anatomy of Criticism,* writes of the *pharmakos* as follows: "In the sinister human world one individual pole is the tyrant-leader, inscrutable, ruthless, melancholy, and with an insatiable will, who commands loyalty only if he is egocentric enough to represent the collective ego of his followers. The other pole is represented by the *pharmakos* or sacrificed victim, who has to be killed to strengthen the others."[5] Frye associates the scapegoat with comedy:

> In studying ironic comedy we must start off with the theme of driving out the *pharmakos* from the point of view of society. This appeals to the kind of relief we are expected to feel when we see Jonson's *Volpone* condemned to the galleys, Shylock stripped of his wealth, or Tartuffe taken off to prison. Such a theme, unless touched very lightly, is difficult to make convincing. . . . Insisting on the theme of social revenge on an individual, however great a rascal he may be, tends to make him look less involved in guilt and the society more so. This is particularly true of characters who have been trying to amuse either the actual or the internal audience.[6]

To make the user of *pharmaka* into a *pharmakos* has required a prefatory demonization. The comic figure of the entertaining, blissfully stoned 1960s pothead or the happy drunk has had to be supplanted by the image of the monomaniacal crack smoker ready to murder his mother or sell his children for another hit of the stuff. And so stories of this kind have been made to dominate both print and the airwaves.[7] Where, in the tolerant aftermath of the counterculture, most drugs (everything but speed and heroin) were thought to be harmless, now the opposite is thought of *all* of them. The "Just Say No" campaign of the Reagan years was formulated because it explicitly called for an end to discourse on the subject. The absence of discussion and hence of any discrimination is necessary for the requisite demonization: during the Cold War it was not allowable to say that there could be any "good Communists," or that there were different kinds of Communists, or that Communism could be anything other than a monolithic conspiracy. It is noteworthy that McCarthy's campaign to shut off discourse preceded the phase of the Cold War when systematic deployment of nuclear weapons began to take place; and so the "Just Say No" campaign prepared the 1980s for the revitalization of President Nixon's old "War on Drugs."

In this next stage, the establishment of the new enemy was completed: the War on Drugs became the "driving out [of] the *pharmakos* from the point of view of society." The sacrifice of the individual in this case was officialized by systematic abridgments of constitutionally guaranteed rights in the name of the war, with the Fourth Amendment in particular negated in practice. One does not have to look to *illegal* drugs to find enforcement practices contrary to the Bill of Rights. Drunk-driving roadblocks, where police stop all traffic, search all vehicles, and administer field sobriety tests, plainly violate any reasonable interpretation of "probable cause." If driving a car is probable cause for the suspicion of a felony, then the next stage must be that walking down the street is probable cause, or eventually that sitting at home is.[8] In foreign policy the change was reflected in the elevation to enmity of "drug states" like Panama, Colombia, Bolivia, and Peru, joining "Communist states" like Cuba and Nicaragua, or the "terrorist states." Just as in the 1950s, when Communists were portrayed as having penetrated the very fabric of American life, now undifferentiated "drugs" were said to permeate every crevice.

The effect of this vigorous coining of a new enemy, and the vitiation of the Constitution itself as a measure of that enemy's internality, has been to render any understanding of drugs much more difficult. One of the reasons for this is the near impossibility of imagining what sort of society should and would exist if all the drugs and users were successfully purged. A society that exists without the influence of any "drugs" must be postulated, yet none is available as an example. Even if such societies existed, they would not be readily accessible or comprehensible to Americans. Let us hypothesize, however, that within the social complexity and diversity of the United States there are social segments that live without drugs altogether. The agglomeration of such segments could then be called "Drug-free America," and this would be the society from which the scapegoat—the drug user—must be purged to ensure collective health. Notwithstanding the fact that this "Drug-free America" would encompass only a tiny minority of the nation's population, let us grant the supposition that this is the "true" society, and that it has both the right and the power to banish those who violate its pharmacological "zero tolerance."[9]

What is missing here is an ideological concept that would unite such a society, apart from its negative definition as a collectivity free of drugs. That would have to be something like "sobriety." But does such a concept have any substance? A mind uninfluenced by drugs can think any thought; conceive, justify, and execute any action (except, of course, the use of drugs); suffer from pathologies and delusions; violate or enforce civil law; foment or suppress revolution. It would span the entire range of human awareness and deed, good or evil, constructive or destructive, and yet remain "sober" if the bloodstream that feeds it is free of external psychoactive agents. "Sobriety" can also mean just "seriousness," but it is plain that drug-free citizens are capable of frivolity and bad judgment anyway, even if we suppose them less likely to be so. "Sobriety," like "freedom," is an empty concept, a null set defined only by what surrounds it, by its various negations.

It is disturbing to think that sweeping legal and policy decisions can be made on the basis of a concept that admits of no definition save the negation of another concept. The next hope would be that the negated concept could at least be made clear; but here too we are disappointed. For if sobriety is comprehensible only by negation, it is necessary to ask what precisely is being negated. If the answer is "drugs," we are no wiser, since that designation may mean anything from aspirin to heroin to cigarettes—substances that have nothing in common with one another in terms of their psychological and physiological effects.[10] This serves to pluralize the concept of sobriety to the point of absurdity: there must be a subconcept for every drug whose absence is being designated. This means that any given human being, even someone under the influence of multiple intoxicants, is still "sober" for the majority of subconcepts. It is possible to offer a concept like "inebriation" as a general antithesis for "sobriety," but that too entails the same unwieldy list of subconcepts. Plainly, the entire dialectic of "sober/inebriated," however useful for public rhetoric, has no ideational substance, and cannot provide the basis for discourse or policy. Indeed, as I suggested earlier, its aim appears to be to end rather than to promote inquiry.

An enhancement of this strategy is to elaborate "drugs" into something even more sinister—a "drug culture." This is portrayed as a unified social body that has grown up around the use of all drugs, and to which all users belong. In truth, no such thing exists. Users of illegal drugs may share a contempt for the laws that interdict their practices, but they haven't much more than that in common. The effects of, say, heroin and amphetamines are so divergent that it is hard to imagine a frequency on which their users could communicate. The social rituals surrounding use also vary from substance to substance, as do the means and places of procurement and administration. And if legal drugs are thrown in with the others, then there is no difference whatever between the phrase "drug culture" and the word "culture" *tout court*. It might seem like a good idea to try to describe a distinct and specific culture for every psychoactive substance. But this would be just as ridiculous, since relatively few people use only one drug.

What happens in real life is that people who like alcohol or cocaine are more likely than not to associate with others who share those tastes. Sometimes patronizing the same dealer may put these people in touch with one another, but in most cases they know each other through some other circumstance and begin or continue using together. But there has never been a mass movement based on drug use and drug use alone. Even the counterculture—often dismissed as nothing more than a marijuana or acid cult—had other defining demographic elements, such as youth, matriculation in college, or opposition to the Vietnam War. That historical anomaly was tinged with old-fashioned Romantic individualism: "do your own thing" as well as Timothy Leary's "tune in, turn on, drop out." If the counterculture was perhaps the last manifestation of Modernism, drug users since that time have followed the postmodern pattern of breaking up into enclaves, one of whose determining elements may be choice of drug. A more legitimate use of the term is in "cyberculture," where there is a unified social structure, even if it is balkanized into a hundred thousand little electronic "rooms."

Yet "drug culture" continues to be demonized as if it actually existed. Images are spun around its lewdest and crudest venues: the crackhouse and the shooting gallery, places with no charm save the availability of cocaine and heroin, respectively.[11] Since neither of these drugs is much concerned with the physical setting of administration, it stands to reason that their emporia can be located in abandoned buildings or half-dead motels, dirty and derelict and easily productive of negative pictorials. The aim is to show how diminished in all other respects is a life governed by desire and/or pleasure, which are conflated into one. We have all downloaded these graphics: junkies nodding out on three-legged couches with ripped cushions spewing their stuffing, crackheads huddled at the end of a half-lit corridor. If the word "culture" still retains any of its etymological sense of "growth," these are images of an anticulture, a social acquiescence to diminution and self-destruction. Crack babies and pregnant freebasers are the avatars of this anticulture, of growth and life denied. Users of unrelated drugs like marijuana or the psychedelics can be depicted in the same great nihilistic tableau. They are "part of the drug culture," after all.

The depiction of a unified anticulture is intended to have the effect of creating the appearance of a unified legitimate culture where there is none. Here there is something to be learned from history. Rock-and-roll culture, a previous anathema, was similarly damned as a direct assault on everything valuable in American life. Its music created "juvenile delinquents" depicted in leather jackets and brandishing switchblades. This isn't to deny that such creatures existed, or, for that matter, that the crackhouse and shooting gallery exist today. The point is that these demons require endless retailoring. Yesterday's monster is today's marketing strategy, and rock and roll has long since been recruited into the service of Consumerism, as official product theme songs sampled from "classic" material or sung by present-day rock stars under contract to corporations. Through intermediate stages like the Fonz, juvenile delinquents were similarly turned into benevolent and instantly recognizable nostalgia items. Perhaps even the crackhead will someday be portrayed as a harmless buffoon, as the hippie is now.

The real enemy is always the antithetical—whatever stands against the values and directions of whoever's in power. Since the concept is too abstract, it needs incarnation to be properly abhorred. One *pharmakos* at a time is no longer enough. There has to be a whole culture of them, a world as close and distant as Bolshevism, with a needle and pipe instead of the hammer and sickle.

To find a way around this impasse, it is tempting to make a case for the diversity of substances commonly called drugs, and call for a better taxonomy upon which to base law and social policy. But drug taxonomies have usually been prepared with some foregone conclusion in mind. Other than serving to exclude certain medicaments from the problem's circumference, however, yet another novel taxonomy does not seem to be a worthwhile end in itself. Biochemical formulas, which describe the physical differences of drugs rather than distinguishing among them by their effects, should be ceded the task of classification. Even this sheaf of molecular diagrams is of transient value, since new drugs are being invented constantly, and since any schematic of this sort should be applicable in unforeseen circumstances if it really has any value for the present ones. Still, in order to simplify this jungle of a problem, it is necessary to exclude certain classes of drugs from consideration. All drugs given by physicians for the treatment of illness will be deleted from this discussion insofar as they address that function. Thus morphine will be considered only as it is administered for its own sake, and not in response to medical exigency. Marijuana's role in the treatment of glaucoma will be outside the present question. If healing uses of drugs are to be disregarded, so too are narrowly poisonous ones. Morphine could be employed as a murder weapon, but that aspect is excluded as well for these purposes. We could say that the criterion for inclusion is self-administration, where the application has no medical purpose nor any deliberately and immediately suicidal intent. This is also an imperfect exclusion, however, since drug users may administer (and in a sense even prescribe) to one another.

What motivates self-administration? Perhaps the solution is so simple as to be almost invisible. The sorts of drugs under investigation here are taken—or at least were initially taken—in the hope of pleasure, or inversely for avoidance of pain in the widest sense. Of all the words relevant to the discussion of drugs, "pleasure" stands out by its very absence. There is a sense in which the War on Drugs

has also been a campaign against the legitimacy of pleasure. Some of
this is probably due to old-fashioned puritanism. Desire for the
kind of pleasure provided by drugs—"drug lust"—suggests a complex relationship, or even a confusion, between drugs and sexuality,
and reticence to talk about sex may carry over. This is strange, since
sexual pleasure appears to be overridden or drastically altered in the
presence of some drugs. But of course it can also be enhanced, and
this may account for the portrayal of users—whether anonymous
crackheads or General Noriega—as habitual participants in orgies,
cross-dressing, homosexuality, or other heterodoxies. This association, however exaggerated by the media and government public-
relations offices, is not entirely groundless, but it is only one possible drug-potentiated alteration in sexual behavior. I will return to
these questions, but for now I need to ask what status pleasure in
general would have in the hypothetical society known as "Drug-free
America."

There are pleasures sanctioned by Consumerism, the principal
one being of course the delight of purchasing and owning an object,
or at any rate of renting or patronizing one. The satisfactions of having a stylish new car, or of watching a movie on video or a sports
event on network TV, or the vanities of improving one's appearance
through the use of beauty products—these are the innocent pleasures
of late capitalism. What they have in common is that they require the
irreversible expenditure of money for their achievement. Why, then,
are drugs so different? They too are costly, and when consumed their
value cannot be retrieved even in part, as a secondhand car's can. I
suspect that the exemption of drugs from legitimate commerce is
based in part on the notion that their pleasures are purely somatic;
and for this reason they become part of larger complex of pleasures
that are considered illegitimate despite their profitability. There are,
for example, certain products that, because of their connection to
very precise delights of the body, are banned from public advertise-
ment although they are still available for sale. I think of dildos and
other sex toys, and of hard-core pornographic videos. These commodities stimulate or intensify bodily pleasures too specific to be
marketed atmospherically or in general terms. Supermarkets can
advertise their commitment to "service" without waxing lyrical
about the superior taste of their produce and meat, but no such general pieties can be invoked to sell instruments that excite very specific
inches of flesh. Similarly, users are expected to know what drugs

do—whether they soothe or stimulate, how much longer an erection can be held, how much more powerful orgasms feel under their influence—without advertising. There is a kind of chronic hypocrisy in Consumerism about what is actually for sale. Advertising apparently has the power to confer public legitimacy upon certain desires and not upon others. What has often been portrayed as an immoral fact of modern life—Madison Avenue's eternal stimulation of petty desire—may in fact be the age's last ethical arbitration. The battle over the marketing of condoms in the AIDS era provides some support for this speculation. Since rubbers were previously thought to permit sexual pleasure without entailing the consequences of venereal disease and pregnancy, they could not be advertised or awarded open shelf space in pharmacies and supermarkets until there was a compelling public health emergency. Now the formerly unmentionable condom has assumed its new role as a primary weapon against an epidemic. It is as if vibrators were suddenly found to prevent uterine cancer. Over-the-counter preparations are usually avoidance-of-pain drugs whose promotion is permissible. But anything that causes or enhances pleasure still cannot be promoted without a good excuse.

Products that encourage heterosexual enjoyment may possibly be more marketable than those that address individual or homosexual delights, on the assumption that straight coupling may eventually lead to big families and stable demand for other categories of goods. But to advertise devices enhancing masturbation would have no such long-term benefits. We no longer cringe at explicit advertisements for hemorrhoid remedies, but we would still recoil from ads for a foam that would sharpen a lonely orgasm. Consumerism, like its ancestor empiricism, has never solved the problem of whether one consumes the thing itself or one's image of the thing. If the latter is the case, then a useful or desirable product would remain useless and undesired if the image it generates cannot be made palatable for aboveboard buyers. A classic example is the current dilemma of cigarette advertising, whose product has lost much of its romantic image in the wake of decades of negative medical testimony, and whose promotions have been banned from television. Even in their packaging and print ads, cigarette manufacturers are required to give up a certain percentage of the space they have paid for in order to reproduce government health warnings. The result has been the gradual erosion of the bon-vivant atmospherics so carefully built up throughout the 1950s and 1960s. The only real argument left for those who sell cigarettes is that the pleasure of their vice is so great that it is dearer than health and life itself. Yet they are aware that any precise depiction or description of this physical pleasure will only seem repugnant. Imagine a present-day ad showing smokers closing their eyes and writhing with ecstasy at every puff.

Drug users have been scapegoated not only because their chemical practices are purportedly antisocial but also because they have been lumped in with the sexually promiscuous and the intentionally obese as proponents of the body as a locus of pleasure. After the supposedly body-conscious 1980s, it may be surprising to think that the flesh is still frowned upon in its pleasure-giving aspect. But it is. The athletic fads of the 1980s were all about *punishing* the body—"No pain, no gain," as one of the slogans went. The body cannot be beautiful unless it is tortured into curves and muscles, never if a life of food, sex, and drugs has rendered it soft and seductively weary. Readers and TV viewers are apparently able to ingest limitless representations of violence and loss, but they cannot tolerate an account of what a hit of crack does to a user. The objection to pornography is not really that it encourages similar behavior. The problem is that it says: this happens, this exists, people do this and enjoy it with no regrets. The authors of Greek tragedy sent all violent actions offstage and out of sight of the audience; but at least the other characters could talk about what happened. We send all pleasurable acts offstage, and then either keep quiet about them or mention them only for condemnation. That which is held to be obscene is any form of discourse or depiction that forces the reader, hearer, or viewer to stare directly at some form of pleasure that they are then compelled to accept or damn or deny.

The drug user is assumed to be someone who has seen these things—who has seen ecstasy and excess, loss of sexual propriety, loss of control of other bodily functions, and the candid and undisguised hunger for the kinds of pleasure drugs offer. Many drugs are unappealing to nonusers in their forms of administration. A full ashtray is a nauseating sight to nonsmokers, but the image of a needle on the point of penetrating an already overpatronized vein makes almost anybody flinch. There is an element of passivity and degradation in many techniques of drug administration: the epidermis must be punctured, the lungs clogged with tars, the nostrils jammed with powders. If pain through overexercise is thought to be beneficial to the body, these exercises of pleasure, we are repeatedly assured, are physically destructive. In the age of cancer, crack, and AIDS there is every reason to suppose this to be true, and so the body must be disciplined like an unruly animal if it is to be considered beautiful. The final expression of this condition comes from a weight lifter whom I once heard rejecting a sexual advance: *"Nobody* gets *my* body." But the inverse applies for the drug user: because of what I do to my body, anyone can do anything they want to it, anytime.

The media present the crackhouse as the final nightmare of pure libido, and so it is in a sense. What they hesitate to tell are the details. That oral sex on crack is more prevalent than genital; that men can ejaculate on crack without getting erections, sometimes spontaneously from the effects of an administration of the drug itself; that gender is not always the determining factor in deciding who has sex with whom; that users can find themselves having the paradoxical experience of sexual "climaxes" that extend for many minutes; or that many users avoid conclusive orgasm at all costs, trying instead to maintain the preorgasmic frenzy as long as possible. These particulars are best trundled offstage, where Sophocles sent Oedipus to put his eyes out. Except that we don't even want to hear about them later. We have drawn a circle of discourse and depiction around the lives of drug users because we would not want to relinquish our own social control to the point of ecstasy, of "standing outside ourselves." And because we do not want this for ourselves, we reject all representations of it, afraid, perhaps, of some involuntary empathy.

Drug users do not always resent this banishment. In fact, they sometimes relish it. The concern for teenagers in a world of readily available drugs has this legitimate element at its core: we know that teenagers' thinking can be a mirror image of their elders', where everything adults think bad is assumed to be good, and vice versa. We know too that teenagers are in the grip of a powerful hormonal drive toward sexual activity. And drug worlds, with their clear but heterodox value systems, may be as appealing as cults to a teen's desire to find an alternative to the parents as explicators of life. In other words, by criminalizing drugs the law has introduced multitudes of otherwise lawful people into the mystique of criminal life, and in many cases forever alienated them from "respect for the law." And if the criminal worldview is free of the scruples about the body that "Drug-free America" purportedly possesses, that only makes it more endurable than the straight one.

In the 1960s the laws that interdicted recreational drugs flowed from the same sources of power that were prosecuting the Vietnam War, and it was easy to rationalize illegal behavior of all kinds if that conflict were the crowning achievement of our lawmakers' deliberation. After the fall of Saigon in 1975, however, came the age of cocaine, when delusions of grandeur (rather than broad moral claims) fortified the societies of users. The petty criminal conspiracies of the 1960s rapidly grew into "cartels." Suddenly there really appeared to be a "drug world" out there, whose antithetical and autonomous nature was by now more than just the revolutionary fantasy of hippies. Along with its moral fundaments, moreover, the innocent pro-body reveries of the free-love sixties were supplanted by an unprincipled drive to give the body greater pleasure. At the outset, the cocaine era believed that its drug made people more intelligent and capable of working longer and more effectively. But as the appetite of users grew, the utility of the drug for socially acceptable goals became less and less arguable. The same users who snorted lines in the stairwells of Wall Street brokerage houses to celebrate their deals and promotions found themselves, a year or two later, cooking up freebase or spread-eagled for anal masturbation. Many of the lies told about marijuana in the 1960s were suddenly true for cocaine—but by then even the liars were tired of talking. Because cocaine is finally about itself and nothing else, its rhetoric imploded and it offered no further rationales. User construction of the high gave way to stark repetition of private reveries and onanisms.

Perhaps the reason why a serious alcoholic like Winston Churchill was able to lead Britain through World War II and thereafter into the era of the Cold War was simply that no one told him that his use of drink was supposed to disqualify him from political leadership. One of the deleterious side effects of criminalizing drugs is that users themselves come to accept their own criminalization, and perhaps even enjoy it. They accept the blanket condemnations, and may believe that they will never be able to contribute anything to society. This phenomenon has now reached the point where even cigarette smokers are liable to resign from organizations that ban smoking at meetings, and where whether or not a prospective employee or volunteer smokes may determine whether he or she will be accepted or rejected by an organization. Since just about every cultural endeavor with the possible exception of poetry is by now a collective (i.e., corporate) endeavor, and since almost every major human achievement is ascribable to the wonders of organization, we should probably assume that most human beings want to be part of some collective enterprise. But if the only organizations available to drug users are the ones that find, procure, import, package, sell, and deliver drugs, hasn't criminalization (again as in the case of alcohol prohibition) led inexorably to the flourishing of criminal activity? Haven't we turned an individualist rebellion into a collective sedition? Haven't we driven people with all sorts of talents into believing that drug organizations are the only ones with any use for those talents?

The generational questions that invaded the presidential campaign of Bill Clinton in 1992—why didn't Clinton serve in the army? hadn't he demonstrated against the Vietnam War? hadn't he smoked pot? and so on—implied a more serious question: can anyone of Clinton's generation, whose best moral instincts once drove them outside conventional politics and the law, be capable of administering that polity and law twenty years later? During the campaign Clinton was occasionally asked about these matters, and his response was that he believed that drug cultures were by their own choice outside even the more inclusive America he was seeking to build. In so saying, he confirmed for another generation the identification of drugs and criminality, and perpetuated the compulsory alienation of users.[12]

Throughout *Ceremonial Chemistry*, Thomas Szasz returns to religious justifications for drugs, claiming that the constitutional separation of church and state has led all sorts of would-be mystics like drug users into compulsory opposition to civil law. I suppose that in due time we will have to accept the notion that what's human is human regardless of race, religion, sexual orientation, gender, physical or mental limitation, or choice of intoxicants. I think we need to ask whether the criminalization of drugs is merely a legal detail, or a summons to an antithetical life that permanently alienates the user from contributing what he or she can to the world. If a worker smokes pot from Friday afternoon till Sunday night, should that disqualify that worker from doing what he or she can from Monday morning until Friday afternoon? Is doing drugs all weekend so much less productive than golfing or watching sports events on television? If we assume that drug use is a personal detriment, will we require that every user quit work and devote full time to recovery?

We must have a scapegoat, though, and no one fits the bill so perfectly as the drug user, who may look just like an ordinary citizen and function just as well, but who has a secret that disqualifies whatever good she or he does in the world. Through this process of scapegoating our prisons are full, and we blame this on the ravages of drugs. But maybe we should blame it on the notion that those who seek to be conscious in a different way for part of their lives can't be granted full citizenship. If users are not alienized, perhaps they will not be relegated to criminal enterprise, so that the criminal world will be the poorer. Again, Northrop Frye:

> The *pharmakos* is neither innocent nor guilty. He is innocent in the sense that what happens to him is far greater than anything he has done provokes, like the mountaineer whose shout brings down an avalanche. He is guilty in the sense that he is a member of a guilty society, or living in a world where such injustices are an inescapable part of existence. The two facts do not come together. The *pharmakos,* in short, is in the situation of Job. Job can defend himself against the charge of having done something that makes his catastrophe morally intelligible; but the success of his defense makes it morally unintelligible.[13]

2 What Is "Straight" Consciousness?

A government legislating and enforcing sobriety must be subscribing, however tacitly, to an implicit model of consciousness that drugs in general are thought to impair and endanger. But what is this model, and where does it come from? If there is no official statement on the subject—and neither corporate boards nor the American state routinely pronounce on matters of metaphysics—then where can evidence be found?

One hypothesis is that the state always uses a model of consciousness that passively reflects the beliefs of a majority of its citizens. The use of the phrase "community standards" in legal decisions concerning artistic censorship suggests that this is a principle the American state occasionally invokes. This hypothesis assumes, however, that the state is actually the *product* of a national cultural consensus rather than one of its creators. This is a difficult proposition to defend in the case of the United States, whose population is as diverse as the entire world's. As its history of antidrug legislation shows, America's state metaphysics, far from reflecting this diversity, tends to assert the values of one of its subgroups against the others. The 1909 opium law was primarily directed against Chinese immigrants in the West, the 1914 Harrison Act against African-Americans in the South, Prohibition against Midwestern brewery owners of German ancestry, and the Marijuana Tax Act against Mexican-Americans living in the Southwest. It is far likelier that the American state accepts a fixed and traditional model that harmonizes with the beliefs and ideals of those whom that state itself promotes, benefits, and serves: the individuals and institutions that own and control the economic and cultural resources of the nation.

In the present age of postindustrial Consumerism, culture and economics have merged into a single entity, as reflected in "advertorial" content in newspapers, commercial endorsements by artists, video news releases, and the common production sources of television advertisements and music videos (to choose only a few examples). All art forms and media are now engaged in sales, and conversely advertising itself is now created and experienced as an art form.[1] Cultural forms or genres without sales potential, like poetry, find themselves marginalized to cult status, so that their public functions now resemble sectarian social and religious assemblies. Whatever tacit view of consciousness can be ascribed to the United States in particular or to the international corporate world in general must be consistent with the endless selling that dominates our discourse and serves as a template for all other relationships. The pejorative use of the term "materialism" in observations about the domination of commercial over spiritual values, like all truisms, contains a core of truth. To sell something, one has to persuade a potential buyer that the commodity is in some sense "real," even if the instrument of the sale itself is only an image or a verbal construction. A correlation between an abstract sales tool and a "real" and marketable material object must be assured and assumed.

Yet, from the marketing side of the relationship there is an apparently inconsistent tenet that "image is everything." A product image formed by advertising is sustained in packaging and in the appearance of the commodity itself. It is as important to chronicle a flow of images and "information" about available manufactured objects as it is to maintain the sales flow of the objects themselves; that is, there has to be an unending cognitive mediation between consumers and commodities. Subjective reactions to advertising and other sources of product image are now thought to be quantifiable—measurable by marketing research and capable of control, able to serve both as predictors and determiners of subsequent purchasing behavior. The official metaphysics of Consumerism and/or the American state, were it made explicit, would therefore somehow have to be idealist and materialist at the same time.

This apparent contradiction can be expressed in mundane terms: a consumer's perception of a product provides the motive in inducing its purchase, yet that perception is nothing if it cannot be translated into a commercial transaction that assumes and delivers a "real" material object as the result of a monetary mediation. The *image* of the product and the product's *reality* are both essential.[2] For a historical model that can accommodate this paradox, one need look no farther than empiricism, whose pragmatic ambivalence has served a useful purpose throughout the evolution of capitalism.

Like John Locke himself, most Americans simply do not care

whether mind precedes matter or the other way around. Although it can be misleading to generalize about "common ordinary speech" with no reference to determinants like class or ethnicity, it nonetheless seems that the bulk of casual speech is devoted to *describing* selected phenomena and the speaker's relation to them: places gone, what was seen, what went wrong with the car or the heart, what was purchased and at what price, who has moved, married, divorced, or died, and second- or thirdhand accounts of what other speakers have reported on the same subjects. Most informal narrative consists of a chronicle of observations and actions in a world whose existence is both taken for granted and yet endlessly noted in meticulous personal detail. No distinction is made between the reporting of firsthand experience and descriptions of movies, television shows, or Top 40 songs. Consumerism encourages a technique of data processing whereby information is received either directly through experience or indirectly through hearsay and/or the various electronic or print media, with no recognition of any differences among these disparate sources. This is a quotidian result of the empiricist inability to determine the source of perception, and therefore the origins of ideas.[3] The relationship between mind and matter is at one and the same time a personal organization of experience and desire *and* the imprinting of matter upon mind in an event *emblematized and celebrated by the act of purchasing*. This reunion of the ideal and the material is evaluated quantitatively and qualitatively by its purchase price and the degree of "customer satisfaction"; it is sustained and sanctified by the condition of ownership. In other words, in the consumerist worldview, the only way to know an object is to buy it.

If this is the model of consciousness that the American state is trying to defend as it pursues its War on Drugs, then what exactly is the objection to these generalized "drugs"? Presumably it hinges on drugs' alleged power to disrupt the process of downloading information, and the action (purchasing) that issues from the processing of that information. For example, the long-standing accusation against marijuana—that it impedes learning and damages recall—is based on the notion that anything that disturbs the downloading/outloading process is bad. There is also, perhaps, a fear that drugs may create in "the mind's eye" a heterodox mode of perception (including cultural imagery) that is not the same as the one downloaded by TV viewers, newspaper readers, and moviegoers. Drugs, in other words, somehow problematize the fluid (that is, creatively inconsistent) relationship between mind and matter. Drugs may tilt this delicate equivocation of idealism and materialism too far toward the ideal. They could encourage the idealist notion that by changing the way perception is received and processed, an individual can actually change the world. In the late 1960s Jerry Rubin is rumored to have said, "Every time I smoke a joint it is a revolutionary act." Some drugs may encourage a contemplative, aesthetic, or otherwise disinterested kind of perception that does not necessarily require the act of buying for its consummation. Or it may be that drugs are thought to skew the perceptual process so utterly that the purchase cannot be competently executed. In the case of cocaine—a drug that acts mainly upon the hydraulics of desire—it can be argued that desire for the drug itself supersedes all other desires, including the desire for acquiring material objects other than the drug itself.

Of course the prosecutors of the War on Drugs have never specified their reasons for fighting it. Here we run across another delicious paradox: even if all the allegations against drugs are true and drugs do in fact interfere with the consumerist model of consciousness, it is equally true that drugs are themselves commodities that may be purchased. What one is purchasing when one buys drugs, however, is not an object for long-term ownership or a product consumable for the sustaining of life and the attendant assurance of further consumption. What one is purchasing is the promise of a change in consciousness—and possibly an alternative to Consumerism. Thus, with drug buys the act of purchasing paradoxically defeats the act of purchasing. The drug transaction is a shadow of a conventional transaction, a spurious substitute for a "valid" acquisition. As such it withdraws energy from the system of ordinary commercial activity. It creates an economy that resembles the official one but also stands outside it. The existence of this black market undermines the mendacious free-market language used to promote state-supported enterprises, particularly in military economies like America's. Similarly, in its supposed wastefulness the drug market mirrors and silently parodies the waste-based national metabolism of defense spending. The contention that drugs are escapist may be accurate. And those who profit from consumer culture do not want anyone to escape it.

The current model of the mind, then, is first and foremost a matter of practical economics. The fact that the 1980s wave of drug testing began in the workplace is indicative of a need to maintain the vocational ideal of a well-programmed mind capable of prospective action based on retrospective knowledge.[4] But since empiricism assumes the validity of perception (regardless of the source of that perception), it is not the place of the downloading mind to discriminate among incoming data except on the basis of what is functionally useful to it. In a more general way as well, the ideological apparatus of the state can program the population with "public information" in the form of words or images. A person who downloads a great deal of this stuff is said to be "well-informed." But since the empirical version of the mind possesses no inherent means of distinguishing between "natural" data (Dalmatians, ottomans, cold weather) and artificial ones like television images, a population that unquestioningly accepts this model is open to ideological downloading as well. An altered mode of consciousness, especially one that reinforces the notion that the mind can actually form or even change reality, might become resistant to an unexamined acceptance of "whatever's coming in." It is precisely that lack of examination which Consumerism counts on for its hegemony. If the subject-object relationship is not problematized, then it is simply not a problem. But drugs threaten to roil these clear waters.

Widespread use of drugs might spawn a class of Others for whom perception itself is variable and capable of operating in more than one mode. It might even (as for an instant in the 1960s) lead to mass apostasy. The idealist/materialist ambivalence of empiricism, when faced with opposing multitudes, can attack them with either blade of this double sword. Hippies, for instance, were damned for refusing to work and for freeloading off the nation's industry and affluence, and also for being physically dirty. Communism, which once governed two-thirds of the world's population, was condemned either as godless materialism or as a colorless material devastation bereft of consumer goods. Drug users in sufficient numbers could become a political force, to be damned because of their greed for the material substance itself, or for their irresponsible behavior toward economic commitments such as job and family. They are depicted as both "out of it" and yet violently effective in assaulting the world and its values in pursuit of drugs and the money to buy them. Drug-generated small business is a "crackhouse" and drug-generated big business is a "cartel," pejorative terms equivalent to the neutral "nightclub" or "liquor distributor." Groups of users barely different from drinkers at bars are "gangs" or "cults," depending on whether the material or antimaterial blade is being brandished. The alternative economy is seen as simultaneously incapacitated and empowered by drugs. The media depict users as losers, but losers who are somehow always winning. Individual users are portrayed either as incompetent at work or as competent only for the purpose of disguising their drug use. They are condemned both for withdrawing from and remaining in the social world. Drug users are antisocial but are continually forging reprehensible social configurations. They are lawless, but at the same time subject to the law's most intimate scrutiny.

Drugs, then, are thought to threaten Consumerism in a variety of ways: (1) by impeding downloading and memory; (2) by supplanting other acquisitive behaviors; (3) by presenting an apparently free market to those who pay lip service to the concept while actually administering state capitalism, and by providing a repository for capital accumulation that is invisible to government by government's own choice; (4) by turning a commodity into a state of mind rather than vice versa ("vaporizing" the commodity, possessing it by literally consuming it); (5) by generally problematizing the subject-object relationship; (6) by circumventing civil law, and creating a de facto political opposition.

A Phenomenology of Addiction

It is a commonplace of official drug rhetoric that there is an absolute divide between "casual use" and addiction. The presumption is that the voluntary use of a given psychoactive drug becomes involuntary after a certain number of administrations, or over a certain length of time. But it is difficult to say where this divide falls, because drugs differ from one another, as do drug takers. It is unlikely that there is a fixed point beyond which a user becomes "addicted" to a drug, because the notion of an absolute divide suggests that the drug's effect then becomes entirely different from what it was beforehand. This suggestion is dubious. The use of almost any psychoactive drug brings some alteration in the conventional workings of consciousness, and what is called addiction is simply a more profound and intractable alteration reaching deeper into the groundwork of cognition.

Once upon a time, philosophy divided consciousness into "faculties": cognition, intellect, desire, and feeling. Cognition received and organized sensory perception, and determined what is real. Intellect, or reason, tried to create or discover some invisible order in the world, and then to elaborate it systematically into abstract constructions like logic, ethics, and metaphysics. Desire was the successful or unsuccessful impulse to appropriate a selected object of the senses by hypervaluing and internalizing it. Feeling was entirely contained within the subject, the quality or atmosphere of consciousness as it engages in other kinds of activity. This philosophic notion of faculties is long gone, and with good reason. It is logically implosive, since it is itself a product of intellect, which is at the same time one of its components. It suggests, on the model of Newtonian physics, that there are certain laws that govern consciousness that are analogous to the laws governing the physical world. Arguably—though the argument is unfashionable today—it survives even into the twentieth century in the Freudian model with its hydraulics of libido, superego, and ego. If the end of the Newtonian universe came with the particle physics of Einstein and Heisenberg, the end of the faculties as a model of consciousness came only with Nietzsche and the phenomenologists Husserl and Heidegger. Yet, in *applied* physics and philosophy, the older schemes survive. It is still possible to do carpentry or nonnuclear engineering in a Newtonian field. And in untechnical discourse about mind—the common ordinary speech of it, as the logical positivists used to say, or what Husserl called "natural thinking"—there are vestiges of those antique diagrams of consciousness.

I believe that some fundamental aspect of cognition is profoundly altered by almost any psychoactive drug if exposure to that drug is protracted or intense enough. What is metamorphosed in repeated drug taking is time, which Kant called a "Form of Experience," that is, an element (along with space) without which nothing, not even dreams, can be called experience. What Einstein did for physics and Nietzsche did for philosophy is recapitulated in every drug-affected mind. Drug consciousness in the twentieth century has reflected and even mimicked changes in the way physics and philosophy have reinterpreted the universe. Repeated drug experience dismantles seamless cognitive fields or wavelike "lines of argumentation" or wavelike vectors of normal appetite into particles or discrete bursts of energy that may be known and manipulated separately. Nathan Adler recognizes this progressive fragmentation, although he attributes it to Consumerism itself, to the "marketing of consciousness" implicit in the sale and use of drugs: "Phenomenology as a reduction or analysis of reality into its constituent bits in consciousness has been an intense preoccupation of German philosophers like Husserl and Heidegger. It took the drug scene and the drug world to make Everyman a phenomenologist, to demonstrate that sophisticated, complex, elaborate procedures of analytic reduction could become a mass-produced consumer product."[1] Once a subject is accustomed to constructing consciousness according to this cognitive quantum mechanics, the return to a Newtonian universe is difficult to achieve. Such a reversion, it seems to the user, would require a renunciation of joy and play, of insight and vision, *and* of privileged knowledge and perception. It would entail a return to mechanized cognition. The discontinuous fields created by drug use become normal as a result of habituation, and stopping the use of a drug is not in and of itself sufficient to restore anterior categories of value and knowledge. Once time has been atomized according to a pattern of drug administration,[2] the very existence of memory prevents an easy reversion to "natural thinking."

There are drugs that alter the relationships among cognition, intellect, pleasure, and desire only temporarily. These are sometimes called nonaddictive, although it is certainly possible for a user to be unwilling, if not unable, to stop using them. A user can renounce these drugs and thereafter carry their quanta without harm. This may be why marijuana, LSD, and the drugs of their respective families do not cause withdrawal symptoms. To "come off" such drugs requires that the former user learn to live with a quantum re*organization,* but not necessarily a complete re*construction* of consciousness, as is the case with stimulants, which subvert the intellect, or heroin, which trumps sexual desire.[3]

The 1960s myth of the LSD flashback was created and publicized to frighten users, but it has a metaphorical veracity, if not a literal one; that is, the affective reconstruction of consciousness that results from using any psychoactive drug (and not just one of the psychedelics) is irreversible, as least insofar as it survives in memory. It is this permanent and, at last, involuntary estrangement from empirical consciousness that Samuel Taylor Coleridge refers to at the end of his opium poem "Kubla Khan":

> And all should cry, Beware! Beware!
> His flashing eyes, his floating hair!
> Weave a circle round him thrice,
> And close your eyes with holy dread,
> For he on honey-dew hath fed,
> And drunk the milk of Paradise.

The flashing eyes are a precise figure for the dismantling of cognition into particles. His floating hair no longer frames his face into a coherent shape—just as there are no more systematic frames for consciousness. As a way of containing this heterodoxy, a circle, the revenge of lost Newtonian coherence, must be woven around the user. The user is *circumscribed,* written into otherness, a condition related to addiction in its etymological sense (discussed later). The dread accompanying this new circumscription is "holy," suggesting the reassertion of a theological order against it. And while one villain of the piece is pleasure—honey-dew, and the milk of Paradise—the other is the man from Porlock (whose knock on the poet's door brings the poem to an end) with his personification of a now untenable sense of Newtonian time. Against whatever is isolated (and externally completed) by the drawing of the circle, only another totalistic order can be arrayed and deployed.

It is for this reason that totalistic or even totalitarian methods are often employed to help people break addictions, and that programs of this sort are usually militantly antipleasure. But it is not the euphoria of getting or being high that must be obliterated and forgotten so much as the purer metaphysical pleasure of reordering time into particles. The insights offered by psychoactive drugs, their new temporal arrangements of seeing, feeling, and thinking, must be *retroactively* expunged, and doing this requires the cultivation and enforcement of a kind of formalized amnesia. What happens, however, in most official sobriety programs is that a third kind of consciousness is imposed as a template not only upon the quantum consciousness of drugs but also upon predrug-"wave" consciousness. The aim is purportedly to reestablish predictable Newtonian fields, and to reassert the notion that cognition, intellect, and desire have "natural" relationships that should not be playfully redefined. But as in the dream of returning to a prelapsarian world, it is inevitable that any paradise regained (if that is what it would be) can't be identical to the paradise lost. The third consciousness of twelve-step groups, for example, is revealing in its emphasis on a redefinition of time, superseding both predrug *chronos* (horizontal time) and the kairotic organization of addicted time (whereby temporality rearranges itself around the moments of the drug's administration). In this third scheme, what is cultivated is a kind of contemplation without pleasure, a passivity in relation to temporal passage. Alcoholics Anonymous slogans like "One Day at a Time" and "Easy Does It" illustrate this.

But just experiencing a drug and its alterations of time and consciousness, and then simply remembering the drug's effects, cannot be the same as being addicted to that drug. Many an adult vividly remembers a single LSD trip early in life, and recollection of that experience may affect all subsequent consciousness even though the drug is never taken again. Addiction's minimum criterion is clearly repetition of the drug's administration. But more than that it involves a constant reemphasis on the subjective reason for taking the drug. An occasional or onetime user of any given drug is likely to be curious about the drug's results, what it does and the changes it brings. An addict, on the other hand, already knows this. What interests the addict is the rhythmic act of administration itself as a device of temporal reorganization. When the next dose comes is as important as what the drug actually does. This is partly because of the diminution of novelty: what began as a *kairos*—a special occasion or privileged moment—through repetition assumes the role of *chronos* or horizontal time. What characterizes the condition of addiction is above all else the atomization of time, the replacement of conventionally measured seconds, minutes, hours, and days with a different chronometry based on the tempo of administration. As a result, the drug's reordering of consciousness loses, over time, the elements of play and pleasure. It becomes as compulsory as a clock.

Addiction can be defined as the chronic atomization of consciousness by drugs or by some other time-splitting obsession. When the drug's administration is halted what ensues is not a new and altered harmony leading (as with nonaddictive drugs like cannabis or psychedelics, or even with alcohol) to a harmless or even salutary "second vision" of the self and the world, but instead an inability to reestablish any harmony at all. The word's etymology points to *addictus*—the past participle of the Latin verb *addicere* (to say or pronounce, to decree or bind)—which suggests that the user has lost active control of language and thus of consciousness itself, that she or he is already "spoken for," bound and decreed. Instead of *saying*, one *is said*. The addict is changed from a subject to an object; at least one aspect of the user's consciousness becomes passive. Intellect (and with it ethics) is broken into discrete moments rather than maintaining continuous or systematic value structures, and these discrete moments are governed by isolated imperatives taken out of any context but that of continuous need.

At least, that is, according to the etymology of "addiction." But it seems strange that origins of words are accorded such privileged status, as if the hypothetical coiner in antiquity possessed some insight that centuries of evolving usage have only served to obscure. Following etymological authority too religiously can cause an investigator to overlook the fact that from the user's point of view there *is* an ethics operating within the condition of addiction: whatever leads to procurement and administration of the drug is "good," and whatever impedes them is "bad." The relationship of intellect to desire is altered in such a way that they become a new compound faculty that replaces social imperatives (the superego?) with another, chemically generated batch. Where "straight" ethics, despite the herculean efforts of philosophy and theology throughout the centuries, has not become more than a set of codifications and collectivizations of social conventions and values, the imperatives of addiction are absolutely objective, with that objectivity reinforced by biochemistry. Indeed, a chemical dependency (or some other obsession) may be necessary to achieve *any* set of imperatives strong enough to compete successfully with social convention. The addict knows that without the drug and its attendant social activities, he or she must revert to "straight" civilizational rules, which are less instructive and certain than the decrees of psychic chemistry. One of the characteristics of drug withdrawal is not knowing what to do at any given moment, or not wanting to do anything.

A number of drugs illustrate the fundaments of addiction. Heroin, an obvious choice, plainly redefines time according to the rhythms of administration and duration, and it ceases to be "playful" as its aesthetic becomes an anesthetic, so that in withdrawal ordinary consciousness is received as pain. Stimulants, as enhancers of desire, certainly involve atomizing consciousness into discrete units. These drugs' "quanta" after long-term use or after a period of intense and frequent repetition are no longer the result of any cognitive/intellectual/appetitive play, but of the utter fragmentation of intellect by temporally disparate surges of desire. Withdrawal is difficult, since consciousness does not return (as with cannabis drugs or psychedelics) to any harmony, however heterodox. Withdrawal in this most traumatic sense occurs when one of the faculties is so disabled by accumulated drug experience that it can no longer function even in altered consciousness and must be rebuilt from the ground up, since it has not only been shattered into particles, but the particles themselves have ceased to relate to one another in any coherent field. A transition from one disharmony to another is terrifying. William Burroughs describes it as "a nightmare interlude of cellular panic, life suspended between two ways of being."[4]

Perhaps the best way to approach the problem of addiction is through considering nicotine, a simpler study than stimulants or heroin. Despite advertising rhetoric about the "pleasures of smoking" (a proposition more arguable for pipes and cigars, perhaps), the cigarette exists primarily to deliver a dose of nicotine. Nicotine is a "transparent" drug that does not distort cognition at all, and, if anything, seems not to inhibit but to stimulate intellectual activity. At the same time, smoking cigarettes entails a suspension of regard for one's own life and health, and to some extent the lives and health of others. The sector of intellect that nicotine stimulates is the one that thrives on the "pleasure of thinking" rather than on ethics. Nicotine has some effect on the appetites, mildly suppressing food hunger but not affecting sexual drive. The temporal "cigarette after sex" and "cigarette after the meal" suggest that nicotine's principal impact on desire is to create the desire for more of itself, so that any interruption of that reflexive appetite, even for food or sex, has to be marked by a ceremonial return to it. Still, cigarettes do not disharmonize consciousness, or make it dysfunctional. Given its transparency, it is at first hard to understand (especially of course for nonsmokers) why the drug is so addictive that it is often said to be harder to give up than heroin. But at second glance it becomes clear that nicotine is a chameleon willing to play any drug role that the user casts it in.[5] It is a kind of template addiction, and this makes it a promising candidate for examination.

Consciousness realizes itself only over time and through space—the media, in effect, through which perception and judgment develop. Again, it is difficult to think of anything that could be called experience that does not take place over time and through space. Even dreams seem to assume both of them, though both are somehow liquefied by the dream state. Cognition works over *chrono*logical time, but intellect has *logical* time in its sequencing of the elements of argumentation. "Normal" desire—that is, desire unaffected by chemical suppressants or enhancements—also has its schedule: three meals a day, patterns of sexual activity, and so on. The temporal rhythms of arousal and satiation are desire's essence. But there are drugs that can break these smooth waves into particles.

The fundamental change that nicotine effects is a fragmentation of the wave motion of time (*chronos*) into discrete particles (*kairoi*). Cigarettes become the commas of daily life, dividing otherwise uninterrupted waves of experience into punctuated intervals or separate temporal units.[6] There is symptomatic evidence of this in nicotine withdrawal, when time hangs heavy and days seem to be endlessly long. An active smoker's cognitive activity is completely divided into quanta. All phenomenal experience takes place not in an undivided Newtonian field but somewhere in Einsteinian relation to the next or the last cigarette. A physical concomitant is the change in the smoker's smooth and unconscious patterns of breathing, which are now reassigned from the medulla oblongata to the cerebrum as inhaling and exhaling become conscious actions. Breathing becomes transitive.

The sensation of intellectual enhancement that cigarettes cause stems from the same "making conscious" of autonomic activity. Patterns of reason, as reflected in patterns of speech, really are different in smokers than in nonsmokers. Smokers chronically hyperventilate, so that there is an "inspiration" to smokers' thought and talk that makes them seem—to themselves and even to others—more alert and intelligent. Conversely, withdrawing smokers have the sensation and appearance of stupidity.

Oscar Wilde wrote that "A cigarette is the perfect type of a perfect pleasure. It is exquisite, and it leaves one unsatisfied. What more can one want?"[7] So long as the smoker is still smoking, an equilibrium develops that incorporates interruptions of chronological time into an alternative but nonetheless stable and consistent pattern, so that the smoker can continue to function normally in all other aspects of desire. But the effect of nicotine on desire can only be known when the smoker tries to stop. In that unhappy state, quanta of desire for nicotine (which are never really satiable even when indulged) now rise up in their habitual rhythm only to be denied; and nicotine desire, like most other desires, is strengthened in proportion to its lack of satisfaction, at least until some kind of amnesia ensues. In other words, no matter whether the smoker indulges or denies a surge of nicotine craving, that desire and its rhythm continue anyway. The difference is that quanta of desire that are indulged cause time to speed up, whereas quanta denied cause it to slow down. Unlike the protractible "privileged moments" of the drugs of play and contemplation, nicotine develops a relentless (if individually variable) rhythm that beats on regardless of whether the drug is readministered or not. This transformation of temporality, when time becomes a slightly lopsided wheel rushing onward in discrete turns, permanently alters the smoker's self-consciousness and consciousness of the world.

Different drugs create different rhythms of desire.[8] There is tremendous individual and generic variation, but in general the cycles of desire for heroin and cannabis are comparatively slow, whereas those for nicotine and cocaine are fast. For amphetamines and cocaine the rhythm of desire becomes so rapid that desire supplants everything else, to the point where it cannot be specified as desire *for* anything, let alone actually satisfied. Cocaine when smoked probably establishes the fastest rhythm of all, so that almost all the user's effort is required to keep up with the process of administration. It is no longer a question of "pleasure"—there is no time for that. In the case of alcohol, the rhythm of desire accelerates with successive administrations so that what may have begun as casual drinking speeds up as the effect of earlier drinks accumulates. But alcohol has the advantage of ending in unconsciousness, which terminates the cycle, whereas stimulant intoxication ends in a sleepless dysphoria.

It would be helpful at this point to establish an etiology of addiction in order to understand how an uninterrupted time wave is first divided into particles. As Nathan Adler says, "One cannot speak sensibly of . . . drugs without examining the selection and induction process that determines who becomes a user and under what circumstances. One cannot generalize about drug effects without differentiating such issues as types of use—is the use experimental, casual, recreational, or habitual? What stage is the user in?"[9] A user's first cigarette or shot of heroin or line of cocaine is obviously undertaken not out of any established desire but out of some other impulse— curiosity, impetuousness, or the pressures of social conformity. The first administration of any of these drugs stands out not only in immediate experience but also in subsequent memory as a unique occurrence, an extraordinary event still located in the medium of ordinary time. The effects of this first administration vary from drug to drug. With nicotine, nausea and dizziness usually result, followed by an uncomfortable increase in heartbeat and respiration. No particular pleasure follows. With heroin, initial nausea and vomiting are accompanied by the pleasure of the first rush—a sensation some say the user is forever trying to recapture. With the first dosage of a stimulant there are usually no initial side effects other than the desired ones (except in those special cases where the first administration kills the user, as in the famous instance of the basketball star Len Bias),[10] but there is usually no hunger to administer more until the effects of the first dose have begun to wane. What makes nicotine particularly interesting for the subject of addiction in general is that the smoker-to-be receives almost no pleasure from the first try. One of the wonders of nicotine is that the desirable sensation a cigarette offers becomes available only to someone already addicted. This means that the neophyte must persevere with little or no intermediate reinforcement until habituation results. This suggests that the preliminary desire that leads to smoking is in some sense nothing more than *a desire for addiction itself*. That is a strange proposition, since it encourages the speculation that there must be something inherently and preliminarily attractive about the condition of addiction per se. What could this possibly be?

The commonplace explanation is that smoking is flatteringly constructed in advertising and cultural imagery. Most of the antismoking campaigns of the past two decades have tried to nullify those enticements by superimposing medical information to the effect that cigarette smoking is not life-enhancing but life-denying. The trouble is that ads promising death are not able to deliver it until much later, and indefinite deferral necessarily makes their threats less potent. Other approaches assume that the more adult and sophisticated demeanor available to a young person who smokes is the main allure for the beginner, and the desire to "be cool" or "be grown-up" is what enables a new user to persevere through the sickening early stages of habituation. Campaigns based on demonstrations of smoking's "uncoolness" would then be expected to achieve a greater rate of deterrence, but oddly most people who have quit as a result of antismoking propaganda are older and have smoked longer. Teenagers continue to adopt the practice in ever-larger numbers, possibly because they cannot credit the idea of mortality, or because the need for a more adult image is simply the most powerful imperative for those on the verge of actual adulthood.

I have a friend who claims that he is a nonsmoker only because he tried smoking and "couldn't stick to it," suggesting that he lacks the persistence to become addicted. This is a joke, but as with most good jokes it has a kernel of seriousness. The difficulty in understanding why nicotine addiction begins undercuts all public efforts to discourage people from starting or to encourage them to quit. It is hard to provide a good reason to stop when there is no knowing why anyone starts.

The following hypothesis will be disheartening to those who wish to see the habit of cigarette smoking extinguished. Drug experiences tend to be predetermined by the user's expectations of them. Nicotine addiction provides an especially clear example. There is some sort of metadesire operating here, some *desire for desire itself* that provides the incentive for the beginning smoker to outlast the unrewarding initial stages of the habit. The only way I can understand this is in terms of the modification of time involved in addiction. Most teenagers experience time as slow and oppressive, since they are imprisoned in schools by day and in their families' houses by night. Time moves for them as it moves for inmates in a prison or mental hospital. Horizontal time or *chronos* dominates teenage consciousness in an inexorable progression of minutes and hours. From my own adolescence I remember a junior high school health class so boring that every time the clock ticked away another minute I made a scratch on a notebook page. Presumably I was seeking to break up the oppressive temporal wave into more endurable discrete and measurable particles. But this was not in itself enough, for measuring *chronos* only describes but does not change its nature. Against the tyranny of *chronos,* the only counterforce is *kairos* or occasion, the privileged moment that interrupts (and doesn't just measure) the glacier of chronometry. The smoker-to-be, in preconstructing the experience of his or her addiction, foresees each cigarette as a *kairos.* Cigarette smoking is imagined as filling the long and brutally dull day with an endless succession of happy occasions. Those who are able to experience these moments are perceived as less miserable and perhaps more complete people than the drudges who simply endure. These drudges, of course, are more often than not parents and teachers, and it is for this reason that their pleas to avoid smoking are all the more ignorable. Why should the beginning smoker not begin? In order to become like these wretched creatures?

Charles Baudelaire's prose poem "Enivrez-vous" describes the desire to get high precisely in these temporal terms:

> You have to be drunk all the time. It's all there is; it's the only question. So as not to feel the horrible burden of Time that breaks your shoulders and bends you to the earth, you have to be drunk without respite.

> But on what? On wine, on poetry or on virtue, whatever you want. But get drunk.

> And if sometimes, on the steps of a palace, on the green lawn of a chasm, in the dull solitude of your room, you awaken, drunkenness already disappeared or diminished, ask the wind, the wave, the star, the bird, the clock, ask everything that rolls, everything that sings, everything that talks, what time it is; and the wind, the wave, the star, the bird, the clock will answer: "It is time to get drunk! So as not to be slaves martyred by Time, get drunk and don't stop! On wine, on poetry or on virtue, whatever you want."

So too in Italo Svevo's novel *The Confessions of Zeno* almost every important event in the narrator's life, whether positive or not, is marked in his diary by the punctuational phrase "Last cigarette" or even the abbreviation "L.C." Additional evidence for this hypothesis is to be found in the reminiscences of former smokers who cannot help thinking that they were happier when they were still smoking. If this is the case, then it is clear that the only way to combat the beginning of cigarette addiction is to make young people's lives less boring, and since this would require nothing less than a social revolution, it is hard to imagine that cigarette smoking will ever be eradicated.

Once a smoker begins, the bouquet of happy occasions that cigarette smoking promised becomes commonplace itself. But the *process* by which the inception of nicotine addiction provided at least momentary relief from "hard time" leads to similar preconstructions of alcohol and other drugs. Another variety of antidrug ad, especially common in the 1960s, suggests that marijuana leads to the use of more dangerous or addictive drugs. It was this line of thought that discredited most of the antidrug propaganda of that era, since cannabis does not necessarily lead to anything beyond itself. But there probably is a progression from tobacco to alcohol to heroin and/or stimulants based on the template of experience that teaches the novice that each new initiation into drugs has the ability to alter the nature of time in social realms (like school or, later, work) where time is unavoidably oppressive.[11] Who wouldn't want to punctuate a desert with oases?

For this reason I concur with those who find that drug use among adolescents is encouraged by boredom, bad schools, parental difficulties, and the lack of subsequent opportunities. But this statement is more or less empty unless it is understood that its quasi causality takes place not in demographic and economic equations but in the very nature of time as a fundamental medium of consciousness. It is possible that addiction is more generally a response to the negative valuation of time in secular world outlooks: that time brings a diminution of capacity and a long decline that ends inevitably in death. The strange popularity of the American bumper-sticker proverb "Life sucks—and then you die" illustrates general agreement, across social classes, with such negative views of time. Any way of escaping or disrupting this degenerative design will necessarily be attractive, and those most attracted may be the strongest and most resistant spirits.

Alcohol addiction also illustrates the intimate connection between drug habituation and an altered sense of time. Almost all alcoholics have a certain hour of the day after which it is permissible to begin drinking, the time when "the sun is over the yardarm." In *John Barleycorn,* his memoir of alcoholism, Jack London describes the way time is continually reorganized for the drinker as the habit deepens. It begins with the desire for a drink at a certain time of day:

> I became aware of waiting with expectancy for the
> pre-dinner cocktail. I *wanted* it, and I was *conscious* that
> I wanted it. . . . The program of my ranch life was as
> follows: Each morning, at eight-thirty, having been
> reading or correcting proofs in bed since four or five,
> I went to my desk. Odds and ends of correspondence
> and notes occupied me till nine, and at nine sharp,
> invariably, I began my writing. By eleven, sometimes a
> few minutes earlier or later, my [daily] thousand words
> were finished. Another half hour at cleaning up my
> desk, and my day's work was done, so that at eleven-
> thirty I got into a hammock under the trees . . . One
> morning, at eleven-thirty, before I got into the ham-
> mock, I took a cocktail. I repeated this on subsequent
> mornings. . . Soon I found myself, seated at my desk
> in the midst of my thousand words, looking forward
> to that eleven-thirty cocktail. . . . But a new and most
> diabolical complication arose. The work refused to
> be done without drinking. . . . I had to drink in order
> to do it. . . . My brain could not think the proper
> thoughts because continually it was obsessed with the
> one thought that across the room in the liquor cabinet
> stood John Barleycorn.[12]

What is interesting about this passage is that London describes not so much an increasing quantity of consumption as a progressive alter- ation of his daily schedule. In fact his consumption does increase with the additional hours of drinking, but that increase is also explained in terms of the schedule: "Once, I was in a rush. I had no time decently to accumulate the several drinks. A brilliant idea came to me. I told the barkeeper to mix me a double cocktail. Thereafter, whenever I was in a hurry, I ordered double cocktails. It saved time."[13] In fact all habit- uation to alcohol involves an ever more refined atomization of time by patterns of the drug's administration. London's book, published in 1913, was a best-seller as America moved toward Prohibition, and it is important to remember that the Anti-Saloon League and other organizations promoting Prohibition often made their arguments against alcohol in temporal terms: husbands stopping for drinks after work were late getting home, or their inebriated arrivals disrupted the household schedule. Since repeal, bar and liquor store hours have generally been closely regulated, so much so that the tempo of life is in some sense determined by this drug even for those who do not drink. This institutionalization of alcohol scheduling has been even more rigorous and elaborate in Great Britain, where for decades pubs opened and closed twice each day. Unless drinking comes to engulf all hours of the day, as it eventually did for Jack London, the division of the day into drinking and sober hours provides a relativity for time atomized by addiction. When one drinks all the time, that relativity is lost, and the drinker is "bottoming out." It is at this stage that drinkers either die or seek help. Drinkers are also prone to quit and resume over longer temporal panels; this is true of London. Here I repeat a popular apothegm that expresses this well: "The good thing about being a drinker is that you feel great when you're drinking and you feel great when you're not." The implication is that a nondrinker suffers from the lack of relativity in his or her temporal sense. A person addicted to any drug may very well come to value the organizational aspect of the habit.

Addiction depends on a willingness and ability to service the temporal rhythm of the drug. Even renouncing, a user is still likely to frame that renunciation by the drug's scheduling powers, or to superimpose another equally rigorous schedule, as is the case in most organizations of reformed users. This must be so because once a drug habit is formed the nature of time is permanently altered, so that it can be difficult, painful, and even lethal to return to unpunctuated chronometry. The chemical and metabolic effects of the various kinds of drug withdrawal have been amply documented, yet no infallible procedure for ending any addiction has ever been found. Purely ethical arguments ring particularly hollow, asking the user to combat habituation by strengthening "willpower"—a rank misnomer, since it is the power *over* will that must be developed. Some therapies substitute one addiction for another—nicotine gum for cigarettes, methadone for heroin, and so on—but obviously this does not alter the fundamental temporal pattern. "Cold turkey" withdrawal is based on the assumption that a former user may be able to outlast and eventually forget the temporal pattern of addiction.[14] But the ex-user never forgets. A person may give up sex, but no one can return to virginity.

The development of the nicotine patch as a tool for stopping smoking is promising because it is the first antismoking device to address the question of time in addiction. By releasing a steady supply of nicotine through the epidermis, the patch prevents the drastic metabolic effects of cessation, and reduces the daily dosage only twice—after the first month and after the second. Because the patch is worn twenty-four hours a day, it addresses the question of fragmented temporality as the primary problem. It allows the user to concentrate on learning to live with an altered sense of time *before* he or she has to learn to live without the drug itself. However, the high rates of recidivism reported with this procedure suggest that there are many users who simply cannot endure the run-on sentence that consciousness becomes without cigarettes. There have been reports of smokers having heart attacks from nicotine overdoses when they put on the first strong (21 mg per day) patch and then keep right on smoking anyway.

There are too many problems with the supposed dynamic of intellect and desire that is so frequently invoked to describe addiction. The assumption is that a resurgence of intellect may occur if its suppression has been definitive enough to cause the totality of consciousness to try to "right" itself. An ex-user's reconstructed ethics must be fortified by a specific proviso against any renewed use whatever of the drug in question; hence the puritanism of a reformed addict of almost any sort. But a reassertion of intellect does not necessarily lead to any diminution of desire. For that to happen, desire must turn against desire. With cocaine users, for example, the desire to eat, have climactic orgasms, sleep normally, and so forth must prove at least transiently stronger than desire for the drug. The problem is once again that it is impossible to restore predrug temporality. Two time-rhythms are asserting themselves at once. If listening to two pieces of music with different tempos is distracting, imagine how disorienting it is when variant temporalities are trying to operate simultaneously within a single consciousness. This is why organizations like Alcoholics Anonymous must completely deracinate the withdrawing user from her or his own drug-restructured mind, referring all metaphysical questions to an *external* "easy does it" God who takes it "one day at a time"—that is, whose chronicity is steady and seamless, and whose balanced intellect and desire may be downloaded whole to replace the user's own. By this approach the user simply vacates her or his own consciousness as if fleeing a burning building. Literal belief in "God" is irrelevant. I once spoke to an AA member who said that she invoked the radiator at the foot of her bed as "God." Any routine object of cognition may be recruited as this new divinity, so long as it is the "not-me."

There is an important social recognition at this creed's core: namely, that an addict accustomed enough to the fragmented temporal and experiential patterns of a drug has already become "the other." This otherness at first reinforces the addiction, since for every drug (as for every hobby and sexual preference) there is always a supportive community—just another of the myriad subgroups in the postmodern social world. This otherness has been eagerly exploited by the generals in the War on Drugs, who have often linked users to *other categories of otherness* in race, sexuality, and class. There are an internal economics (in the etymological sense of "housekeeping") and semiotics in drug communities that mirror the consciousness modifications of their particular high. These social factors affect everything from drug-specific behavior like buying and selling (think of the utter dissimilarities among cocaine, nicotine, marijuana, coffee, and alcohol transactions) to housekeeping to dress to speech patterns to toilet hygiene. The uncanny ability of the habituated to recognize strangers in the same subgroup is reminiscent of the vampires' mutual recognition in an Anne Rice novel. There is a certain delight in finding oneself no longer part of a bland and amorphous mainstream, but the member of a smaller and more intimate community of "others."

There is almost always an internal vocabulary in these communities. It takes time to learn all of it, to achieve initiation, to speak the language effortlessly. For those without a strong identification with any previous language group, drug acceptance can be empowering. Twelve-step organizations achieve much of their success by replacing the language of these communities with still another "initiated" speech, and by constructing their own litanies to replace the stock recognition phrases of addiction. They provide a meeting place to supplant the bar or crackhouse, and even encourage the use of a sanctioned drug: black coffee. This strategy is often successful in part because it recognizes that the *quest for* otherness is a strong secondary reinforcement to drug use. Members are reassured that they cannot be expelled from this society; they are required to identify themselves as alcoholics or drug addicts even when they have not touched an intoxicant in years. The sort of consciousness AA and related organizations offer is not billed as a return to predrug consciousness, but instead as the advent of a whole new state: "Today is the first day of the rest of your life." These programs know that once something as fundamental to experience as time has been altered, any illusion about returning to some anterior and hypothetical "sobriety" is permanently obliterated.

The addict, then, is "spoken for," is pledged to his or her drug. Language and consciousness are caught in a narrowing circle. The view that a given set of addicts all have the same personality,[15] and are therefore of no clinical interest, is more arguable for alcoholics and heroin users than for tobacco smokers, but even for the latter it could gain some currency as cigarettes come closer to prohibition. Set conversely against the "spoken for" model of addiction is a null set: the unaddicted who are "free" to use language without commitment, as if there were no factors governing language other than drugs or their absence, or as if the putatively "sober mind" were not also free to think itself into some other kind of unfreedom. There is, by this token, a loss of freedom in every sentence we say or write, because in saying or writing any one of them we preclude saying or writing any of the infinity of other sentences we might have written. And so "diction" requires the same narrowing as *ad*diction.

The difference lies in the possibility that diction can go on and construct another sentence entirely different from the first one, whereas addiction in effect writes the same sentence over and over again. What is regrettable about addiction is precisely that it is a condition that resists change. It requires the addict to relive and retell the same ritual tale of acquisition, administration, euphoria, and withdrawal day after day after day. Addiction, like any system of belief or survival, is inherently conservative: it would like to keep the same schedule, the same supplier, the same price, the same location, the same strength and quality, and the same setting for administration. Under such repetition, cognition is dulled and ethics frayed, pleasure (if there was any to begin with) thins, and desire is ritually aroused and then either served or frustrated. Memory becomes indistinct, because there is only one thing to recollect, and its daily variations are unimportant and forgettable. Anyone who is committed to any ideology, social relationship, habit, or course of action is also "spoken for," and so it is possible to see in addiction a reflection of anyone's ordinary commitments. If the heroin user's commitment seems more onerous than others, it is not difficult to imagine that to the same heroin addict marriage and parenthood may appear to be abject slavery, and home ownership not so different from any other junk that cannot be stopped at will.

To be sure, an addiction can be ended. There are a myriad of possible scenarios in which users of all sorts give up drugs or replace one drug with another simply because the force of change—pressure from that noumenal fourth dimension, the future—can be stronger than all the things we can actually know about consciousness and ourselves, or stronger than addiction's resistance to change. For one thing, external circumstances can vary: a drug to which one is habituated can become unavailable because of the vicissitudes that govern any market. Or an addict can have a spontaneous remission, as heroin users are sometimes said to experience if they live into their sixties. Or the user can get busted and undergo forced withdrawal in prison, or overdose and withdraw in the hospital, or seek treatment, as William Burroughs finally did.[16]

But regardless of the direction in which a recovering addict goes, the time of addiction remains in a particular and self-contained precinct all its own, so that it is impossible to forget. Solomon H. Snyder blames the tenacity of heroin on the inherent rewards of "drug-seeking behavior":

> Simply put, an addict will relentlessly seek out his
> drug, regardless of whether or not he is experiencing
> any withdrawal symptoms. The drug-seeking behavior
> seems to be totally independent of the presence of
> tolerance or physical withdrawal. It has been the bane
> of physicians trying to curb opium addiction. . . . Some
> authorities (including myself) argue that compulsive
> drug-seeking is sociologic . . . The culprit is mental set
> and physical setting.[17]

To overcome an addiction completely would mean at least partial amnesia, the obliteration of whole ranges of recollection. It would mean forgetting people, places, and years. This would disrupt time as radically as addiction itself. A woman in a TV antismoking spot says of her "new life" as a nonsmoker, "It's a lot different." Different from what or whom? Addiction, even when inactive, causes recognition of the differences within oneself, within a single consciousness. One becomes more than one. One becomes a plurality of creatures living under different calendars, consulting different clocks, living in different time zones.

If the rhythm of supply were matched to the rhythm of an addict's desire, servicing the habit would not require all of life's energy, and the addiction would recede almost to transparency—as has until recently been the case with the legal sale of tobacco. It will be interesting to see what happens when and if cigarettes are interdicted completely, since the *social* problem with addiction lies not so much in drugs as in the lack of them.[18] If cigarettes disappeared from the planet and decades went by, those old enough to remember the habit would still be craving cigarettes—more so than ever, for if addiction is so intimately entangled with the sense of time, one of the fundaments of consciousness, then the old smokers' attenuated craving would become indistinguishable from their nostalgia for youth and yesterday, and perhaps indistinguishable from whole sectors of memory itself. Since an addiction atomizes time from hour to hour and day to day, it also divides long-term memory into similarly discrete zones, mapping the past the way all great commitments do: when the baby was young, when someone was dying, when Dad was in the service, when we smoked cigarettes on the library lawn during lunch break at school, when the evening's baggie was bought through the facade of a ruined church.

Although it may appear from an external vantage that an addict's habit is "out of control" in that the addict cannot stop it, in fact the management of a drug habit confers on its owner at least an illusion of control. There is, for once, a concrete reason to live. The fragmentation of temporal consciousness that characterizes addiction may eventually prove to be no worse or no different from the general fragmentation of consciousness in a world of electronic phenomena and domestic and workplace complexities. I do not mean this line of reasoning to recapitulate the weary liberal nostrums about "society" as the root of all evil. But just as it is possible to tell something about an organism from examining a single cell of its body, it is often possible to see analogies between apparently isolated conditions like the lives and minds of addicts and the parameters of wider frameworks of action and belief. Although an individual is powerless to control the plagues in the world at large, an individual drug user can at least take the daily measures required to service a habit, even if frustration may follow on any given day. The only recognized remedy for addiction, then, is to acknowledge that everything is out of control, including oneself, and to become passive and quiescent. In this way one escapes the altered temporality of addiction, but also the privileged moments and daily coherence that it confers. Not everyone is willing to do without these, even if survival itself is at risk, since the other options are either attenuated versions of the same (consumer desire and its privileged moments of buying) or the abject surrender of whatever narrow order and purpose there may be in addiction. It is a rare addict who expresses joy in ending the habit. Pride is a more common reaction; and despair more common than pride. The appetite for taking up residence on an unpunctuated continuum of time and space—a place resembling more than anything else a desert of boredom and anomie—may be slight.

PART II

What Drugs Do and Don't

What Drugs Do and Don't

Generalized "drugs" are often said
to interfere with mental functioning,
especially where that interference may impede
the mind's adherence to the consumerist paradigm:
download, remember, desire, and purchase. But most psychotropics do not have the simple effects that are usually ascribed to them. Perception, emotion, intellect, and memory are changed in certain users under certain circumstances, but none of these elements is obliterated or disabled short of unconsciousness or death. Here again the experience of users is different from what is imputed to them.

The notion that drugs cripple the mind is something of a joke to users. I can remember when smoking a joint was prefaced with the exhortation "Let's get stupid!" or when cocaine snorters joked about finally having found a purpose for the unemployed six-sevenths of the human brain—getting itself killed. Users tend to incorporate public antidrug rhetoric into their self-appraisals, much as hippies once adopted the pejorative word "freak" as an honorific, or the way homosexuals appropriated "queer." The present generation of druggies takes similar pride in being called "slackers" or "stoners." Users think that the real brain death is located not in their own crania but in the language and institutions of straight consciousness. If drugs simply killed the mind and/or brain, why would anyone take them? Most common psychotropes bring changes in mental operations as certainly as they alter brain chemistry. But change is not death. Death is school, political discourse, censorship of recorded music, "Just Say No," and compulsory asexuality in the face of the AIDS epidemic. To think creatively, any person, high or sober, needs to transform the fixed counters she or he inherits from the previous generation and its political and cultural establishments. Since substances like cannabis sativa, psilocybin, and Ecstasy seem to rearrange Consumerism's carefully compartmentalized model of the mind, it is difficult to distinguish their agency from that of imagination itself.

I am not arguing, however, that any of the self-administered drugs necessarily "improve" consciousness—sharpen perception, deepen feeling, hone logic, or secure memory.[1] The point is that the problems raised by autopharmacology are so complex, and the number of variables so large, that generalization becomes dangerous and inane. The effect of blanket assertions about drugs' deleterious actions is to obscure what they can teach us about the nature of consciousness. Psychiatrists and biologists are the first to admit that knowledge of brain chemistry has been significantly furthered by the employment of drugs as research tools. Why shouldn't the same prerogative be available to investigators outside the natural and medical sciences?

Whatever learning can be gained by these examinations will be possible only when the user's perspective is taken as primary. Since users are usually discredited as too "other" to add anything to our knowledge of ourselves, it may be that some of the following discussions will seem skewed because they keep returning to that interdicted point of view. I hope to throw the terms of the present debate ever so slightly off-kilter, so that philosophers and literary theorists will discover that they do have something to contribute to it after all.

4 *User Construction*

If a man "whose talk is of oxen,"
should become an Opium-eater, the probability
is, that (if he is not too dull to dream at all)—
he will dream about oxen.
THOMAS DE QUINCEY

The life of the senses is not passive. What I perceive right now—the long view over a cow field to the hills, smoke from my neighbor's woodstove, the thunder of an Acid House CD, the discouraging clutter of an academic's desk—are not here just by accident. I prearranged them. I bought the house with this view and neighborhood, I put on the CD, I chose university life. What I sense, its joys and disgusts together, has been preconstructed by some earlier me. I see it now because it somehow resembles what at some point in the past I thought I might want to see "in the future." The same principle holds for ephemeral perceptions. In the most cursory of social interactions, I choose where I focus my eyes, how I hold my head, which conversations I start or overhear, whether or not I establish touch by shaking hands or kissing hello. Although sense organs are simply receptors, there is an element of volition in the ways I direct and deny them. I *look* where I want to, even though once something *is seen* I see it necessarily.

Even in involuntary situations, there is control. The car breaks down in a part of town I don't know. In the garage where I'm towed, the odor of grease and cigarettes is strange. My time frame is skewed. I don't know how long I'll be here, or when my car will be fixed. Yet even here my perceptions are not merely forced upon me. Perception is affected by memory, anticipation, fear, pleasure, and desire. I can look out through the station's glass front into a street of strangers—or I can implode in a cyclone of misery and fear. The way I order the alien perceptions of such an afternoon is a result of who I am, and what my history of ordering novel experience has been, and what expectations that history causes me to bring to new surroundings. If the past has given me fear, I will bring fear to the present. But if I have ever received novel and alien sights as pleasurable or engaging, then I can leave my guard down and participate in the day's creation.

These mundane illustrations lead to a commonsensical proposition: that consciousness is a collaboration between the individual and the universal, between subject and object; and that this is an active relationship on both sides. Although this seems obvious enough, from the neo-empiricist perspective of Consumerism it is outright heresy. Consumer culture is founded on the notion that the mind is passive, first downloading and then data-processing external "ideas" without adding anything of its own.[1] Its mode of logic, inductive reasoning, leaves consciousness incapable of determining truth or fact, since there can never be enough evidence to reach a conclusion. Induction is endless, so that even if an interim conclusion could be reached it would quickly be swept away in the next tide of data. Consumerism, in the corposant flux of its images, tells us that just as desire is insatiable, so too there is never enough information. The result is a "cult of the new," a systematic personal and historical amnesia that denies perceivers any role in the creation of the world.[2]

A collaborative model affords several advantages for studying drugs. If consciousness is a *relationship* of subject and object, then it is possible to imagine an almost infinite number of "possible consciousnesses," whereas Consumerism (as a mass empiricism) has only one: the mind receiving information about the world and then intelligently and profitably recombining it. Anything that interferes with the functioning of this empirical process is in some sense bad, like a defect in the operation of a machine. From this it is impossible not to see the "Just Say No" campaign as essential to the consumerist agenda: it means "reject all heterodox consciousness." In a collaborative model, in contrast, there are only more and more configurations of consciousness across time and space, and each one of these could be discussed and described (given world enough and time to do it). Each one could be approached on its own terms, and not prejudged according to its compatibility with a single predetermined standard. There is no point in making diagrams of these, or enumerating the many schematics that centuries of philosophers, psychologists, and biologists have introduced. The less systematic the system, the more flexible—and flexibility is a prerequisite because of the exploratory nature of any discussion of drug consciousness. A rough vehicle is best for rough terrain.

It is said about LSD that the user's expectations before tripping always come true. If you expect a living demonology, then Hell will open beneath you. If you prevision Paradise, then you walk in the privileged gardens. In the language of psychology, "Findings to date seem to confirm that there is no drug-specific behavioral response in the use of LSD; the behavioral effects are a function of predisposing personality, the situation and setting in which it is administered, the orientation and expectations of both subject and operator, and the induction procedures involved."[3] Nathan Adler's notion is more usually expressed as "set and setting," meaning the user's mindset before taking the drug, and the circumstantial setting in which the administration takes place. Although for many years now these terms have provided the variables for sociological studies like Norman E. Zinberg's *Drug, Set, and Setting*,[4] they had their origins in the early research on psychedelics conducted by Timothy Leary and Richard Alpert at Harvard University. Andrew Weil defines them as follows:

> Set is a person's expectations of what a drug will do to him, considered in the context of his whole personality. Setting is the environment, both physical and social, in which a drug is taken. Leary and Alpert were the first investigators of the hallucinogens to insist on the importance of these two variables. Without them, we are unable to explain simply why the drug varies so unpredictably in its psychic effects from person to person and from time to time in the same person.[5]

While these terms gained currency in acid research, Zinberg and others have extended their applications to heroin and marijuana. Although they may indeed help "to explain simply why the drug varies so unpredictably," in so doing they invoke the nearly infinite number of possible drug experiences considered as the mathematical product of people multiplied by places multiplied by times. They reveal a "garden of forking paths" that opens up when anyone tries to generalize about drugs.

I am more interested in the problem of expectation or "set" than I am in "setting," although Zinberg and others are persuasive in their view that managing the setting may help the user control and determine the effects of the drug.[6] By a system of rituals and sanctions, limitations are placed upon the use of any substance to prevent the user from simply doing the drug all the time and sacrificing life or livelihood. The conclusions of this research are quite at odds with the all-or-nothing rhetoric of the War on Drugs, which equates even casual or occasional use with utter perdition. There is something intuitively obvious in the assertion that a person is more likely to have a pleasant experience with a psychedelic drug in a firelit study than in a fluorescent CIA interrogation chamber, or that one is likelier to enjoy smoking pot with friends than with enemies. But the same thing could be said of playing cards. It is "set," or the conditions of consciousness that preface an administration, that raises more difficult and interesting questions.

All experience is to some degree prevalued. The funeral was "not as bad as I expected." The anticipated "party of the year" ends with disconsolate personages trawling the halls of a loft. When expectation is not socially formulated, as it is with parties and funerals, we can deliberately construct it. We can lower our hopes so far that whatever eventuates seems fresh and surprising, or we can exaggerate our positive expectations in the hope that the event will somehow rise to the occasion — at the risk of having our boredom exacerbated. But even without conscious forethought, we invariably bring some sort of anticipation to the doorstep of every moment. It is not exactly that we form our experience in advance. The future, that nonexistent thing, consists only of whatever we think about it in the present. More to the point, every moment of the present is informed by pieces of the past that try to preconstruct it. Ordinarily, the event in question either confirms or disconfirms the anticipation even as it is partly created by it. But the event also supersedes the preconception, as the present always supersedes the past. With drugs, however, the threshold one crosses into intoxication can change the dynamic of sight and hindsight. The early determination, now on the anterior side of getting high, can be as irrevocable as the onset of the drug.

Let's say an emergency medical technician reaches someone in the throes of a bad acid trip. He or she may administer a counterdrug like thorazine, or try to "talk down" the user, giving assurances that everything is all right or that the apparitions that now seem so threatening are actually nothing but ordinary phenomena. But no matter how well the medical technician succeeds in relieving the immediate symptoms, the predicament of the "bummer" is fundamentally irremediable. This is because it goes back to the time before the drug was ingested, when the user consciously or preconsciously foresaw what was going to happen when it took hold. Expectations are in some sense permanent, and the same sorts of chronic memories that haunt psychiatric patients for life may engorge the acidhead in an acute and intimate nanosecond. Each trip has its own prehistory, as potentially deterministic as childhood is upon maturity. And now the only cure for what is really a temporal dislocation is the passage of yet more time, since time cannot be reversed.

In the bum trip, the past—what the user brings to the experience—in overdetermining the present suddenly and inexorably conjures up a future that becomes identified with death. Hyperawareness of mortality is a major part of every negative drug experience; a user can feel it like a fist in the stomach. Death is no longer a deferrable abstraction, but an immanence. To the degree that human misery stems from prescience of mortality, the user can foresee a bad end even in the face of acid's dazzling immediacy. The same is true with other drugs. Marijuana panics are similar to acid bummers, but with less intensity. Bad moments with cocaine usually come as the drug first begins to wear off, when the user feels the "death of the high" as identical with death per se. In all of these cases, a drug experience negatively prefigured causes the user to be bound by the past, to deny the present, and to be swept into a projection of coming disaster.

A bum trip is sandwiched between discrete zones of bad memory and destruction, but a good trip brings past, present, and future into a single and uninterrupted field of time, centered in the present. The advice of Richard Alpert to "Be Here Now" is a prescription for positive psychedelic experience. If, before taking the drug, a user is at peace with self and personal history, there will be no need to escape the immense power that the present acquires for the duration of the experience. The less baggage carried on, the easier the travel. A positive drug experience can confirm the collaborative model of consciousness, since the user relates to objects not as if they were dialectically opposed to his or her subjectivity, not as if they were immovable counters for memorization or purchase, but as if they were cocontributors to the creation of the world.

Within the consumerist framework, all that can be said is that a given drug has certain empirically observable biochemical effects. These cause the user to veer off the true path of desire into what can only be regarded as madness. But in fact even the commonest pharmaceuticals do not work autonomously. Aspirin has relieved my pain in the past, and when I take it now I expect my headache will soon disappear, and I expect this will be true every time I take it "in the future." If I say that aspirin "usually" cures me, then I am falling back on the empiricist trust in habit. It is better to say that there exists an ongoing relationship between aspirin and myself that, upon taking the tablet, I am reaffirming and renewing, and as a result of which reaffirmation and renewal I "feel better." Aspirin, in other words, *cannot cure me in my absence*. So too, psychoactive drugs are just physical substances (the object or the unconscious) that interact with my metabolism, and as they cross the blood-brain barrier they enter into or confirm a relationship with the consciousness that is already there — the same one that has decided to take the drugs and that now awaits, with specific expectations, the onset of their effects.[7]

It is the remarkable facility with which an object (like an amphetamine tablet) collaborates with a subject that gives drugs their epistemological interest. Taking a pill may resemble (or parody) consumerist downloading, but the view of consciousness on which it depends is different. Consumerism believes that consciousness is empty (the tabula rasa) until an idea arrives through the senses. It does not then transform the idea, but merely registers it and combines it with previous ideas. In this view, neither the idea nor the awareness that receives it is changed in its essential nature, though consciousness may be thought to grow quantitatively with the addition of the new information. In collaborative views of consciousness, both the input and the nature of its receiver are transformed. Drug use provides both a dramatization of and a metaphor for this process. In taking a drug into consciousness, the metamorphosis of that drug is inevitable. This happens chemically in the physical metabolism, but *meta*physically the drug's transmutation from object to partial subject is a fundamental one. And symmetrically, in the process of appropriating the drug into subjectivity the user's consciousness is also changed. It too becomes part of an altered relationship or redefined collaboration.

Internalizing a drug synopsizes the process by which ordinary sensory perceptions construct and alter consciousness. A perception enters the brain and thereafter is always a part of what has been experienced, changing the subject forever. Taking drugs and perceiving the world have this much in common if consciousness is defined as "the ongoing relationship between subject and object." But there is a difference, too. To internalize a drug generally involves using a sense or other organ for some purpose other than that for which it is biologically designed. To ingest drugs the user must supplant a portion of the lungs' capacity that is ordinarily used for breathing air; or must employ the alimentary canal for some purpose other than nutrition; or must violate the membranes of touch with points of needles; or must reverse the eliminatory processes of bowels or sinuses, and so forth. Drugs are introduced into consciousness, then, through what amounts to an alternative array of receptors. In the brain, psychotropics change the activity of neurons by altering the chemical media that control their firing order. These substances mimic chemicals found in the undrugged brain, just as their ingestion in some sense mimics perception. This mimicking effect is one of the characteristics that makes most drugs seem unnatural or perverse. To lump them together under the single rubric of "drugs" makes these mockingbird effects more sinister by hinting that throughout all the myriad and protean chemistries and circumstances of psychopharmacology only one thing is happening: the spurious IT has returned in some new and unrecognizable form, a novel event that takes place in the same way over and over again. The simulacrum has come, threatening the integrity of the "real" the way a counterfeit twenty-dollar bill causes all the genuine twenties to become suspect. If this great interloper is granted the least shred of toleration and respectability— if IT too can be called consciousness—then *anything* can be, and consciousness itself is depreciated.

On what basis can it be decided which consciousness is legitimate and which is the interloper? At the heart of Consumerism is the notion that consciousness has a *purpose:* to learn, to rearrange, to act and produce, and above all to purchase. This is the basis of Consumerism's affinity with traditional capitalism, which valorizes growth for its own sake, productivity no matter what is produced, and short-term profit no matter what the long-term loss. The next why must never be posed: Why growth rather than stability? Why profit instead of survival and breaking even? Why fuel and run this machine of consciousness if it cannot ascend to a level beyond the practical, if it must only desire, work, and buy, and never find surcease or contemplation or beauty or religion beyond the marketplace? For the consumer, everything taking place outside the busy commerce of goods and ideas has no actual existence, unless a marketing strategy can be formulated for it—as telereligion markets spirit, or Warner Brothers sells aesthetics.

The collaborative view, on the other hand, sees consciousness as an end in itself, and as a matter for study even and especially if—as is the case with some drug users—a particular awareness is "dysfunctional" according to the transactional criteria of Consumerism. Consciousness considered quite apart from any end it might be made to serve, or from any utility it inherently possesses, is the nearest thing to supernature that can be directly known. "Supernature" in this sense is used etymologically, to mean "exceeding nature." Although consciousness is (probably) natural, it exceeds the sum total of nature (where nature is understood as "all possible experience") since it can at least theoretically encompass all possible experience while still superadding its own experience of itself. Since this state of supernature far outweighs the more partial empiricism of purpose (because it encompasses it and more), there is no need to assign a function to it. It exists, and that is sufficient.

It can be objected that such a model cannot permit value judgments, that it cannot even argue that rationality is preferable to the pinball game of desire that is played in the skull of a crackhead. Maybe this is true. All assignments of value to states of consciousness are social judgments, and devolve from the configurations of manners, ethics, and laws that societies use to create and regulate themselves. To think that every drug constitutes an absolute state regardless of its social contextualization leads to what Adler calls the "pharmacological fallacy":

> We cannot speak of drugs as if the issue were merely
> the ingestion and incorporation of a chemical substance
> which invariably elicits the same predictable response.
> Such an approach distorts the facts, leads to pseudo
> issues, and creates the base for the futile polemics which
> have dominated the discussion. Such a restricted focus
> is based on a pharmacological fallacy. The consumption
> of drugs is not merely a physiological event. The drugs
> we use, whether as beverages, pills, injections, or
> smoke, exist within a matrix of psychological, cultural,
> and social values; and it is the roles and meanings of
> these that we incorporate with the drug. The pharmaco-
> logical fallacy is the assumption that there is a single,

specific drug effect independent of the individual's set
or the setting in which the event occurs. . . . One cannot
legalize or prohibit drug use and abuse by fiat alone without attending to the normative systems that establish
the built-in control and that institutionalize both the
use and abuse of the drugs.[8]

Andrew Weil confirms this proposition: "I have repeatedly stressed
that drugs are merely means to achieve states of nonordinary awareness and must not be confused with the experiences themselves.
They have the capacity to trigger highs; they do not contain highs."[9]
What Adler calls the "pharmacological fallacy" and Erich Goode calls
the "chemicalistic fallacy" and Weil calls "materialism" all designate
more or less the same metaphysical trap that I call Consumerism.

Comparisons can be made to tot up the similarities and differences between any two awarenesses, but this should be a descriptive
rather than a judgmental task. If a value judgment emerges, it should
be based on the criterion of which is the wider and more inclusive
state of mind. Unfortunately, most twentieth century discourse
about drugs has been based upon one or another of the Modernist
metanarratives. Modernism was characterized by the drive to place a
wide variety of phenomena within a single analytic framework that
would apply in all instances. Collapsing the potential infinity of drug
experiences in a universe of individual users, a discussion of "drugs"
in an absolute sense is plainly useless from any point of view—legal,
therapeutic, or theoretical. What is needed to accompany a more
flexible and relational model of consciousness is an understanding
that the fragmentation and complexity of postmodern society and
thought require an acknowledgment of yet another diversity: diversity of consciousness. If postmodern sociology has learned that the
world has become a matrix of numberless self-contained ethnic, economic, and sexual communities, then it is time to add to that list
those subgroups characterized by particular kinds of socialized consciousness: heroin addicts; meditators; alcoholics; recovering alcoholics; or religious groups, like Rastafarians and members of the
Native American Church, whose worship uses drugs as sacraments.
Until these social clusters can be recognized and approached without
recourse to a prejudicing metanarrative like the one imposed by state
and corporate Consumerism, all discourse on drugs will be reductive
and oversimplifying.

Maybe it is easier to think of it this way: the drugs we take, and our anticipation of what they will do to or for us, are expressions of who and what we want to be. Embedded in our choice of highs is the question of our aspirations, fears, and identity. An opiater I once knew divided drug users into augmenters and diminishers. The augmenters want to live faster, telescoping the consumerist process of desire and acquisition into the course of an evening or an hour. And so they shoot speed or snort cocaine. The diminishers want to defeat the process by leisurely patterns of dosing and contemplation, and so they shoot heroin. In both cases what is at stake is an idealized version of the self. The drug a user takes to assume an ideal self may have as much or as little significance as the clothes he chooses to express his character, or to costume the role she hopes to play each morning. People for whom drugs have deadly consequences are usually those who seek to play a role they are unsuited for, whose choice of drugs is based not on who they ideally are, but on someone completely different whom they wish to become. They lack the resources to construct the high they have chosen, and they experience madness.

Character really *is* destiny for druggies.

From the days of antihippie proselytizing comes the image of the stoned-
out freak stumbling into furniture, mistaking
one object for another, or seeing things that aren't there.
Although this made for good situation comedy at the time, it
has left in its wake all kinds of misapprehensions about the effects of
drugs—particularly cannabis and the psychedelics—on perception
and the higher cognitive functions. It may come as a surprise that
social and natural scientists generally agree that these and the other
most commonly used recreational chemicals have almost no impact
on the physical operation of the senses, and relatively little on the
brain's interpretation of sensory data. Some, like nicotine and the
stimulants, are "transparent" and don't affect perception at all.[1]

Cannabis is a special case, since it changes the physical mechanism
of vision by lowering the internal pressure of the eyeball. This is why
it can be used as a treatment for glaucoma. Erich Goode, who finds
only three universal drug effects, lists as one of them the fact that "in
almost every case the whites of a person's eyes will become blood-
shot after he has smoked a sizable quantity of marijuana."[2] Marijuana's direct influence on the eye may help explain why vision
appears stretched and grainy to the pothead. It sometimes promotes
an isolation of phenomena that the undrugged eye automatically
integrates into a visual field. It problematizes seeing by estranging
perceived objects from each other and from the viewer. But the eye
itself is not suspect. It still sees what it sees. In fact the pot smoker's
vision might seem clearer, assessing objects one at a time and perceiving them as sharper and better defined (positive figure-ground
distortions). But cannabis is an exception; few other drugs have a
direct effect on the sense organs themselves.[3] There are no drugs that
disable the sensorium *at the point of collection* unless and until they
cause unconsciousness—alcohol, sedatives, or heroin, for example,
at their extremes. In most cases the mechanics of sight, touch, sound,
taste, and smell are unchanged by psychoactive substances.

Even if the physical capacities of the senses are intact or enhanced, there is still the possibility that drugs cause sensory information to be reinterpreted at a later point in the cognitive process. For example, LSD brings about closed-eye kinetic hallucinations for many users, and alcohol in excess can make a drinker see double or think the visual field is spinning. There are also withdrawal conditions that precipitate sensory disturbances.[4] However, these distortions are located not in the inputting process but in the program that orders perceptual data into coherent fields. No matter what we call this software function, it sorts the chaos of multisensory perceptions into a matrix that aligns, justifies, and harmonizes them.[5] It gives a preliminary reading of temporal and spatial relationships among phenomena, so that an integrated field, and not just a ragbag of images, is forwarded to the cerebrum. This field can be formatted and reformatted in a multitude of ways. Emotional conditions—fear, anger, jealousy, lust—can affect it. So can peer pressure or consensus. And so, conceivably, can some drugs. One sense can be isolated at the expense of others, or synesthetic realignments can be created. The five senses can be conflated into one, or detached into entirely discrete inputs. The connections among them can be either tightened or loosened.

As any computer operator knows only too well, a programming error or faulty disk can disable software and prevent it from performing the function for which it was designed. What results is an interruption of the program's routine, so that disorder follows. Similarly, however unimpaired the functioning of the senses, without some sort of preliminary matrixing the brain cannot process their data. If this capacity is conceived as formatting the raw material of the senses for the brain, then it is reasonable to think that some drugs may impose an alternative ordering that influences, biases, or reprioritizes reception. Perhaps psychedelic drugs intervene at this point in cognition. They seem to remove perceptions from their context, giving a sensation of narrower focus compensated by depth of insight. Psychedelics reveal the microstructures of phenomena that in nonpsychedelic consciousness are unnecessary or even distracting, and are ordinarily subsumed into panoramas, noisy soundscapes, or integrative tasks like driving. In other words, the complexity of psychedelic microimagination renders the amount of information in a matrix too enormous to be conventionally ordered. This is sometimes received (as by Aldous Huxley in *The Doors of Perception*) as a refreshment, a liberation of the senses from dull empirical function-ality.[6] But it is also possible to feel it as stark horror.

Intervention by drugs may also take place at the subsequent point of highest cognitive integration, when the brain interprets the world around it and uses that information to think, act, or react. Kant called this capacity "Judgment."[7] Judging at the cerebral level deter-mines which perceptions are universally and objectively valid, that is, are accepted as "real" for anyone under the circumstances. It imposes the time-space grid, and also submits perception to a variety of other relational criteria. Now drugs are often said to "impair judgment." In this locution judgment refers to the ability to make ethical or safety decisions. Cocaine users, for example, may find themselves having sex with people to whom they wouldn't otherwise be attracted, or in circumstances when they might not choose to have sex at all if they weren't under the influence. Alcohol impairs a drinker's judgment of his or her own motor skills. But even avoiding the word "impair," it's likely that under some circumstances some drugs do alter *cognitive* judgment. Even though an LSD user knows that the cobwebs in the corners of the room were not there before the onset of the drug, they are still perceived as if they were real. Part of the attraction of psyche-delics is their ability to widen perceptual validity, to augment the real. Similar suspensions take place in relational elements like causal-ity. Cobwebs are spun by spiders; removed from that cause, they are not cobwebs at all. But under the spell of a psychedelic drug, they can still be cobwebs despite the disjunction. Existential concepts are similarly susceptible to subversion. What is impossible is suddenly possible; what cannot exist exists anyway. There are also instances where a spontaneously generated perception (a hallucination) is momentarily validated—squadrons of police pulling into the drive-way during a cocaine crash. These short-circuitings are vivid exam-ples of a cognition whose rapport with the sensory world has been rearranged, but which still attempts to carry on its operations.

The consistency of cognition through a wide range of drug intox-ications is quite astonishing. Despite some reordering, the funda-mental structures of perception are not overridden by drugs. The mind under drugs does not delete any sensory inputs or thwart any cognitive processes. Time and space do not disappear; their fabrics are stretched but not rent. However distorted they become, they persist as necessary components of experience. No drugs that I know of can eliminate or override any of the four dimensions. But they can certainly alter their proportions. Cannabis drugs make time pass slowly; cocaine and amphetamines make it move faster. The tempo of administration of a particular drug can become a more valid chronometer than a clock or watch. Psychedelics can make shallow spaces appear deep, or two-dimensional representations extend over three. Static two- or three-dimensional images can appear to move, thus assuming the additional dimension of time. But although drugs may promote these changes, short of the point when they cause unconsciousness they do not have the power to suspend perception altogether. The problem is quite the opposite: that more rather than fewer phenomena are apparently "real."

This, of course, is not necessarily a good or desirable thing. A person having paranoid delusions from cocaine withdrawal or LSD, for example, might wish that cognition were working as it did before the drug's administration. But the terrors that bumming and crashing users feel do not have their source in perception so much as in its interpretation. Coordinated systems are not, after all, unrelated. If indigestion speeds up the heart rate, we are not surprised. If a car overheats we are not surprised when it loses oil pressure. And so it is less than amazing that an ethical conflict, say, might disrupt cognition. The cognitive effects of drugs are simply not their most important. If we invented a drug that caused perceptual transformations but left the user appetitively and aesthetically indifferent, this funhouse mirror would be of little interest, since no one would use it.

Particularly for unaccustomed users, changes in cognitive integration can give a feeling of estrangement from quotidian perception, a liberation from deadening habits that suppress the wonder and pleasure of seeing, tasting, touching, smelling, and hearing. Undoubtedly this is one of the gratifications for users of certain drugs. This "creative alienation" may help to explain the historical association between drugs and the arts, for one of the traditional missions of art is to reinvigorate the senses by a "making strange." The evolution of the word "imagination," from the Kantian "arranger of images" to the current "creator of images," may reflect this. Drugs mimic inspiration in the artist even as they can cause, for the art consumer, the world itself to mimic an artwork's novelty and transformative power. With drugs, however, the requisite suspension of disbelief, not always easy to accomplish at will, is reinforced by changes in the blood and brain.

If the effect of drugs on cognition is found mainly at the more

evolved and integrative stages rather than at the point of physical collection, the next question is *how* this takes place. There is always a
temptation to cede this field to physiologists and clinicians with their
empirical studies of body chemistry, neural activity, behavioral deviation, and so forth. But the limitations of empiricism are never more
obvious than in these exercises. To describe the metabolic action of a
drug simply does not say anything about what it feels like, whether it
is pleasurable or not, or why a user might or might not want to repeat
the administration. Consciousness, because it resists quantification,
can be "measured" only by behavioral events whose correlation to the
mental state that supposedly produced them is entirely speculative.
Also, because empiricism in principle can never have enough evidence, to follow an inquiry through the jungle of variables that a topic
like drugs generates condemns the investigator either to an incomplete report or to a maddening confrontation with infinity. Skewing
cognition is not, despite official rhetoric on the subject, a simple
event. It is an endless series of possibilities, given the number of factors involved. These include (1) the nature of the drug in question;
(2) the amount of the drug administered; (3) the general physical and
psychological character of the user; (4) the circumstances in which
the individual takes the drug; and (5) the "squaring" and "cubing"
effects of simultaneous multiple drug administrations. You don't need
to work through the calculations to see that generalization is impossible, even if the number of variables is as small as those just enumer-
ated. Any list of typical scenarios (or a collection of "case histories")
would be ridiculously partial. No wonder public manipulation of slogans and images has tried to simplify the problem until there is almost
nothing left of it.[8]

The "funhouse mirror" drug I hypothesized (one that "left the user
appetitively and aesthetically indifferent") would distort perception
but bring no alteration of feeling—that is, it would not get the user
high. This suggests that cognition is not the real issue. The power of
drugs must lie elsewhere. But where? What do psychoactive drugs
do? Getting high isn't simply a matter of distorting the phenomenal
world. It has more to do with what we feel about what we perceive:
a drug's affect outweighs its effect. Doesn't it promise pleasure?
Don't we suppose so? Aren't drugs about feeling good—about that
interdicted topic, pleasure?

Why is pleasure forbidden when desire is encouraged? Because unlike desire, feeling does not seek to appropriate an object. It wants, rather, to establish an empathetic or antipathetic (but never apathetic) relationship with it. The English language is notoriously sloppy in making this discrimination. For example, "I love New York" and "I love ice cream" appear to be establishing the same alignment of subject and object, but the first is, let's say, *contemplative*, while the second is *appetitive*. Feelings like pleasure are entirely contained in the subject. They do not alter the object in any way. New York is unaffected by my love. But ice cream can be eaten.[9]

Let's assume that pleasure is a kind of feeling. So how can it be distinguished from desire? Desire is forever constructing a future out of the present. Desire that finds satisfaction is annihilated; yet it always seeks its own destruction by picturing a satisfied future in which it will no longer exist. Pleasure, on the other hand, is contained within the present, and would completely stop the movement of horizontal time, if it could.[10] It may occur spontaneously, without first having been desired. It is a harmonious state, whereas desire is dissonant. In some cases pleasure ensues when desire is satisfied, "all passion spent." But desire just as often engenders nothing but more desire, unavoidably followed by one of two displeasures: satiety or frustration.

There is a relationship, then, between pleasure and desire, but it is not a fixed one. Pleasure may arise when not desired, and desire once aroused does not necessarily lead to pleasure. Virtually any object can occasion pleasure, according to the nature, character, and circumstances of the subject in question, but only something that can potentially be appropriated can become an object of desire. There are, however, certain objects that *promise* pleasure. Artworks are in this class, as are all games, sports, and entertainments. Drugs too, since pleasure is the nominal reason for their existence and consumption. This expectation of pleasure, if unfulfilled, can be *un*pleasant, that is, can result in an antithetical feeling. This is certainly true of art. There is nothing so displeasurable as a dull movie, for example, which has soured our expectations of being entertained. With drugs too, anticipation—user construction—can directly control feeling. A person who self-administers a psychedelic drug expecting to be terrified by it will almost always be so. But someone expecting pleasure and not finding it will be frustrated. And so there is a paradox: only someone open to the possibility of pleasure has any chance whatever of finding it, although desiring pleasure seems to lessen the possibility that it will occur.

The difference between at least some drugs and other objects promising pleasure is that a drug itself does not necessarily remain the object of pleasure. An ice-cream sundae promises to delight the taste buds if it can be acquired and appropriated. It doesn't promise anything to the sense of touch, or present the hope of a visual transformation of the world, and the pleasure it offers will last no longer than the final bite. The sundae, then, can give pleasure only according to the limitations of its existence as an object. Without that object, there may be desire for it (wanting ice cream when there isn't any in the house) but there cannot be the delight of eating it. To be sure, there are drugs (such as cocaine) that like the sundae are largely about themselves and the consumption of themselves, whose promise of pleasure comes entirely from the anticipation of their own effects, and that accordingly do not "expand consciousness" but instead contract it to the point where all other objects are only facets of itself. But there are other drugs, such as psychedelics and hemp, whose ability to give pleasure lies in their power to transfer the pleasure-giving or pleasure-enhancing capability to *other* objects, or to enhance whatever capacity for giving pleasure was already present in those objects. One might as well do heroin in a shooting gallery or crack in a crack house as in a mansion or an idyllic landscape. But with LSD, for example, the environment is of the utmost importance. A dismal surrounding is almost certain to lead to displeasure. And marijuana, more an enhancer than a transformer, is best used in conjunction with a place or activity that would have been pleasurable in any case, although its capacity to elicit pleasure responses to the quotidian world is strong enough that it can sometimes make tedious tasks or obligations more tolerable.

Stimulants are different from other drugs in that they are not about pleasure at all. Cocaine promises the greatest pleasure ever known in just a minute more, *if* the right image is presented to the eyes, *if* another dose is administered, *if* a sexual interaction is orchestrated in just the right way. But that future never comes. There is a physical pleasure to the drug, to be sure, but it is incidental, trivial, compared to what is always just about to happen. Even at its most intense, when it expands into a great horizontal orgasm, the climax *as a climax* cannot come. A sensation driven out of the present into the past or the future cannot be pleasurable. With psychedelics or cannabis, however, the drug is taken to achieve a state that is sustainable as such. It turns one's attention away from the drug itself toward a contemplation of the drug's affects/effects, one of which can and should be pleasure. Obsessing over the white physical substance is a large part of the cocaine high. But no one passes an acid trip staring at the envelope the drug was delivered in.

Drugs of pleasure and desire are restricted by law, but not for the same reasons. This is a result of Consumerism's tacit metaphysics. Pleasure, self-contained in the present as it is, does not motivate the subject to work, spend, or otherwise engage the phenomena except in contemplation. Pleasure, unlike desire, does not appropriate. Its existence is based upon a provisional escape from economics, whereas desire in Consumerism is the economic drive wheel and the engine of consciousness. If the recipient is capable of anticipating (rather than desiring) it, pleasure can come from natural beauty, domestic tasks, friends and relatives, conversation, or any number of objects that do not need to be purchased. Pleasure can be found as close by as one's own body, or in objects that one already owns. The demonization of marijuana in America is based on this element of its character: it enables the user to take pleasure from ordinary objects already within the range of perception.

The particular opprobrium reserved for cocaine by American law is based on the notion that a drug that diverts desire from the conventional appetite for consuming objects is the most dangerous of all, since it mimics ordinary capitalist appropriation. It takes the motive force of Consumerism—desire—and renders it reflexive, depriving the aboveground market of revenues. A person using a great deal of cocaine is likely to buy little else but the drug. Cocaine capitalism (at least in the view of the conventional capitalist) is to conventional capitalism as cancerous cell growth is to normal cell growth in the body—the same thing only faster and deadly. Cocaine must be combated on a war footing for precisely this reason.

One convenient way to dissuade consumers from entering cocaine's world of accelerated desire is to deliberately confound the drugs of desire with drugs of pleasure, even though they have almost nothing in common. The traditional aversion to "unproductive" pleasure may be harnessed in this way without requiring an attack on greed and desire, the forces that motivate both the conventional and the cocaine markets. If cocaine is portrayed as a drug of unproductive pleasure rather than a savage mimicry of consumer consciousness, Consumerism can attack it without attacking itself at the same time. The term "high" as a synonym for "intoxicated" suggests a rising above, the obtaining of a superior overview. The person who is high on a pleasure drug stands above consumerist metaphysics, above the getting and spending, above what William Burroughs calls "the algebra of need." By asserting a heterodoxy of consciousness, the user represents a serious challenge to the prevailing metaphysics, because he or she has found a way around its dependency on insatiable desire.

Drugs of feeling entail a provisional modification of the structure of perception. This means that time and space are graphed differently. Robert Ornstein recounts that "Albert Hofmann, the discoverer of LSD, had no expectations and thus provides the clearest recorded summary of the experience: '. . . I lost all count of time, I noticed with dismay that my environment was undergoing progressive changes. My visual field wavered and everything appeared deformed as in a faulty mirror. Space and time became more and more disorganized.'"[11] With cannabis there is a particularly pronounced extension in the fourth dimension, time. Both drugs diminish the "objectivity" of the object—that is, de-emphasize its cognitive "reality"—and prioritize the subject's feelings about it. Both dramatize the condition of disinterestedness, or distancing from appetite. They accentuate the feeling of playful estrangement that is central to all aesthetic experience.

The affective authority conferred by these substances disrupts the "seamlessness" of cognitive experience. There is a physical analogy to this change. Newtonian physics viewed the electron waves emitted by radioactive atoms as a smooth continuity, whereas quantum mechanics has come to view them as a series of intermittent bursts. Psychedelics and cannabis drugs precipitate an analogous transformation in modes of perception. The uninterrupted flow of time or the seamless extension of the three spatial dimensions is divided by these drugs into distinct and perceptible quanta, capable of provisional isolation and separate contemplation. In parallel with this cognitive play, pleasure itself is divided and differentiated, no longer generalized to amorphous sensation or dependent upon totalistic fields. The eyes may see the universe in a grain of sand, and correspondingly pleasure may be found in a single flower or photograph or blade of light. An affective universe constructed through cognitive play does not have to be totalistic, even if it is self-contained; that is, pleasure does not need to be preconceived as a single, undivided, and general condition to which some state, experience, or activity gives (or fails to give) access. Pleasure results from a certain disposition of quanta abstracted from "all possible perception." LSD can make a snowbank sparkling in moonlight into an autogenous solar system, even though it is at the same time bounded and contained in a cognitive field. The pleasure of contemplating it is the same as that of contemplating the universe as a whole, despite its boundedness and "quantification."

Certain drugs facilitate the construction of pleasure by cognitive play. Perhaps it is for this reason that drugs of the cannabis family seem to heighten the user's sense of humor. Objects become funny (that adjective of play) as their estrangement from mechanical cognition is accentuated by the drug. They seem awkward and out of place in their momentary oneness. All humor depends upon similar detachments, whether accomplished by words or images, and accordingly it is a kind of pleasure. Cognitive play, as an unpremeditated rearranging of phenomena, may generate harmonies reached by roundabout and improvisatory means. Marijuana, hashish, and related drugs facilitate this process by suggesting to the user that since the very existence of any object is a caprice (and is funny), then all social and natural order is arbitrary. By highlighting the incongruity of a single object these drugs can make all ideas of order crumble in a sort of ontological slapstick. But pleasure may also intensify the poignancy of a phenomenon's isolation in space, time, or both. LSD, for example, seems prone to provoke this negative pleasure. Quanta of pleasure may be so vivid that their unavoidable transience causes sadness. This sensation does not require the intervention of drugs, of course.

Still, there is a persistent confusion in the West between pleasure and desire, leading to traditions that hold that pleasure is anti-intellectual, and even damaging to the intellect. One difference between pleasure and desire is that the *latter,* not the former, is antithetical to ethics and the intellect. If this is right, then it is also true that drugs of pleasure like marijuana and mescaline do not pose as great a threat to society or the individual as do the drugs of desire. To legislate against drugs of pleasure is like legislating against music, chess, golf, or any other form of play; it is arbitrary. At least with crack the law can claim to be combating a full-blown antiethics. But the conflation of pleasure and desire into an indiscriminate category of "highs" is at the heart of the fundamental and deliberate misunderstanding of drugs that Consumerism requires for its privileging of the commercial subject-object relationship above all others.

Drugs
6   and
Thinking

There is a Buddhist proverb that
goes: "The mind is like a wild monkey."
When consciousness is idling, disengaged from
any particular task, its attention tends to jump from
branch to branch in capricious patterns. Any systematic and
orderly movement from one to another can only be the result of
deliberate discipline and effort. This may take the rudimentary form
of a meeting's agenda or a list of phone calls to be made, or it may be
a grand ideological scheme like Marxism or Christianity that tries to
provide a strong central trunk for all the monkey's business. Whatever degree or kind of ordering is deemed necessary to constitute
"thought," there is general agreement that the monkey must somehow be trained to take its branches in a certain order. This training
can be given majestic names like acculturation or education or even
civilization, but there is never much accord on the right way to
orchestrate the process. Profound differences on how to school the
monkey have fueled the ferocity of recent debates on pedagogy, and
the increasingly politicized controversies over university require-
ments and curricula.

In the rhetoric of abstinence, (undifferentiated) drugs are said to
undermine *any* ordering of consciousness, causing the mind to
become "wild" again. Virtually all psychoactive substances except caffeine, nicotine, nootropics, and some antidepressants are widely held
to disorganize thinking, thereby endangering education and culture
itself. The focus on children in drug-war initiatives like DARE is a
product of this assumption: that drugs keep the monkey wild, and if
that simian isn't trained in youth it will remain feral for life. Such a
mind is "blown" or "killed" in its ability to accept and promote order,
but it may be alive and dangerous in other ways. Fear of the irrational,
the "uncivilized," especially when it is projected onto young people,
provides the emotional ambience of the drug war, and a good deal of
its imagery. The wild monkey of the mind becomes less innocent
when it makes its capricious leaps in the grip of drug desire.

I want to consider the narrowest and broadest paradigms of thinking, as if that could make the others fall into place. The narrowest I can imagine is logic, which for centuries was enshrined as a kind of metasyntax governing the organization of sentences into arguments. Logic exerts the tightest control over the monkey's motion. Ideally it would predetermine each new leap by the sequence of leaps that have come before. For this purpose it establishes syllogisms, which are templates of permissible movement from branch to branch. Excluding emotion or any other extraneous interest, it wants to be able to label lines of reasoning right and wrong, as if thinking could become a precise science. And in fact the technical study of logic resembles nothing so much as mathematics. At the same time, logic is completely neutral about the content of thought. Its templates should apply to the elaboration of the most heinous blasphemy as much as to close philosophical reasoning.

Are there drugs that destroy logic? Or do certain psychoactive chemicals so warp its traditional templates that its claim to neutrality is undermined? Here again, there are profound differences among the various substances known loosely as drugs. Some apparently abridge logic's patient connectors, causing the deletion of middle terms whose sequencing is the bone and blood of argumentation. In the case of psychedelics, there appears to be a teleological race, a rush to reach sweeping conclusions without the labor of logical development. The user has the *experience* of achieving enormous metaphysical insights by posing a question and then, in two or three steps, reaching a conclusion of such startling and revolutionary import that it verges on the inexpressible. The abridgment of intervening steps seems justified in light of the weightiness of the outcome—the logical end justifying the means, as it were. The result is like a connect-the-dots puzzle whose solver, seeing the intended course of the line, skips from number 12 to number 23, approximating but not duplicating the intended contour. Soon the picture is completed, but without the detail of the design. A generality is traced, but like all generalities it may assume the grandeur of a universal. The illegitimacy of this telescoping becomes apparent if the user attempts to record the results in a sentence or two. As logic's syntax disintegrates, so does language's, and the conclusion feels too complicated to record in full. If it is recorded at all, the likelihood is that it will read like gibberish the following morning.

With cannabis drugs, whimsical steps give reasoning a cavalier quality, introducing extraneous variables as if they followed necessarily. Distorted reasoning is one of the commonest traditional devices of jokes and humor in general, and the propensity of pot smokers to break into uncontrollable laughter is often a result of pretzel logic leading to hilariously unexpected conclusions. The progression from A to B may be effected not by the obedience of the two propositions to some template that orders them to follow each other, but instead by puns, non sequiturs, or obscure and distant correlations. Reasoning forms knots, obsessive pursuits of linguistic and associative connections that possess only the most local excitement. Where psychedelics give the user the sensation of reaching cosmic conclusions, cannabis drugs can produce trains of inference that simply lose steam and eventually stop dead in their tracks.

Alcohol erodes the dispassionate and disinterested nature of inference by dissolving it in emotion, by breaking down barriers between thought and feeling. This can power the most trivial ratiocination with an urgency far beyond its importance. In fact it is symptomatic of alcohol's dangers that a disagreement about the proper next step in a syllogism can end in fisticuffs. Alcologic quickly abandons the supposed neutrality of reasoning, and with it all necessity in the progression from A to B. By this suffusion of feeling contraries cohabit and inconsistencies pile up. If the line of thought had any teleology to begin with, the user may strive to reach that point regardless of any obstacles that logic may throw in its path. This drug's hostility to logic is perhaps the most complete and intractable.

The drugs that appear to be the most transparent for cognition—tobacco and coffee—are usually harmless to or even beneficial for logical thought. The family of nootropics—piracetam, Hydergine, choline, ginseng, and the like—are used primarily because they are supposed to enhance memory and logical functioning. They too are almost completely transparent. It may be that this transparency is salutary because it mimics the disinterestedness of logic, permitting intellectual activity with a minimum of distraction. In this the nootropics differ from the amphetamines, which were once used widely for stamina in intellectual labor. At small doses they appear to aid logical thought, but they tend to make the labor too interesting in and of itself.

The effect of stimulants on logic changes through their three stages of toxicity. In the first stage, the user relishes the careful development of an argument from point to point. One of the great difficulties in discouraging the use of cocaine and amphetamines arises from the fact that the people who most value orderly thought feel that it is being reinforced and even congratulated by the early action of the drug. During the first stage users can work productively, and perhaps accomplish more than they otherwise would. In the second stage, however, there is a tendency to get lost in the minutiae of logical steps so completely as to forget the argument's teleology. The realization of the enormous number of steps to be covered causes the user to talk or write faster, and hurry to process these steps as quickly as possible. When the user loses sight of the general aim of the argument, attempts to recapture it may lead to meandering, pausing, and asking listeners (if there are any, by this time) how this point was reached. In the third stage the number of possible continuations is so vast that no one of them could possibly be chosen above all the others, and the user sinks into the thoughtlessness of pure desire (or despair).

Syllogistic thought is so artificially rigid that it is quite brittle, and apt to break when subjected to powerful outside forces that shake its delicate disengagement. But these outside forces need not be drugs. Being in love or in mourning, or suffering from a physical or psychological malady, might be enough to disrupt it as utterly as that third martini does. It is nonetheless hard to escape the conclusion that drugs are among these disruptive forces. But does the hostility of some drugs to logic also entail hostility to *all* rational activity? How useful is a syllogism as a criterion of thought? Is there such a thing as reason without logic? Does the defeat of logic necessarily entail the defeat of the intellect as a whole?

For better or worse, postmodern thought is more accustomed to alogic and fragmentation than earlier Western thinking. The fear of error is accordingly diminished, since truth is no longer a fixity. Seeing the world as a plurality of discrete and hermetic discourses opens the possibility that thinking may take place in language environments that are organized by a potentially infinite number of internal systems that may or may not resemble logics. By this standard it is feasible to see the changes wrought in logical thinking by various drugs as resulting in another group of equally valid narrative structures. The absolute identification of thought and language that characterizes postmodern philosophy would then presumably necessitate a rhetorical analysis of each such state of consciousness, or of each drug. From a sociological perspective, adherents of one or another of these heterologics would then become demographic subgroups in an increasingly diverse world. Something like this is depicted in William Gibson's novels, where users of a particular drug become a social heterocosm, like an ethnicity or a religious sect or a street gang or a political party.

Those who believe that thought and language are identical do not regard the monkey's preverbal leaps as thinking, and by denying it that designation fall into a tautology: only syntax creates thought, and thought is recognizable only by syntax. Vague and functionally interchangeable words like "mind," "reason," and "intellect" can be clarified by some proposition like "the phenomenal apparition of consciousness is language." This can be codified into doctrine (the Word or Logos) or taken simply as the development of a grammar that orders and valorizes what might otherwise be nothing more than the grunting of beasts. Language is clearly intended to save us from the body. Its manifestation in speech is as a perennial outflow of air from flesh, formed by a voice synthesizer located close to the brain. Its manifestation in print promises permanence, even eternity, as an alternative to the brevity of physical life. Print is another physicality, a second body that does not change and therefore cannot perish. Audiorecorded language has a limited temporal existence, but it can live that short life over and over an infinite number of times. Language videocast to satellites and back again is language that has momentarily escaped from the earth's own body.

If language is posed against the body, it follows that there must be a relationship between an acquired ethics and a learned syntax. If a drug restricts or simplifies the user's range of available verbal constructions, this is an indication that it is tilting the balance in the wild monkey's favor. It is often said in popular discourse that the use of drugs induces or constitutes "immoral behavior," and if certain drugs do in fact compromise the intellect then it follows that ethics itself is endangered; for reason—the intellect—is the only impediment to the direct translation of desire into action. This formulation could just as easily be made in Freudian terms: if drugs erode the superego, then the id threatens to become identical with the ego, so that either civilization is imperiled or the drug user is maladjusted to it. The same result could be foreseen if drugs strengthened desire so as to enable it to overrun the intellect.

Conflict between drug desire and rational scruples may be found even with the most transparent drugs, such as nicotine, which both users and nonusers agree "does nothing" but which is at the same time extremely difficult to give up, perhaps more so than heroin. Tobacco's deleterious effects on health are so widely acknowledged that cigarette packaging carries warnings detailing them and suggesting that the user abandon the drug. Yet tobacco smokers plainly find the desire to keep smoking more than a match for whatever opposition the rhetoric of labeling can muster. In no other case (except for the more recently introduced warnings on alcoholic beverages) is the conflict of desire and language so graphically displayed. The brevity of these admonitions tries to digest libraries full of medical literature into a single sentence. As if so brief and direct a piece of rhetoric could be arrayed against all drugs, on this model "Just Say No" was contrived as the portmanteau antidrug slogan of the 1980s: it is the simplest possible distillation of the syntactic opposition to desire. "Just" emphasizes that very simplicity; "Say" underlines the reliance of reason on formulated language; and "No" carries the traditional message of reason in the face of desire. It is the voice of a child's conscience enforced by police and soldiers and the full brunt of public language and the law.

But how *do* the various drugs affect language? Here again there is a dizzying range of possibilities, too many factors to be taken into consideration. Probably some drugs do affect language, not only changing the tempo of thought and utterance but altering sentence structure as well. In some cases syntax is simplified to its most basic elements; in other cases sentences become more and more complex; in still others silence reigns and nothing more; and sometimes there is no discernible change. We could make a list of which does which, but that would be a misleading exercise. Too many variables would have to be introduced. First there is the question of an individual user's pre- or extradrug language group, by which we mean not only his or her native tongue but also any professional, class-based, or ethnocultural universe of discourse. Then there are questions of the individual's proficiency or dexterity within her or his group(s). And then, of course, there is the question of which drug has been administered, and how much of it for how long, with this factor squared or cubed to account for simultaneous administrations of multiple drugs. Finally, we would have to consider the specific sociolinguistic situation, including the interaction of many people, each one of which would have to be appraised for all of these variables. Here again we face the garden of forking paths, the empirical chess game with infinity that always ends in checkmate.

So discouraging a realization undermines generalizations about the "effect of drugs on language." To say that drug discourse falls between the extremes of silence on the one hand and that of asyntactic babble on the other is really only to describe the possible range of all language itself. To assert that people under the moderate influence of amphetamines talk more rapidly, or that marijuana users talk more slowly, is not to say anything about what these users talk *about*, or what kind of vocabulary and syntax they use. Furthermore, there is no reason to suppose that these alterations would take place in every case. An empirical survey, if one were possible, could be made to provide a counterexample to any hypothesis.

A putatively narrower approach would not necessarily remain narrow. It might be instructive to study drug-specific vocabularies among certain groups of users, for example, but this would almost certainly implode the inquiry, entertaining though it might be. An analysis of the specialized terminology of English-speaking marijuana smokers, say, might reveal something about the sort of consciousness induced by the drug. It would certainly be possible to collect words for a marijuana cigarette—joint, doobie, reefer, mezz, splif, number, blunt, bone, stick, and so on—and study the connotative fields they generate. There would surely be something to learn from this, perhaps even an inkling of the drug's action as it is interpreted in this special lexicon. Promising though this approach may be, it could illuminate such vocabularies only by reference to others. But which others, out of the plethora of available language universes? And are the available ones the *only* ones? And what language would the analyst use to analyze the language? And how would that choice bias the inquiry?

No matter which strategy is deployed, the best that can be hoped for is a partial insight into a microscopic bit of the question. And so most vocabularies used for discussing drugs presuppose a conclusion, like the discourses of law enforcement or the social and medical sciences. But as long as they are predicated on the antithesis of "drugs" and "thinking" they are on shaky ground, since both terms of the antonym are indeterminate. If logic serves as too narrow a criterion, so language is too broad. The condition of being high on a drug is not a static one. The high has its history and immediacy, and is no more likely to freeze than other any state of consciousness. Similarly, thinking is a process that runs through that special case of *chronos* known as "logical time." At various times these two processes—being high and thinking—can pass through antithetical phases, but at other times they may be harmonious. It is possible to think about being high, or to get a kind of high from the exhilaration of reasoning.

Drugs,
7 Regression,
and Memory

If there has been so much effort-
ful writing on drugs, it is in part because
writers tend to overcompensate in various ways
for taking up the subject at all. There is often a half-
conscious desire to prove to the reader that the narrator is not
now and has never been, or at least is no longer, a drug-using Other,
but a peer who somewhat abashedly happens to know something
about, well, this. It is rather like confessing that there is syphilis in
the family; one would never do so unless it were cured long ago.

Often the quickest way to accomplish this simultaneous assertion
and denial of one's text is to express disgust and regret at ever having
had anything to do with psychotropics. So Charles Baudelaire condemns opium and hashish while writing lengthily about them, and
Henri Michaux presents himself as loathing every one of his psychedelic experiences—making the reader wonder why he keeps enduring them. The "I snorted the house" narrative so popular in the late
1980s is part of this tradition. In all of these cases the writer aims for
a complementary deconstruction and reconstruction of his or her
own truthfulness in order to set up a moral paradigm, playing simultaneously on the reader's presumed double interest in "sin" and
redemption. This presumption makes these confessions dull, since
none of them is grounded in anything but a supposition of regret:
that all of us are sorry for our misdeeds, and that all of us are therefore sympathetic to other transgressors because they are like ourselves, even if our own sins are not specifically the sins of having used
drugs and enjoyed them.

Given the guilty magnitude of many of these literary tracts on
drugs, it is noteworthy that the most moving and heterodox text of
"drug memory" is only three pages long: the "Author's Note" that
concludes Philip K. Dick's novel *A Scanner Darkly*.[1] In it Dick
identifies the drug user's motivation as a willful regression to childhood, and an ominous aspect of childhood at that—its inability to
recognize danger while in the thrall of play.

This has been a novel about some people who were punished entirely too much for what they did. They wanted to have a good time, but they were like children playing in the street; they could see one after another of them being killed—run over, maimed, destroyed—but they continued to play anyhow. We really all were very happy for a while, sitting around not toiling but just bullshitting and playing . . . There is no moral in this novel; it is not bourgeois; it does not say they were wrong to play when they should have toiled; it just tells what the consequences were. . . . If there was any "sin," it was that these people wanted to keep on having a good time forever.

He then gives, by first names only, a list of casualties:

To Gaylene	deceased
To Ray	deceased
To Francy	permanent psychosis
To Kathy	permanent brain damage
To Jim	deceased
To Val	massive permanent brain damage
To Nancy	permanent psychosis
To Joanne	permanent brain damage
To Maren	deceased
To Nick	deceased
To Terry	deceased
To Dennis	deceased
To Phil	permanent pancreatic damage
To Sue	permanent vascular damage
To Jerri	permanent psychosis and vascular damage

and so forth . . .

This clinical list includes, by his earlier admission in the text, himself, the third from the end. In comparison with the conclusiveness of the others' fates, Phil's pancreatic damage seems like a light sentence. Nonetheless it establishes the narrator as a voice of the dead and unconscious, shouldering the trope of "I alone have returned to tell you." (In fact, Dick lived only a short time after this 1977 novel; he died in 1982 from a stroke that was probably related to his long-standing amphetamine habit.) Side by side with his metaphor of street children a nostalgic military analog is running: "In Memoriam. These were comrades whom I had; there are no better. They remain in my mind, and the enemy will never be forgiven. The 'enemy' was their mistake in playing." Dick, like a post-Nietzschean theorist of tragedy, is refuting the equation of hamartia (fatal flaw) with sin, presenting it instead as an error in judgment.

Still, there is something uncomfortable in the way these metaphoric layers finally meet. The enemy is not drugs, nor are these soldiers victims merely because they fought on the wrong side in the War on Drugs. The fallen, instead, are soldiers of *play*. That they "remain in my mind" has the double force of memory and internalization. As the narrator internalizes them, it becomes clear that their tragedy has been "played" when it ought not to have been: the drama shouldn't have been put on in the first place. There shouldn't be a choice between drugs/death and not-drugs/life. There ought to be a world of joy and play, a neo-childhood, accessible to all and not punishable by the forfeiture of health or life itself.

Play and war are joined this way only in tragedy. But if the conventional tragic hero distinguishes himself or herself by individuation and by entering a realm of conflict and war, Dick's tragic heroes distinguish themselves by sacrificing their individuality and immersing themselves in the danger of the play itself, embracing a choric anonymity as they lose their last names and are drawn into the centripetal annihilation of "the play's the thing." The first-name-only relationships of young children are revived, and the chorus closes tightly to encompass them. By knowing only the last name of "Phil" on the list of the fallen, we are aware that all of them must once have been fully named. Unlike real children in their first childhood, these tragic children have chosen—by an error in judgment, to be sure—to return to a world of play potentiated by the drugs they take. By moving against the flow of conventional chronology, they are *contra naturam*, heterodox, and Other.

It is characteristic of many types of drug experiences that they entail a revision of temporality, whether a speeding or a slowing, or a dislocation of the user in the unfolding matrix of time. But Dick's view of the matter identifies this temporal dislocation specifically with a conscious, willful, and usually fatal retreat from adulthood. In *A Scanner Darkly*, a drug called Substance D causes the individual user to schism (slowly and eventually) by severing the left and right brains and granting autonomy to each. This is a figure for regression, for the renunciation of the whole complex of individuation that is called "adulthood"—including surname, productive labor, and concern for self-preservation. The characters in the novel are, therefore, all very partial. "I myself," Dick writes, "I am not a character in this novel; I am the novel." And so the narrator establishes the author as the hypothetical totality where all the novel's fragments are united. But then the narrator goes on to list the author among the casualties.

Regression is not simply a developmental failure, the retardation of psychological growth at a certain moment in an individual history of consciousness. Instead, it is an antichronology, a withdrawal from an advanced to a less advanced stage of maturation. In the involuntary world of mental illness, it often marks an unconscious but calculated return to the point where development began to go wrong, as if the patient could, by revisiting that crossroads, correct whatever went wrong and resume growing in the right direction. Like a physical symptom, like a fever, regression is an impulse toward healing, even if that impulse can be (considered) deadly in a different and unexpected way. But the *voluntary* regression of drug use attacks the holy principles of Progress and Development. Adulthood is found to be an accommodation to a world of toil and compulsion. In the reversal of development, then, there may be a restoration of the free play of cognition, desire, and intellect that characterizes the less developed consciousness of children.

In *The Doors of Perception*, Aldous Huxley argues that psychedelic drugs can cleanse cognition to restore some of its infantile immediacy. In the work of William Burroughs, and particularly in *Naked Lunch*, drugs are seen as stripping away the civilized mannering of desire, reducing social *inter*actions to the arrangement of libidinous or drug *trans*actions, thus returning the user to a state not unlike a baby's polymorphous perversity. But the regressive content of much drug use need not be elaborated so grandly to be obvious. A smoker is visibly fixating in orality. A beer drinker is still pulling at a nipple, as is a coke snorter, mutatis mutandis. Drug shooters and coke smokers are aiming for the earliest kind of erotic experience, full-body rushes detached from any particular organ or orifice. The fact that heroin may negate genital sexuality and that other drugs like the stimulants may sometimes deflect it to oral, anal, or "full-body" expressions is clear enough evidence for proposing regressive theories.

This Freudian recitation, like all truisms at least partly true, is also incomplete. It may also be disingenuous. It could be incanted to scold drug users for being babies, to order them to grow up (or to send them to boot camps). But expressed in language more distant from the clinic's, there is clearly something in the drug user's character that refuses the labor, fatigue, jadedness, and cynicism of adulthood. A person high on a psychedelic, for example, moves from object to object in the thrall of transient fascinations not unlike an infant's. A stimulant user lying back-down during oral sex flails like a baby on the changing table. A drunken party can resemble scaled-up preschool play. The question lies not so much in the existence of these analogies, but in their motivation. If drug use is a voluntary regression, why does a user want to move backward to an earlier phase of development?

One answer is simply resistance to adulthood in a society enslaved by a remorseless work ethic and an economy where unceasing labor is not enough to ensure survival. The same society, however, observes the converse: the more desperate adult life becomes, the more Americans romanticize childhood and indulge their children, even if this indulgence only encumbers their adulthood with yet more labor. In the depression of the early 1990s, when virtually all businesses suffered significant declines in profits and volume, manufacturers and retailers of toys and child-care products reported stable or even increased levels of activity. The worse the world becomes, the more parents who are capable of shielding their children are inclined to do so. The result is a perpetuation of what is really a *pre*-Freudian view of childhood's innocence.

This "toyland" syndrome, where early life is viewed as a privileged state of being, affects the adults who believe in it just as profoundly as it affects their offspring. The supposedly "normal" adult response to it is to deny oneself in order to give the children everything. Childless adults are always assumed to want children, and are made to feel incomplete or selfish without them. Obviously this sentimentalizing is promoted by advertising for children's products, as well as by a variety of conservative social forces that wish to control the adult population by guilt and an exaggerated sense of familial responsibility (as well as by overwork). One possible subversive response to this privileging of childhood is to want to return to it oneself, or at any rate to incorporate into the misery of grown-up life some element of play. The word "recreation" synopsizes this feeling, suggesting as it does some kind of rebirth or redevelopment. In the glossy magazine version, this means playing *along with* the children:

taking them to theme parks, bowling, circuses, and so forth, and sharing the kids' supposed delight in these templates of fun.

At the same time, during the 1980s a great deal of publicity was given to various threats against this reasserted sanctity of babyhood. Photographs of missing children were reproduced on the packaging of many products, principally milk (the food most commonly associated with infants). Sexual abuse and violence directed against children were publicized ritually on the evening news, as if these things had never happened before. Mutant types of baby "others," like "crack babies," "AIDS babies," "welfare babies," and "children of children," were depicted ceaselessly as reminders of the disgraces that follow when the adult world intrudes into the Edenic gardens of infancy. Antidrug advertising tried to achieve maximum effectiveness by continually reducing the age of purported victims: twelve, ten, eight. Presumably this concentration of media-generated information and imagery, accompanied by horrifying statistics about infant mortality and malnutrition in the "Third World," was intended to augment the value of childhood by showing it to be imperiled from all sides.

As it pertains to drugs, there is a sharp paradox at the heart of this apparent campaign on behalf of children. On the one hand, drugs are consistently represented as threats to the competence of parents as well as to the mental, physical, and pedagogical well-being of children themselves. On the other hand, drugs are shown as an abrogation of maturity and a retreat into the irresponsibility of childhood. What reconciles the paradox is the implicit notion that adults should be adults and children should be children, so that any intrusion of adulthood into children's lives is as lamentable as any manifestation of irresponsible or childlike behavior among adults. The wall between these stages of being is supposed to be impenetrable. For this reason teenagers, as transitional beings, are the focus of considerable attention just as they were in the 1950s, the era of "juvenile delinquency."

Teenagers are thought to be especially vulnerable to drugs because they are caught in a developmental limbo from which there is no real escape. They cannot be adults and live on their own, but they needn't be cared for constantly like babies. Their manifestations of adult behavior—carrying guns or having sex—are viewed with horror. Lacking the economic basis for adulthood, they are prone to use drugs out of a feeling that since they are condemned to childhood anyhow, they might as well try to prolong its playfulness. The danger attributed to this impulse lies in the fact that although teenagers cannot be adults, they can still perform some adult acts like sex and driving, but being sealed in childhood cannot perform them with adult responsibility, as part of an integrated and laborious life. This combination of drug regression and adult capacity leads to the images of disaster so familiar to viewers of television news: traffic wrecks, overdoses, botched abortions, disappearances.

The traditional lament of adolescents is that there is "nothing to do"; that is, there are no immediate adult options when childhood activities have receded into the past. There are no social structures like nightclubs; there are no homes of their own to entertain in; there are few opportunities for civic engagement. What social platforms do exist have been constructed by adults: youth organizations, drop-in centers, no-alcohol concerts, and the like. Drugs present themselves as something autonomous to do, a complex of quasi-adult behaviors that encompass the perquisite autonomies of childhood. For teenagers, drugs are regression and progression at once. The point is that drugs cannot literally return the user to infancy. What they do is to establish a second and voluntary childhood that has significant differences from the first. Because adolescents are still adept at being children, they can adjust quickly to this neo-infancy, and do so in a different and less critical way than a thirty-year-old executive using cocaine for the first time. This is part of the template fear: it is easy for teenagers to enter and navigate the drug world, so much so that the adults in their life may not even be aware that they are doing it. Antidrug propaganda is like missing-children pictures in this regard: the children have been taken to some unknown and unrecognizable place by a sinister and invisible stranger, so that one doesn't even know how to begin looking for them. This world is an unperceivable noumenon for anxious parents, a place where they cannot see their children growing, and where parental influence is replaced by alien values. It is a place where their intimates become Others.

This standard scenario of fear has an adolescent socializing with older people, mainly older men, as she or he becomes involved with drugs. There is, in the antitemporality of drug use, a certain disregard for chronological age as an important determinant of character, as long as someone sells or shares the goods. By the same token, association with the denizens of the drug world may involve knowing people of other ethnicities, classes, races, and sexual orientations than those of the parents and their social circle. It is assumed that the love of drugs violates every conventional social boundary line. And so "drugs" becomes a code word for the child first associating with and then turning into the Other, and triggers parental fears of their once-dependent infant becoming independent. What runs through this skein of public imagery is not regression, then, but the opposite: the prospect of premature adulthood.

So which is it? Both, perhaps. Regression and prematurity are both temporal dislocations; drugs promote temporal dislocations; therefore . . . "Drugs," in that undifferentiated usage that renders discussion nebulous, make children of adults and adults of children, dissolving the supposedly impermeable barrier between the human ages and taking with it the legal fictions that embellish it: majority and minority, the age of consent, the age of responsibility for criminal actions, the drinking age, and so forth. This is more than a simple disruption of *social* categories. It represents an attenuation of every kind of order and value.

One mutation of fear about children growing up is that they may adopt a value system greatly disparate from that of their parents. Certainly an early involvement with drugs would be likely to precipitate this process, since nearly all drugs (and this is one of the few things they have in common) tend to valorize and ritualize the processes of their own acquisition and administration. The value that drugs acquire with habituated use may be strong enough to replace or at any rate *dis*place the values inculcated during childhood. "Straight" or sober consciousness, empty signifier though it may be, is easy to associate with family morality. In fact, one of the attractions of drug use for adolescents is that it provides a clear, immediate, and incontrovertible alternative to Mom and Dad's musts and mustn'ts. Once a chemical commitment has been made, the user's fear may be that without drug *x* or drug *y* she or he will revert to parental rules. This is true for older users as well. The material existence of psychotropic substances, and the physical effects they potentiate, lend them a kind of objectivity that something so murky as a "value system" can never quite achieve.

A mirror image may be found in the figure of an older user regressing in some unseemly way. The sight of Silenus as a superannuated reveler disgusts Pentheus in Euripides' *Bacchae,* just as a drunken "young-old man" horrifies Aschenbach in Thomas Mann's *Death in Venice.* Those who mistrust pleasure as a human legitimacy find it the most reprehensible in people old enough to know better. Regression as a psychoanalytic concept may be a rational hypothesis to be considered and tested, but as a series of images it is something else altogether. What rises to the mind's eye partakes of the horror of diapers for the incontinent geriatric: an unholy and entirely ghastly mixing of ages, but this time under the aegis of delight. The physical and behavioral similarities of infancy and extreme old age are often noticed, but this seems to strengthen the resolve to keep them rigorously separate. The notion that they might be one and the same is profoundly disturbing, closing life's apparent linearity into a circle.

When nonusers think about drugs, or when ex-users remember, they may experience some of this autonomic revulsion. People under the influence do not act their age, and so much social order depends precisely upon acting one's age. So much of our identity now comes from demographics. We define ourselves by age, weight, ethnicity, income, and other griddings. A force like a high, powerful enough to render all that unimportant, would imperil the template values that societies depend on for survival. Each drug entails its own order, an order certain to deviate in some way from boilerplate consciousness. When a user subscribes to one of these heretical orders, it is with an implicit rejection of the parental (or, should we say, ancestral) world. From a conventional perspective, an undifferentiated "drug world" exists just over the visual horizon, and by squinting hard at it there arise images of a complete meltdown of values and categories, images of young and old in one another's arms, of inexpressible pleasure somehow finding its hideous expression, of miscegenation, of wasted time and lost labor, of appetite that cannot discriminate among its objects.

So the problem is not regression but transgression. Just as it makes no sense to discuss "sin" without reference to any particular sins, so it makes no sense to talk about "drugs" indiscriminately. There is no single Dionysian landscape, but an infinite branching of possibilities. The interdiction of this discussion during the "Just Say No" era has reinforced the general hysteria about drugs, which, like all hysteria, is inflamed by ignorance of what it fears. However moving Dick's paean to regression may be, there are ways to explore this subject that avoid such reductions even as they also avoid the conflation of transgression with sin. The word's forebear *transgredior* means "to cross over." It does not suggest that it is wrong to do so, nor does it indicate where one is crossing from or to. It is wrong to cross over into this particular unknown with a single paradigm, since consciousness is so malleable a substance that it will fit every method, and be encompassed by none of them. Inconsistency is the only hope. We can learn more about this subject from stumbling around then we can by traveling in a straight line.

This brings us to the question of memory. A common side arm of the antidrug crusades has been the speech given by the reformed user who wishes to deter others from following in his or her regrettable footsteps. Here memory is raised ostensibly as an occasion for contrition. But how often the speaker involuntarily relishes the recollection. The gray face of mea culpa moves forward over the lectern, and its eyes flare into life as it recounts with barely bottled delight some anecdote of excess and recklessness. What is happening is that drug memory is exaggerating the action of memory itself: the selection of certain incidents for revivification through narrative. "The Past," wrote Vladimir Nabokov, "is a constant accumulation of images. It can be easily contemplated and listened to, tested and tasted at random, so that it ceases to mean the orderly alternation of linked events that it does in the large theoretical sense. It is now a generous chaos out of which the genius of total recall . . . can pick anything he pleases."[2] The difference between memory and drug memory is simply that the latter's selection of events is influenced by the superadded memory of being high. The recollecting user or former user is likely to have this choice of images affected by a second kind of memory: the metamemory of the high itself.

The images that comprise memory decay at different rates. Last summer's weeds are all but gone when the snow melts, but a tree trunk takes years to decompose, and a boulder seems to last forever. The mental snapshots of a year ago are abundant and varied, but those of ten years past are few, and usually (differently for each rememberer) of a certain class. A commonly privileged class of slow-decaying mnemonics are erotic incidents, and these are similar in some ways to drug memories in their resistance to the erosion of time. They may also bring in their wake more detail and atmosphere than an anerotic recalling of a journey, say, or a social event. There is a special reason to retain these photographs, an association, perhaps, with pleasure or desire. Drug memories also "bracket" cotemporal occurrences. To remember walking into a shopping mall in 1983 is one thing; to remember doing so while high on desoxyn is something more. For some people these memories are Technicolor while the rest are black-and-white. Charles Baudelaire's only happy memories were of early childhood, and the times he was high on opium.

But already there is an objection to this line of speculation. It seems as if I am about to argue that "drugs" (undifferentiated) are an aide-mémoire, rather than (as "everyone knows") the cause of forgetting what happened even last night. Alcohol in toxic doses often causes "blackouts," lapses in recollection that can be terribly frightening, causing the drinker to inquire how she got home, or wonder how he wound up sleeping where he did. This phenomenon can be accentuated when heavy drinking is accompanied by stimulant use, for this combination can cause revelers who by all rights should have passed out long ago to carry on for many additional amnesiac hours. These animated corpses move through the halls till dawn, when they drop, sleep, wake, and remember little. But the same users can probably remember in maudlin detail ancient binges of equal fortitude. Cannabis is also routinely accused of causing memory loss, particularly in young users, and it is blamed for faltering performances in school. The assumption is that the drug erodes the capacity for getting things by rote; the deeper, empiricist assumption is that education is primarily a matter of brute downloading. But the same drug can "privilege" the afterimage of a visit to an art museum, a concert, or a poetry reading.

Many propositions in the philosophy of drugs are self-contradictory, and this is one of them: most heavy users, regardless of which drug is in question, either forget almost completely, or can never forget at all. There is an affective contradiction in memory that lies at the heart of this paradox. Unhappy recollections—that grab bag of faux pas, mortuary, and error—are both painful and durable. They have a way of coming up, like undigested bits, with little prompting from the circumstances of the present. They make the rememberer wince, like a chronic physical pain that stabs with no discernible pattern of recurrence. But memories of happy occasions are not so purely what they seem to be. They bring with them their own kind of pain. A happy event remembered is at the same time equally unhappy, because it is gone. The pain of a painful memory may attenuate, but it never dies. The pleasure of a happy memory, on the other hand, is self-negating. The shades wandering the floor of the old Greek Hades had forgetfulness as the object of their quest. Blackout—what many of us fear most among the myths of death—was previsioned as a state of grace for them. Their condition is a metaphor of memory. They miss the sunlight, that is, the present. And lacking that light, memory is a constant reminder of their alienation.

As often as not, drug metamemory is experienced as a failure of forgetfulness. Since blackout, with certain drugs under certain circumstances, is held out as a possibility, remembering in spite of that potential grace can make the recollected material all the more painful. A *partially* blacked-out night, whose sequence of events must be reconstructed as if from architectural fragments, is especially prone to cause the user to wish that he or she remembered nothing. The border of the reconstructed image that memory displays is etched in a thick black line that protects it from erasure. It also has the effect of accentuating the removal of the image from its context—something that occurs anyway, but not so definitively as it does in pharmacological metamemory. The change the drug potentiated in the consciousness of the user while its chemistry lasted is reflected, mimicked in the mode of its remembering. A rose preserved in plexiglas is clear, but there are also roses laid in amber. The images left by metamemory have a suggestive discoloration that lends them a fine illusion of permanence, like a yellowed photograph half a century old. Their persistence is accentuated by the feeling that they ought to have been forgotten, that they should have been discarded or lost, but by surviving become almost indestructible.

Their fixity changes the landscape of the past. Where conventional memory puts all things up for revision, metamemory establishes indissoluble points that are not subject to the kinds of changes that narration always wreaks upon the past. If memory presents us with snapshots, these are the pictures that cannot be deleted from the album. Is this a good thing? Does metamemory tie the story of the self too closely to a certain class of experiences? Or does it accomplish the ancient poetical project of the quest for permanence? The steles in Philip Dick's potter's field work both ways at once. The "In Memoriam" keeps them fixed in our recall, but without last names they can never regain their individuation. In this way the images of metamemory lodge in recollection as both ineradicable and incapable of resurrection. They are "our" memories, but at the same time belong to a different and higher history that imposes them upon us whether we want them or not. The reformed user is therefore put in a position of accepting this with the attendant sense of loss, or of rejecting his or her own past, lock, stock, and barrel.

PART III

*Five
Drug
Studies*

The following group of studies is
not inclusive. The most obvious omission
is an essay on the opiates. I have felt unable to
write on this subject because I do not completely understand the way these drugs work. They have the reputation of
being soporifics, more or less, but this is simply not the case. There is
an element of stimulation to them, an excitement that comes of
being impervious to pain. There is a misapprehension that opiate
users cannot function in the world, and this too is untrue. I admit to
feeling a terrible respect for users of these drugs, particularly heroin,
because of the extraordinary sacrifices they make for gaining and sustaining their high.[1]

Thomas De Quincey dominated the literature of opium until the
advent of William Burroughs. De Quincey's laudanum landscapes
inform Baudelaire's and even Cocteau's. He constructs its etiology in
his depiction of an unhappy—really a horrifying—childhood, and he
provides the moral dialectic that characterizes so much of the literary
and popular drug narrative: that the extent to which the drug provides pleasure or surcease of pain is matched by the extent to which it
ultimately inflicts pain. He supplies all the *splendeurs et misères,* the
lavish constructionism and the abyss of contrition, that become the
genre's conventions. At the same time, he divulges a contradiction
that hints at the complexity of these drugs, and suggests an alternative way of reading them.

The intimacy of the opium eater's visions seemed to provide cor-
roboration for the nascent individualism of the late Enlightenment.
Opium's journey into the labyrinths of the unconscious proved in
time to be one of the hallmarks of Romantic imagination.[2] The
apparent autonomy of its hallucinations gave evidence of the existence of a transcendental realm, confirming the heterocosmic
impulses of neo-Kantian users like E. T. A. Hoffmann and Samuel
Taylor Coleridge. At the same time that the drug seemed to confer a
kind of objectivity on private dreams, there is in the content of these

visions a recurrent geometrical bent. A reader of "Kubla Khan" may spend a great deal of time trying to map out the shape and boundaries of the protagonist's domain. It is suggestive more of a neoclassical than an English garden, with the wilder manifestations of nature banished to its periphery. In his opium poetry, Baudelaire refers constantly to configurations of precious stones. I think it is possible that at the same time that use of opiates provided confirmation of an otherworldly individualism it kept alive the antithetical possibility that neoclassicism was right: that the mathematical recombining of beauty was something not to be written off easily by the new expressionism. The conflict between poet and philosopher in Coleridge is indicative of the same paradox, as are De Quincey's protestations of philosophical seriousness.

The mathematical and scientific side of the opiates was overlooked as long as the drug was invoked as part of the project of Romanticism. Only when William Burroughs posited heroin's "algebra of need" did this other side come to light again. The asexuality of heroin has frequently led to a kind of studious asceticism among its partisans. I have known junkies who were virtual encyclopedias of pharmacological information. Partly this is true because, as De Quincey points out, reading is a congenial activity during an opium high. The drug confers an ability to sit still and do one thing at a time, and can even encourage concentration. There is an orderliness to it that stands as a counterweight to its reputed flights of fancy. And that orderliness is only emphasized by the chaos that habituation often strews through the worldly lives of users. The fall from order into the shambles of quotidian life is one of standard motifs of literary opiation, from the knocking of the man from Porlock to Baudelaire's rendition of his wretched apartment in "La Chambre double." Even in Burroughs's work, a systematic social analysis governs the manifestations of his Boschian hells. "*Naked Lunch*," he wrote, "is a blueprint, a How-To Book."[3]

It is not only respect for the commitment of heroin users that deters me from writing on the subject. It is also that I am intimidated by the precision of their scholarship. Far from constituting a withdrawal from creative life, use of opiates can often potentiate great *formal* innovation in the arts, as evidenced in the work of Charles Parker, Charles Mingus, and John Coltrane as much as in the protean versatility of a Jean Cocteau or an Andy Warhol. But it can also be the dumb kick of silence, like the shot that killed Janis

Joplin. For all the vital external manifestations of opiate vision, that silence is solidly embedded at its core. And so Burroughs continues, "How-To extend levels of experience by opening the door at the end of a long hall. . . . Doors that only open in *Silence*. . . . *Naked Lunch* demands Silence from The Reader."[4] And that is all I am equipped to give it.

The essays that follow are predicated on the fiction that drugs are taken only in isolation from one another. The praxis of use testifies that someone doing a drug at any given moment is more than likely to be doing another drug at the same time. The last essay in this section investigates this problem, but in so doing doesn't quite invalidate its predecessors. Think of them as bracketings, as "as ifs."

8 Cannabis and the War against Dreams

But events took place in such a way
that the appearance of things touched me with
a magic wand, and I sank into a dream of them.
WALTER BENJAMIN   "Hashish in Marseilles"

Cannabis, a drug as protean as alcohol, always brings about some sort of fusion between cognition and dream. It never defeats the cognitive mechanism—as LSD, for example, can sometimes at least threaten to do. High on pot, a user can generally function adequately (and sometimes more than adequately) in the waking world of objects; can work, parent, soldier, write; can certainly even shop. But every object perceived under the influence has a simultaneous existence as dreamwork, and can be contemplated *even though* it can also be bought. However, the point of intersection between these discrete epistemological planes is extremely mobile; it can be fixed almost anywhere. This has made cannabis sativa an extremely difficult drug to understand. It has been called both "killer weed" and "the dropout drug."[1] It is associated etymologically with assassination (hashish) but for a time became a cultural emblem of peace and love. The reason for all this ambivalence is that cannabis is a drug that alters a *relationship* without predetermining that relationship's altered form. As such it is (along with the stronger psychedelics) an excellent example of a drug whose effects are almost completely user-constructed. The character of the user is not obliterated or standardized, as may be the case with stimulants, but remaining quite itself it responds to the social and physical contexts of the drug's administration. If a person smokes cannabis in a situation where violence is condoned or expected, violence will proceed as it would have anyway. If the user is expected to join others lying on a pile of pillows listening to records, that too will transpire according to anticipation. This explains why it is often difficult to know whether someone is high on pot or not—unless appearing or acting high is part of an individual user's particular construction of the experience.

Cannabis doesn't implode the world into the drug, as stimulants do, but instead remains a refracting lens through which phenomenal experience is accessible in all its range and complexity. Instead of breaking awareness down into discrete and discontinuous quanta as addictive drugs do, cannabis maintains, reinforces, and perhaps exaggerates the "Newtonian" model of consciousness as continuous waves. Lester Grinspoon, in his encyclopedic 1971 study *Marihuana Reconsidered,* cites several sources who note this "wavelike aspect." R. P. Walton in particular notes that marijuana induces "a continuous change between the dreaming and waking state, a lasting, finally exhausting alternation between completely different regions of consciousness; this sinking or this emerging can take place in the middle of a sentence."[2] Whatever cannabis does, then, it is not reductive. Given the enormous (or even quasi-infinite) number of possible experiences by different subjects over the range of all possible time, it is as difficult to generalize about the consciousness of a pot smoker as it is to generalize about all-possible-consciousness itself. This makes it hard to say what, in the abstract, the effects of cannabis are. Still, it is important to try to determine whether or not there is any common thread along this web that seems to spin in all directions at once.

First of all, with cannabis there are *subjective* changes in cognition, despite the fact that the inputs of the senses are still received and accurately ordered. The world is seen as if under a very clean pane of glass that distorts nothing but confers on phenomena a certain feeling of distance. This attractive alienation resembles the necessary strangeness of objects of beauty. It is a kind of estrangement that idealizes the object, or archetypalizes it. Every object stands more clearly for all of its class: a cup "looks like" the Platonic Idea of a cup, a landscape looks like a landscape painting, a hamburger stands for all the trillions of hamburgers ever served, and so forth. Even as this distancing seems to separate the user from the quotidian world, however, a second factor brings about a simultaneous reconciliation. This is a privileging of affective power, or the subject's attachment to the idealized object so created. The alienation of the seer from the seen is no sooner broached than it can be breached, and there is pleasure in this breaching.[3] This dialectical pattern of reconcilable estrangement—experiencing first a new distance and then a new relationship that closes the distance—is central to cannabis, and applies equally to the aesthete who smokes pot before going to the Guggenheim and to the hit man who reefs up before executing a victim. Cannabis's mutation of feeling toward the perceived world, then, does not alter the ethical and intellectual parameters that governed the user's behavior before the administration of the drug. This suggests that intellect plays only a small and secondary role in the transformations prompted by cannabis, although there is also the special case of the thinker who uses it to aestheticize and energize ideas, giving familiar concepts a suggestive distance.[4]

Some classes of sensory experience provide particularly good evidence for this pattern of contrary motions. The effects of marijuana on the audition of music were widely celebrated by users in the 1960s. Here the drug's usual pattern of estrangement and reconciliation is quite clear. First the fabric of the music comes apart, with each instrumental or vocal line momentarily isolated and alone, standing out in the sharpest clarity. Then, when the movements of the various parts have been made separately observable in this way, their relationship is freshly perceived on what feels to be a more complex level. A harmony greater than that of pitch alone seems to be developing; a harmony of purpose, timbre, and denotation replaces the narrower original technical unity. Music thus becomes spatialized, synesthetically displayed as a field with discrete vectors of energy moving through it. While much of the literature on the subject reports only a heightened sensitivity to sound—that is, an intensification of its unaltered order,[5]—what in fact occurs is more like a reordering that somehow exists side by side with the predrug arrangement without superseding it. This superposed order suggests an affinity among the senses and leads to descriptions of sound in visual terms. A similar interchangeability may develop among the other senses as well.

Synesthesia of this kind is a common symptom of cannabis intoxication. It seems to involve the reduction of sensory data to quanta that can be reformulated in ways slightly (though not completely) different from their original configuration. As Nathan Adler observes: "There also occur synesthetic crossovers from one sense to another so that, for example, one sees sounds as color and translates sensations from the dimension of one sense modality into another. Percepts of color, space, size, and time become deranged and intensified."[6] Adler's irate skepticism about drugs allows him to see the quantum nature of the new perception, the "digitizing" of sensory information that enables it to be downloaded through any of the senses, but not the possibility that synesthesia under cannabis may be as Baudelaire described it:

Like long echoes from far away which melt
Into a shadowy and profound unity,
Vast as night and light,
Odors, colors and sounds correspond.

Adler acknowledges the initial quantification but not the subsequent reassertion of unity.

The notion of a synesthetic "metasense" that underlies sight, sound, smell, taste, and touch is closely related to the process of archetypalization. Through the senses the user (paradoxically) feels as if he or she has obtained some consciousness of a "thing-in-itself" or transcendentally "real" object whose essence and existence do not depend upon the partial and incidental evidence of any particular sense, or indeed of the combined senses together. Awareness of beauty, which arises from the free play of the senses, and which permits some translucence from a noumenal world, works in much the same way without drugs. From this it is possible to deduce that the effect of marijuana on cognition is allied generally to aesthetics, and this helps to explain why it leaves ethics unaffected. The notorious moral detachment of the aesthete, who seeks to harmonize sensual input no matter whether it is by other criteria creative or destructive, loving or hateful, silent or violent, is not far from the ethical transparency of the cannabis user's contemplation. For this reason it is possible to attack cannabis from almost any moral viewpoint. For those who love work, pot makes people lazy. Those who love peace can always find a hashhead whose especial contemplation is of weaponry and slaughter. Those who love order can find pot users slovenly, while those who love disorder can find them obsessive.

Cannabis, then, permits the same sort of cognitive resynthesis as does aesthetic experience in general; that is, it brings about an alienation from perception followed in most cases by an affective reconciliation. It is also transparent as far as ethics and the intellect are concerned. But just as aesthetic play doesn't take place in a void of feeling, so the affective aspect of cannabis is the essential element in the attractiveness of the drug. Still, feeling is the most difficult element of consciousness to discuss. Because feeling appears at first gander to belong wholly to the subject, all discussion about it threatens to become subjective itself—or arbitrary. But certain physically fixed polarities of feeling suggest otherwise. There is, on the one hand, pain beyond the subjective, as the now quite scientific art of torture illustrates. Some things *must* be painful, regardless of the character and sensibility of the feeler. On the other hand, there is probably something like unavoidable pleasure—in orgasm, for example; for although orgasm can sometimes be delayed or avoided, once it begins it is almost impossible to undergo without pleasure, even if that pleasure is for whatever reason unwelcome and undesired. Between these quasi-absolute poles of pain and pleasure fall most of the mixes and gradations that comprise the life of the emotions.

By "digitizing" sensation, cannabis enables the user to assess the state of her or his feelings from instant to instant. In this way this family of drugs intensifies self-awareness even as it intensifies awareness of the world of and beyond the senses. There is a relentless self-monitoring in this intoxication. The moment opens up and takes on the characteristics of eternity, so that something found beautiful seems beautiful forever, and sadness or horror seems like eternal perdition. Contemplating death in this condition is probably closer to actually experiencing it than anything short of the event itself. Feeling is turned upon itself: how do I feel when I feel this way? The refraction of sensory input into this loop can turn autistic, particularly in very young users, and may cause learning difficulties because one cannot learn whatever feels bad. The user wants to take control of his or her consciousness, and what it contains at any given moment. The 1960s phrase of dismissal "Get out of my movie!" expresses this heightened stewardship of internal life. What offends must be avoided, and what pleases can be enjoyed instant by instant with contemplative exactitude. Pot smokers may be deemed antisocial or irresponsible because they are reluctant to tolerate duty and displeasure, or sometimes social niceties, if these things moil their state of mind. Dismissal of such burdens can be accomplished by the use of any of several dispositions: humor in its ability to distance the dire and the inevitable; a placidity related to meditation; or an active discourse that asserts what has become a kind of affective imperative.

Intellectual constructions and ideologies may go the way of imposed social obligation. Whether liberals, conservatives, or Stalinists are in power does not matter to distant trees or the sound of wind chimes blowing over the night water. The world of the senses is made mysterious by affective play, so that all explanations fall patently short of sufficiency, just as all interpretations necessarily fail to touch a dream's essence. The ability of cannabis to metamorphose quotidian experience into a synthesis of dream and wakefulness can apply to any sort of experience, from hard physical labor to making war to walking in the city to sitting still and observing a rural panorama. Just as one can dream anything, one can do anything while high on pot—so long as one acquiesces to it in some way. A worker who tokes up on lunch hour is not trying to avoid work, as the cliché suggests, but to do precisely the opposite: to make alienated labor bearable for a time by allowing a fascination with its physical details to override the boredom and futility that can become disabling if the worker allows them to, as she considers the work's reasons and purposes in relation to herself. Of course the worker may be more likely, if there is any choice, to do pleasant tasks rather than hated ones, or to make mistakes when the affective aspect of the experience comes in direct conflict with some other enforced order of things.

Nonetheless, the rhetoric of the industrial age still prevails, wherein a worker using cannabis is said to be unproductive, a student incapable of learning, a driver more prone to accidents. These conventions are relatively easy to maintain, but they no longer serve as accurate indicators of Consumerism's objection to the use of marijuana and related drugs. The real heterodoxy lies in the fact that cannabis's oneiric or aesthetically disinterested consciousness can momentarily detach the user from the consumerist matrix on which both the postmodern economy and its social order depend. It is for this reason that after a period of toleration that lasted through the 1970s, marijuana has been demonized anew by the law.

The economic foundation of marijuana use seems to reinforce the need for this renewed intolerance, for hemp is notoriously easy to cultivate. Although most pot smokers procure the drug from shadow retailers who in turn obtain their produce from domestic or foreign growers, all a user really needs is electricity and a closet, or an accessible patch of woods, to circumvent the commercial process altogether. In the 1960s pot smoking became a symbol of the counterculture's anticapitalist bias; the drug was *supposed* to be free. Rastafarian culture maintains this position to the present day, attaching the drug's contemplative properties to a political program derived from the thinking of Marcus Garvey. Increased aerial surveillance by state police and the National Guard during the past decade may have stopped some North American rural growing for individual use, but curtailing cultivation only drives users back into the black market. One wonders if this was its aim. In this way users are at least compelled to reenter a consumerist arena of some kind, even if an illegal one. The skyrocketing cost of marijuana during this period suggests that its economic nature has been redefined: from "free herb" to a luxury consumer item.[7] This metamorphosis aligns marijuana more closely with other drugs that cannot so readily be produced privately for individual consumption, and facilitates the notion that "drugs" are in some sense all the same. Like the convictions in the widely publicized illegal arms sales of the 1980s, the clampdown against pot smoking can then be understood as Consumerism policing itself, rather than Consumerism policing the world to protect it from anticapitalist "others" like Communists or neutrals. This reformulation is plainly in keeping with the changes necessitated by the end of the Cold War.

The result has been a secretiveness among marijuana users more profound than at any time since the 1950s. This return to silence seems particularly dramatic after the widespread tolerance for hemp smoking during the 1970s. The fact that none of the many medical and social problems ascribed to the drug during the long history of its suppression have proven to be valid or even consistent has reinforced the long-standing view among users that the laws against it are groundless and capricious. From this it can be extrapolated that all laws are equally arbitrary, so that a continuing feature of the cannabis subculture is an unshakable contempt for the authority of straight society and its metaphysics. Since the nature of the drug's effects is such that it does not encourage greed for its own consumption in the way that stimulants and (to a lesser extent) opiates do, pot smokers continue to represent an almost invisible political opposition. In the "Just Say No" climate of the 1980s, this opposition was prohibited from entering the political mainstream even under the guarantees of free speech, since a letter to the editor or membership in an organization like NORML was simply a provocation to the police to take notice. This led to new cycles of alienation and repression, since the harder the crackdown the greater the confirmation of the law's irrationality.

By smoking pot, the user enters a realm of illegality that, depending on that user's temperament and general attitude toward the law, may be frightening, titillating, radicalizing, or all three at the same

time. The fear that someone will detect, report, and punish this contemplative high enters into its internal makeup. If the fear of apprehension is strong enough, it can dominate the experience. But if the
user mistrusts authority and enjoys transgressing against it, and generally feels superior to good citizens who lack the courage to break
the law, then the drug's illegality can become a positive element of its
makeup. There is an old joke among pot smokers that legalizing it
would cause it to stop working. In the user's fantasy the minor
infraction of smoking marijuana can put her or him in the figurative
company of bank robbers and gunmen, or at any rate somewhere on
that side of the barrier. And once that sensation has been harbored, it
is true (as both proponents and opponents of toleration have
argued) that "respect for the law" per se cannot remain intact. The
internalization of this condition, especially during the high itself,
lends the experience some of the romance of outlaw life.

But since there is no *necessary* connection of cannabis to violent
crime, or to any breakdown of family life of the kind precipitated by
alcohol or stimulants, or to the escalation of medical costs or harm to
other people like that caused by alcohol and tobacco use, the illegality
of this group of drugs has become a sort of prolonged test case: can
some activity be permanently illegal simply because the law declares it
so, in the absence of any cogent rationale? The more one considers
this problem the more certain it becomes that it is not so much the
drug that must be outlawed as the antithetical state of mind that its
administration encourages. It is illegality itself that must be made illegal; this tautology, like all tautologies, is self-sustaining, and flinches
before no known logic. Yet the protean cannabis high varies so much
according to the cultural and individual construction of users that it is
necessary to conclude that it is its *potential* for allowing the user to
escape the consumerist worldview that must be interdicted. The
specter of a recent counterculture of mass contemplation must be
somehow unremembered, or revised into a trivial peccadillo of a generation's common past. Since there is no drug more susceptible to
user construction, one way to combat it is to obliterate its anti-
consumerist history. If, in the 1990s, there is no longer any such thing
as an aesthetic response that isn't expressed in a purchase, then there
can be no basis for constructing the marijuana high aesthetically. And
so the high loses its inherent character, and pot becomes just another
reason to put people in jail.

Another crusade of the 1980s was the War on Sex, precipitated by the advent of AIDS and an unprecedented increase in teenage pregnancies. This campaign was attached to the War on Drugs, since it is a constant truism that "drugs" (in that undifferentiating locution) cause inhibitions to crumble, leading to heightened sexual activity, lack of discrimination in the choice of partners, and carelessness about birth control and safe sexual practices. Yet early studies of cannabis found that it inhibits rather than encourages sexual behavior. "The Indian Hemp Drugs Commission of 1894 reported that hemp drugs have 'no aphrodisiac power whatever; and, as a matter of fact, they are used by ascetics in this country with the ostensible object of destroying sexual appetite.'"[8] More recent studies have shown that chronic cannabis use results in a sharp decrease in testosterone levels in male subjects, suggesting that for one gender at least long-term marijuana use could cause some loss of interest in sex.[9] Still, pot consciousness is apt to make the sight of a potential sexual partner more alluring as the gaze "feeds back" synesthetically into the promise of touch. The commonplace of the matter is similar to that so often put forward for cannabis's effect on taste or hearing: that it makes the sensation more intense, or renders the user more sensitive. As distinguished from drugs of desire like the stimulants, hashish and pot are more about the affective concomitant of an anticipated experience than about the privileging of sexual desire per se. Cannabis anticipates a sexual act in an aesthetic context; where and how it is hoped to transpire is more important and interesting than the fact of its happening, or than the previsioning of an intensified orgasm. The act itself is contradictorily described in clinical literature as lasting a shorter or longer time; as entailing the loss or prolongation of erection; or as making the participant more or less aggressive in performance.[10] What these results suggest is, once again, a high degree of user construction of the experience. Whatever a user would make of any sexual encounter will be true of a cannabis-influenced encounter, only more so. Like the sound of music under the influence, the complex of haptic sensations is likely to break up into discrete components. A fingernail down the thigh can be distinctly felt even though another finger may be depressing a nipple. But as with all user constructions under cannabis, the estrangement of experience can in good circumstances lead to its reintegration. In other words, cannabis can lead to the disintegration of sex into a plethora of unrelated sensations, but it is more likely to lead to a reintegration of that panoply into a unified experience that is aesthetically and affectively different from sex without the drug. One cannot sensibly think of this as "contemplative" or disinterested, since orgasm is the very epitome of interestedness. But even while the drama of desire and satiation is acted out, there is, once again, a descant of aesthetic play orchestrated out of the direct experience and superadded to physical sensations.

It may be that this prospect makes sex more attractive, and may therefore lead to promiscuity. But it is unlikely to lead to lack of discrimination in the choice of partners, since the sharing of flesh under these circumstances would subvert the aesthetic and atmospheric patina if attempted with a partner whom one would find repulsive under undrugged conditions. In the 1960s the ideological association of sex and drugs, particularly pot, was related to the other ideological pairing of love and peace. Pot was thought to lead to gentler sex, and the drug's affective enhancement of sex was supposed to approximate love, even if that love's duration were less than eternal. However unkind history has been to this line of argument, it is nonetheless reasonably certain that the cannabis drugs do not alter the user's sexuality in any appreciable way, neither in frequency of activity, nor quality of performance, nor choice of sexual partner. This is in sharp contrast to the erotic mutations of stimulant hypersexuality, which probably contributed to the spread of AIDS and syphilis during the 1980s.

All the authorities agree on one thing about cannabis: the cessation of its use causes no "physical withdrawal," but only some sort of adjustment to the end of a "psychological dependence." But there is something terribly wrong with this distinction, which appears to depend on an absolute division of mind and body. The "physiological withdrawal" of a heroin addict is accompanied by terrifying spiritual and psychological revelations, when ordinary consciousness is suddenly experienced as pain. Anyone who has ever been seriously ill can testify that the intellect, even in its most practical applications, is profoundly affected by a virus or bacterium that is ostensibly working only on bodily tissues. Any drug that passes the blood barrier into the brain to emulate a substance in the predrug chemistry is changing not only consciousness but also those neurological networks where flesh and spirit are delicately and mysteriously indistinguishable. Similarly, the supposedly "just psychological" stimulant crash is coincident with fatigue, headache, back pain, shaking extremities, and the inability to urinate or sleep. Those who use cannabis in isolated administrations are always delighted that there is no hangover; they usually evaluate it on the model of alcohol, and confuse the nature of those intoxications. But when hemp is no longer smoked or ingested according to a *long-standing* pattern, something happens that is neither exclusively psychological nor physiological; and what this is reveals something about the character of these drugs.

Regular marijuana smokers generally agree that when use discontinues night dreaming resumes. In other words, the synthesis between dreaming and waking that cannabis effects breaks down, and each of those modes of awareness returns to its prepharmacological nature. Often the sense of it is that night dreams are coming back with a vengeance, like a dam bursting, or more like a sewer backing up. The narratives and imagery of night dreams, which under the influence of cannabis spiced and colored waking life, now leave that waking untouched and reappear in the undeniable presentations of the unconscious. Those who believe that these manifestations of the repressed serve a hygienic purpose must then regard the cessation of cannabis as a return to health and normality. But there is also the possibility that repressed materials are repressed for a purpose: to remove from daily awareness their useless, constant, and crippling reminders of childhood, mortality, and forbidden sexual activity. Without putting a positive or negative valuation upon this change, it is still necessary to recognize that having gone through a period of rapprochement between dreaming and waking makes their renewed separation that much more problematic. To speak of a drug as having no withdrawal symptoms when that drug has so flagrantly surfaced and revealed what was, before the drug, an unexamined or "natural" relationship between consciousness and unconsciousness is obviously silly. The question then becomes whether the examined or the unexamined life is more worth living.

The revelations offered by any drug may or may not be welcome or valuable, may or may not empower the user, may offer knowledge or illusion. A reformed user of opiates or stimulants, for example, may look back upon the former habit with melancholy wisdom about human greed and obsession. A person forswearing cannabis looks back too, either with nostalgia for the integrated life of dream and waking, or with the sense that such a playful version of cognition is, in its regressive aspect, not a fit deployment for a maturity where dreams are only dreams and therefore ignorable, and where daily life's demands should be met without affect. It is said that once the back of a fine watch is opened for repair or examination it can never again run in the same way, for a fleck of dust will always lodge invisibly in the works and provide a stress, albeit incalculably small, to the functioning of the mechanism. So too when a drug opens the clockworks of consciousness for examination, that awareness thereafter becomes ever so slightly more self-aware. Self-consciousness becomes a slightly greater part of consciousness. And so the question finally becomes: how intimately do we want or need to know ourselves?

Runaway
9 Engines
of Desire

Impulsion by appetite alone is slavery.
ROUSSEAU   On the Social Contract

Because Consumerism relies on the engine of desire to
power its economic and social vision, it cannot tolerate the traditional ethics of the earlier culture. Old virtues like restraint, thrift,
and temperance would subvert the paradigm of wanting and buying
on which it depends, and are reinterpreted as stinginess and timidity.
Images of the body dominate the promotion of consumer products,
generalizing sexual desire, and endowing every purchase with the
gratifications of an erotic conquest. Instead of the intellect serving its
old role of tempering desire, Consumerism requires that it give its
assent. This devaluation of the mind to a post facto signatory to
appetites is a marked reversal of the ethical traditions of the West.
Even the natural sciences have adopted materialist visions of the
mind, believing, for example, that most madness is chemical and that
even mildly deficient personalities can be improved by drugs like
Prozac.[1]

At the same time there seems to be a hesitation. In order not to
appear to be the radical departure from Western ethics that it really is,
Consumerism has developed a certain *pudeur* about its activities.
There is an element of self-censorship in product promotion, if not
in what can actually be bought. Objects like dildos and bongs can be
sold but not advertised. Government can commandeer space in cigarette ads for medical warnings. Carnal and violent movies can be
released but have to be rated. All of these halfway measures are permissible so long as they are really irrelevant and do not impede sales.
The old ethics is dusted off so that the new one cannot be grasped in
the fullness of its novelty. The result is a confusing set of signals: you
should abstain from sex but buy ribbed condoms; smoking will kill
you but buy Winstons anyway; this CD contains explicit sexual
material you'll want to avoid, so buy it right away; these are the best
rolling papers, which you'll be needing even though, of course, mar-

ijuana is illegal. These ambivalences might be a cause of wonder to a logician, but they are simply part of the empiricist tradition of having it both ways.

The demonization of drugs can be seen in part as a function of this promotional self-censorship. It enables consumer society to say that there really *are* desires that it denies itself. Not that these substances aren't really for sale. They are said to be available only through a sinister and parallel "black market" that, good gracious, has no relationship whatever to the mainstream economy. This way marijuana can be at the same time illegal and (by some estimates) America's second-largest cash crop. On one level, the illegality of drugs is nothing more than a special case of the advertising self-censorship that is found in the market for condoms, legal drugs, and sex toys. During the era of tolerance that followed the countercultural period, possession laws for cannabis drugs were mostly unenforced, or in some cases radically modified or even repealed. But laws against sale always remained in place. It seemed for a time that pot, at any rate, was destined for some form of legalization. The turning of the tide against it is often attributed to the advent of cheap mass-marketed stimulants. As one resident of New York City said to me, "Crack really ruined the pot thing." The stimulants hold a particular horror for Consumerism because they resemble the macroeconomy so closely, because they are a kind of parody of the routine engines of desire.[2] They present a kind of allegory of a world driven by appetite alone, and point out all too clearly the way in which the intellect can be recruited into the service of desire.

Although corporate and state rhetoric usually maintains that *all* recreational drugs are *always* subversive to the intellect, the conflation of too many substances under the rubric of "drugs" makes this proposition indefensible. Caffeine and nicotine are almost never thought to impede mental functions. In the 1980s there was a series of advertisements on American television showing vigorous young men and women in work settings swilling coffee and transacting the day's business with gusto. The voice-over announces them as the "coffee achievers." At the very least, caffeine and nicotine are agreed to be transparent as far as mental functioning goes, but there are also many users who claim an intellectual enhancement from these substances. Yet these drugs are not alone in this transparency.

At the early stages of their intervention in the brain, almost all drugs—alcohol, cannabis, hallucinogens, opiates, stimulants—seem to leave intellectual operations intact, or even seem to excite a heightened activity that users are prone to articulate and sometimes to record. Records of this kind suggest that the *sensation,* at any rate, of improved language ability under the various influences is quite strong. Yet its persistence through subsequent or chronic stages of intoxication may be fragile. Last night's drug-induced "break-through," written down in the wee hours, all too frequently reads like blather the next morning. But although the *sensation* of improved mental powers may be similar (or similarly false) for the initial effects of a variety of drugs, there are significant differences, which become apparent only over time and increased dosage. Stimulants provide a lurid example of this. Their effects can be divided into three distinct stages. In the first, there is a transparency where language and thought appear to be unaffected and often strengthened. In the second, the mind seems to be running too fast, so that narrative and logical connectors begin to disintegrate. And in the third, where there is only the ecstasy of absolute desire, thought and the tongue fall into silence.

Cannabis drugs are known to increase the appetite for food, particularly for salty and sugary snacks. "The munchies," as this effect was dubbed in the 1960s, heighten not only the sensation of hunger but also the sensitivity of the taste buds. A person who thinks that he ought to be dieting is likely to find his self-denial overridden by marijuana or hashish, which render a rational abstemiousness arbitrary, and then hilarious. Partly this is the result of the "precinct" created by being high. Pot increases not only the desire for food, but the pleasure food brings, and pleasure is not the same thing as desire. Marijuana enhances the pleasure achieved by an appropriation of an edible object, which as a result becomes more desirable. And so cannabis desires can be pleasurably satisfied. The stimulants, on the other hand, have no time for pleasure, nor for specific objects of desire. They are about desire itself, and nothing more.[3]

In the first stage of the stimulant high, the result of an oral or intranasal (and not a smoked or injected) administration, the drug is perceived as nearly transparent to both cognition and intellect. The user is able to function well in almost all physical and mental activities—better, indeed, because she or he is oblivious to hunger and fatigue. Truck drivers and graduate students have long been aware that occasional and carefully measured doses of speed can help productivity. One of cocaine's nicknames in the late 1970s was "Peruvian marching medicine," a tribute to its ability to enhance stamina. At this first stage the user seems to be not only in control of all his or her usual capacities, but indeed in superior command of them. Often people *feel like working*. In psychoanalytic terms, the activities of the superego seem as immediately self-justifying as those of the libido, that is, motivation to work seems to be conflated with or empowered by a sublimated mechanism of desire. It is because of the basic compatibility of stimulants at this level with work and ordinary social life that these drugs were at first thought to be relatively transparent. Even the exit from stimulant intoxication at this stage is not necessarily unpleasant. Although insomnia may be experienced as the drug wears off, there is no monumental "crash" with serious psychological repercussions. Fatigue eventually prevails, and the user is able to sleep after a relatively short interval.

But even in stage one, there is a clue to what's ahead. Should the user's setting be more conducive to sex than to labor, some changes may already become evident. Erotic desire can sometimes be strengthened, if not fundamentally transformed. Male sexual performance is often enhanced. "Summaries of interviews with cocaine users . . . note initial cocaine-induced sexual stimulation, including reports of spontaneous erection, prolonged priapism, and multiple orgasm."[4] Effects on female sexuality are more ambiguous. Clinical literature, while sparse on the subject, seems to suggest that women experience first-level sexual arousal less frequently than men. But there is conflicting information. The study just cited finds that "women also reported increased libido and prolonged pelvic thrusting at low doses."[5] Although at this stage the user is only somewhat more likely to follow his or her usual sexual predilections, there is already a sense that this particular arena of desire is, as it were, being cordoned off.

At the second stage of stimulant intoxication, usually the result of a larger (but still not smoked or intravenous) dose, confidence is succeeded by overconfidence. Speech becomes rapid, and logical lines of reasoning are forever overreaching themselves. The user may become obnoxiously talkative, and be prone to plan projects and activities in great detail rather than actually attempting to execute any of them. Malcolm X describes this experience as follows: "It was when I got back into that familiar snow feeling that I began to want to talk. Cocaine produces, for those who sniff its powdery white crystals, an illusion of supreme well being, and a soaring overcompetence in both physical and mental ability. You think that you could whip the heavyweight champion; and that you are smarter than everybody."[6] An overwhelming obsession with the minutiae of thinking may prevent the apprehension of any larger or comprehensive argument, and the forest is lost in the trees. Second-stage consciousness may still seek to apply itself to work or creative projects, but the results are likely to be damaged by the overheating effect of the drug.[7] Interest in sexual activity—or any other normal desire—seems to be replaced for a time by compulsive logorrhea, so that although sex may be the subject of conversation there is seldom time to act upon *its* project any more than any other one.

The "speed rap" or "coke rant" is inherently fascinating to the speaker, but not necessarily to the hearer. This is particularly true if the listener is not high, in which case the driven discourse of the user is generally intolerable. Among the characteristics of these tirades are (1) an obsession with recounting detailed episodes from the past, especially the distant past; (2) tackling enormous issues like world peace or environmental degradation with groundless and sweeping confidence; (3) becoming absorbed in purely theoretical considerations; or (4) beginning any of these sorts of discourse only to abandon them midway and switch to another line of thought. Each cadence the speed rapper reaches opens up a limitless number of possible continuations. When one of these is pursued, the criteria for choosing it are not always obvious to the talker (let alone the listener), and the impression is often one of disjointed babbling. But the mere formation of sentences is exciting to the speaker, who is always convinced of their urgency. Second-stage users often recollect their highs as cheerful parties full of glittering and significant conversation. When the drug runs out or the episode continues to the point of fatigue, a dispiriting letdown is likely.

Many of the ambiguities and uncertainties about second-stage stimulant intoxication stem from the fact that it is actually a period of transition, which may account for the magnitude of disappointment when the supply runs out at this point. In stage two, the user learns the failure of the drug's association with work, culture, and productivity, and has a premonition of the third stage's ecstasy that may be left tantalizingly beyond the reach of the supply, or beyond the reach of the night itself. Again, the nature of the metamorphosis can be seen mostly in sexual arousal and action. The clinical data provides a clue:

"At moderate doses, increasing sexual dysfunction occurs among both men and women. For men, this takes the form of inability to achieve erection and orgasm; in women, higher amphetamine dosage also prevents orgasm (although for some men and women, multiple orgasms are experienced)."[8] As this self-contradictory report suggests, sex at this point is either too distracted and difficult to perform or else it is a raging success. The distractions are formidable: first the compulsive chattering, then the danger of the drug wearing off. Setting— whether or not the circumstances are right for sex—also has a great deal to do with it; there is still some decorum left at this level. As a transition, it can point either forward or back. This depends on whether there is a prospect for continuing on into the third stage. If there is not, disappointment may thwart arousal. But if there is, eagerness to get higher may be far more urgent than sex itself. Despite these obstacles, stage-two sexual activity may be very intensely desired and felt, if it finds just the right moment between logorrhea and despair.

Some users never attain the hypersexual stage of stimulant consciousness, but even after years of use remain firmly within stage two. They may simply never "find" stage three, since usually the ascension is discovered by chance, as the user crosses its threshold by dint of a careless or unpremeditated readministration. The drug's fluctuations of energy (stimulants don't simply turn on and off, but are prone to wane and then reassert themselves several times during the course of a high) may lead the user to try to maintain second-stage euphoria by additional dosage. A symptom of the impending transition comes when desire begins to be felt strongly and almost exclusively as desire for more of the drug. Then the third and most interesting stage of stimulant euphoria is at hand.

How does it manifest itself? First of all, as the user transcends the sexual ambivalence of stage two he or she also moves beyond the obsession with speech. To an external eye it seems as if the user has fallen silent out of fatigue or disorientation, and is no longer capable of making the interpersonal contacts and verbal constructions that form the nucleus of stage-two behavior. The transition from stage two to stage three, in other words, is obvious not only to the user but to any observer as well. Once stage three is located, a user who "knows where it is" will never again have much interest in stages one or two, but will always seek to move there as quickly as possible when beginning an encounter with the drug. This subjective fact is no doubt associated with the clinical finding that a kind of "reverse tolerance" exists for stimulants, so that the user becomes *more* susceptible to the drug's most radical effects the longer he or she has used the drug at high levels. To anyone who "knows where" stage three is, stages one and two become quite uncomfortable because of their transitional—and thus inherently uninteresting—nature.

The user's mode of administration also affects movement through these stages. Intravenous dosing or smokable preparations—freebase, crack, or ice—make the user leap over the first two stages, and can bring even a neophyte directly to the most intense degree of intoxication. But a user who has developed this reverse tolerance or "supersensitivity" by chronic or very heavy habituation may subsequently jump directly to the third stage even by modest oral or intranasal dosages.[9] It is widely held in clinical literature that some fundamental change in the brain's dopamine processing is responsible for this effect of prior upon present experience. In other words, knowing "where" stage three is found seems to expedite reaching it. This also suggests that stimulants cause some permanent alteration in the physical operations of the brain, and in the nature of memory.

Stage three is of paramount interest since here the intellect appears to become almost completely subordinate to the body, leading to the wholesale dissolution of ethics. In stage three the drug seems to have its own agenda, which supersedes the preintoxication values of the user. Richard Smart's *The Snow Papers: A Memoir of Illusion, Power-Lust, and Cocaine* recounts a conversation between the narrator and a therapist:

> "Cocaine totally killed my conscience," I said. "I had
> never considered myself a thoroughly honest person.
> But before cocaine, I was always able to check myself
> before doing anything outrageously out-of-line; I
> always cared about honor, and I generally was able to
> keep within the bounds of common decency. After I got
> deeply into cocaine, there *were* no bounds. It wasn't that
> I didn't know when I was lying, but that I felt I could lie
> with moral impunity. I was specially endowed and
> specially empowered; I was embarked on great causes,
> and the ends totally justified the means. My conscience
> was simply dead." Dr. Pollin's expression told me that it

was an answer he had not heard before, and that it had struck a chord of recognition. His reply was short— "The death of the superego."[10]

Stage-three stimulant consciousness is quite different from anything produced by other highs, yet it is often misrepresented as typical of all drugs. Clinical literature variously describes this stage of stimulant intoxication as schizophrenic, psychotic, or autistic. Laboratory observation pinpoints several identifying behaviors as criteria for this diagnosis. Stereotypy, or overly formalized and repetitive movement, is usually followed by hyperactivity. In animal subjects this may take the form of compulsive grooming or chewing, or an inflexible pattern of rearing, kicking, or twitching, with an ensuing period of pacing. In human subjects stereotyped behavior may involve meaningless tics like those seen in animal subjects. But repetitive movement in humans may have an apparent rationale, like adjusting eyeglasses over and over, or clicking a ballpoint pen, followed once again by pacing. To the clinical observer, these behaviors closely resemble the compulsions of psychotics. On the basis of this resemblance, amphetamines have been used to generate experimentally controlled models of psychosis, so the analogy clearly works both ways. Since stereotypies are quantifiable, they are well suited to empirical research, which cannot account for the affective component of an experience unless it is first translated into manipulable data. The question is what this state feels like from the inside, and for this there is no data save the anecdotal. Clinical vocabulary is not well suited to this task, but on the far end of the literary spectrum there are only autobiographical and fictional accounts that cannot claim any universality. This kind of evidence is regarded as unimportant in clinical literature, if it is not dismissed altogether.

The term Nathan Adler uses to designate the third stage of stimulant intoxication is "hypersexuality":

> The use of drugs is one way of manipulating the body
> image and of shifting the relations between the self and
> world. . . . Perception of the genital area as part of the
> body image may in some persons be repressed, become
> peripheral, or remain ambiguous. Compulsive mastur-
> bation and the use of drugs or other devices may serve

to cope with this aspect of the body image. "Speed
freaks," using amphetamines, often do so for the
experience of hypersexuality. Exhibitionism or hyper-
active, polymorphous sexual activity are ways to induce
and maintain euphoria and to construe the body.

Although the assertion seems dubious, Adler goes on to claim that
"users of speed, even in the milder dosages, report continuous secre-
tion of smegma and semen."[11]

The hypersexual stage of stimulant intoxication is characterized
by an apotheosis of desire that is as intense as it is narrow, and that
transcends and trivializes any specific sexual act. "At high doses, particularly when the route of administration is intravenous, a 'pharma-
cogenic orgasm' occurs for some users which acts as a substitute for
sex. In some cases, where both men and women were injecting the
drug, sexual activity may be replaced by mutual amphetamine injection."[12] The following narrative comes not from popular but clinical
sources, and is vivid in its description of the hypersexual state:

> Indeed, the "rush," as the initial effect of intravenous
> stimulants is called, is a highly prized and psycho-
> logically potent effect that often profoundly alters
> much of a user's subsequent relationship to the drug.
> Intravenous phenametrazine is described by Rylander . . .
> as follows: "One of the addicts . . . said that at first he
> feels numb and, if he is standing, he goes down on his
> knees. The heart starts beating at a terrible speed and his
> respiration is very rapid. Then he feels as if he were
> ascending into the cosmos, every fiber of his body
> trembling with happiness." This experience, frequently
> explicitly described as "full body orgasm," usually
> becomes autonomously desired.[13]

This, the sort of anecdote that clinicians usually mistrust, must
have struck the author of the study sufficiently that he momentarily
left his text of graphs, experimental data, and brain chemistry to
report it. The first striking detail is the user's numbness, as if he is
clearing out all other sensations in preparation for what he is about
to feel. Second is the gesture of falling to the knees, which suggests
many things. It can be read as an abrogation of the essential human

posture of standing, as a movement toward a more animal position, or as preparation for oral sex. At the same time the gesture recalls kneeling in prayer. By this token the user is preparing himself for an encounter with something quasi-divine. He is plainly subordinating himself. He is also, in another nastier sense, literally knocked to the ground by the force of the ecstasy that is about to be. Cardiovascular function and respiration accelerate as the body asserts itself, but the heart's speed is too great and "terrible," as if it were straining to attain the next moment in time. The description of the rush itself is cast in religious and bodily terms at the same time. "Ascending into the cosmos" is felt through "every fiber of his body." A spiritual event becomes identical with a physical one. Between the drug's administration and the onset of the rush, consciousness leans forward in time as it anticipates. This anticipation has a value all its own.

The phrase "full body orgasm" luridly expresses the displacement of stimulant sexuality from the genitals to the body as a whole, and perhaps even beyond the body (to the cosmos?). A sensation ordinarily localized in the genital area can now expand outside the body to fill the entire universe. In Richard Smart's memoir, this is put as follows:

> I relit an expired joint of marijuana, took the smoke
> deeply into my lungs, had a couple of snorts of cocaine,
> and slipped my hand beneath Barbara's mauve silk
> blouse. A responsive nipple hardened; she took a couple
> of quick tokes of the grass and went for my crotch. . . .
> With our drug-besotted brains churning out myriad
> erotic fantasies, it was all ravenous mouths, licking
> tongues, and heaving flesh, with every cell of skin
> vibrantly alive to the touch and every orifice given its
> due. With the coke and grass, the sensuousness quickly
> transcended the identities of the lovers, and the result
> was the astounding knowledge of lust as pure
> abstraction.[14]

In many cases the initial rush evolves into compulsive and indiscriminate sexual activity. The introduction of crack during the 1980s contributed to an epidemic of syphilis as a result. Hypersexuality leads to desire for a range of sexual objects wider and much different than what the user would experience when not under the influence of the drug. "Sexual activity that deviates from an individual's normal sex-

ual behavior may emerge, such as group sex, marathon sex, or homosexual sex."[15] Thus a heterosexual may know homosexual drives, and
vice versa. Some users even experience the sensation of changing
gender. Adler claims that "a case can be made that the female speed
freak can be experiencing the body as phallus in a masculine mode."[16]
Almost any available human body becomes a potential object for
looking, touching, and tasting. A person who because of appearance
or gender would be of no interest to the user when not high may
now provoke the most urgent appetite. The mode of sexual relationship may also be changed, allowing sadistic and masochistic elements
to develop. One can escape one's own sexual nature and accede to a
"higher" hypersexual condition, while not being completely responsible for the changes. As Adler says, "To be high is not to experience
something transcendent and extrapersonal. Rather, it is to be able to
attribute the apprehended experience to a factor external to the
responsible self, to take distance by making the experience a function
of an outside agent, instead of one's own. The drug user attributes
his internal stimuli to the drug."[17]

With sustained or repeated entry into the hypersexual state,
specific sexual activity may actually decline. Compulsive masturbation may be seen as an interim stage, as desire is concentrated in the
user's own body to the exclusion of anyone else's. This is because
desire under the influence of stimulants cannot be satisfied by sexual
activity so long as the drug's primary effects are still strong. In men,
orgasm is difficult or even impossible to obtain during the high, or
ejaculation may occur without erection. In a sense it is undesirable.
Even if achieved, it does little to slake the hypersexual will, which is
almost immediately revived. But it is the *specificity* of orgasm that is
unwanted; a single orgasm is trivial compared to the cosmic expan-
siveness of hypersexual desire. Any single sexual act seems trivial
beside the gigantic generality of lust the drug creates. Since erotic
frenzy can be stimulated by apparently nonsexual acts such as walking, dancing, touching oneself in neutral zones like the arms or legs,
or moving body parts rhythmically, in some cases the principal
erogenous zone is transposed from the genitals to the nipples or the
anus because they are susceptible to hours of erotic stimulation, but
are less likely to hasten orgasm. Especially in cases where marijuana
is mixed with stimulants (as in the passage from Richard Smart just
cited), the nipple becomes a particularly privileged zone. Many stimulant users rub their nipples raw in the course of an episode. Among

male users, masturbating on the tip of the penis, too high up to provoke orgasm, is common. One of the remarkable qualities of stimulants is that they may be applied to any mucous membrane and still
be absorbed into the bloodstream and brain. Almost all the erogenous zones are therefore possible areas of drug application. Sometimes masturbatory activities are enhanced by applying more of the
drug to the stimulated area. Anal masturbation is particularly
favored among users of cocaine, who use the drug in a creme or partial solution as a lubricant, or who concoct enemas by dissolving the
drug in warm water. Stimulants may also be applied directly to the
genitals or nipples, with orgasm-like results for those particular areas
as well as for the body in general. When sexual contact with self or
others is initiated, it may last for long periods of time in a *maithuna*-
like avoidance of climax. It is as if the sensation of orgasm were
removed from vertical time (the *kairos* or privileged moment) and
sustained over *chronos* or horizontal time. The hypersexual state can
give the feeling of "living inside an orgasm," as if a sensation so
intense could be permanently maintained. It is like standing perfectly
still on a wave that is just about to break.

Stimulants are the triumph of polymorphous desire. Desire
becomes so generalized that it is the interest itself that matters, and
not the object, whose purpose is now to ground desire even if only
for a split second (as if desire must always at least pretend to be
desire for *something*). At the outer reaches of stimulant intoxication,
objects of desire succeed one another at a rapid pace, defeating the
ability of syntax to order and express them before they have passed
and been supplanted. Neither any individual libidinal image nor the
racing sequence of them can be perceived for more than a nanosecond, let alone be "appreciated," savored, or even named before disap-
pearance and replacement. A compression takes place that (unlike the
talky earlier stages of intoxication) leads to silence. Some clinicians
compare this condition to autism.

With the suppression of language, the intellect is defeated, and
ethics ceases to exist. This accounts not only for the hypersexually
thrilling notion that anything is permitted, but also for the willingness of stimulant users to do anything necessary to obtain more of
the drug. This is doubly true because of a second displacement of
desire that occurs in the hypersexual state, as the desire for more and
more of the drug itself becomes conflated with the sexual excitement. It is like being in the thrall of a god who offers a supernatural

reward for only two kinds of awareness: anything having to do with more of the drug, and anything having to do with sexual sensations. The reward is a desire so intense it causes panic. It can make people cover themselves in blankets, hide their heads, and bolt their doors lest anyone else see how wildly and profoundly it is affecting them.

There are other examples of drug-induced desire for the drug itself. Nicotine suppresses the desire for food to some extent, but otherwise it requires no other rearrangement of interests. The only desire that nicotine stimulates is the desire for more nicotine, and that not during the period of drug's influence but only when that ends and the user wants to renew it. This is also true for opiates, to some extent. Drug lust in absentia is something that all drugs generate, least markedly in psychedelics and cannabis and most markedly in nicotine, caffeine, and opiates, with stimulants and alcohol somewhere in between. For stimulants, however, drug desire is not only present but intensified *during the course of the high,* as is often true with alcohol too. It is sometimes said that desire for more of the drug is one of the principal symptoms of stimulant intoxication. Given the panerotic indiscrimination of sexual objects that stimulants engender, it is not surprising that desire for more of the drug is subsumed within that same hypersexual matrix. Hypersexual desire is merged with drug desire to the point where they become indistinguishable. Mutual injection as a substitute for sex would be a fit emblem for this. Since satisfaction is impossible and unwanted, drug lust (which in the case of stimulants is insatiable) may indeed prevail over sex lust, since by administering more of the drug the user can experience both the consummation of an urgent appetite and the assurance that the precious appetite will continue. This is why stimulants are so medically dangerous. The more you use, the more you want. And since the drug is "stimulating," there is no escape from it when the body and brain are exhausted and have had enough. There is none of the unconsciousness that succeeds heavy doses of alcohol, for example. The only thing that can break the whirlpool of desire is the physical inability to continue. This may be a simple collapse, or a crash too final to be postponed by further administrations. Or it may be seizure and death. Knowing the possible consequences cannot deter the user, however; risking death only enhances the excitement. The recklessness of the situation has a romance all its own.

The powerful imaginings that replace action in advanced stimulant intoxication mix sexual with pharmacological fantasies, sometimes tingeing them with sadomasochistic tones. Such reveries tend to be very fragmentary, since a single sexual fantasy cannot last long in a universe of infinite desire and infinite possibility. And if one internal narrative were to be carried through to a conclusion—what would conclusion mean? Not orgasm, which is dreaded because its finality suggests that the high itself may also eventually end. A hypersexual fantasy may be framed like an ordinary sexual reverie, but before the narrative can be elaborated the fantasy passes on to another scenario. Fantasized sexual acts are interrupted for fantasized administrations or readministrations of the drug to the subject, the object, or both. Sometimes the subject imagines administering the drug to the object against the object's will. In any case, by its very nature the narrative cannot conclude with a unitary sexual consummation, like an ordinary fantasy. Another imaginary participant may intervene, or the original object may be replaced by another and another. There is an appetite for sexual imagery as great as that for physical contact, and if the user is employing visual pornography to stimulate fantasy, flipping from image to image rapidly is symptomatic of the inability to settle upon a single object of desire.

To make matters still more complicated, stimulant intoxication increases the desire not only for the drug in progress, but for other drugs as well. If the user already smokes cigarettes, the pace of smoking is likely to increase. Often cigarettes are lit only to be put out after a couple of puffs, indicating a desire whose satisfaction is too specific, and therefore uninteresting. Many oral amphetamine users are prone to drink coffee to heighten and hasten the speed's effects. Marijuana is often smoked as a way of intensifying the effects of hypersexuality by doubly sensitizing the user, or perhaps by slowing down the feverish pace of desire just enough to permit a slight appreciation of it. For some users, marijuana can catapult a lower stage of intoxication more rapidly into hypersexuality. Opiates are also used, but not out of desire but as a means of mollifying the crash. And of course alcohol's relationship to stimulant use is undeniable. In many cases users drink before the administration of the stimulant, breaking down whatever scruples might have deterred the start of the episode. But during the course of the stimulant high, alcohol consumption tends to diminish. Users who begin stimulant administration after they are already very drunk may remain awake after the point when they would ordinarily have passed out. These users, like animated corpses, are often the very image of mindless desire. Frequently they have little or no recollection of how their hours of intoxication pass. But they have a better chance of falling asleep, rather than continuing past the point of exhaustion and experiencing a definitive crash.

The utter suppression of the mind during the hypersexual state, visible in the disintegration of language, may account for its tyrannical reassertion when the high has run its course. Clinicians who observe stimulant dysphoria compare it to paranoia; this is part of their analogy between stimulant intoxication and psychosis. Both human and animal subjects exhibit symptoms of epinephrine surges, jumping to defensive postures when there is no immediate threat in their environment. They are unable to sleep or even rest despite the fatigue that many hours (or, in the cases of freebasing and crack, days) of chemical stimulation must inevitably cause. In human subjects, the universe becomes a conspiracy against them. They develop "ideas of reference" where incidental elements in the environment seem to concern them and them alone. The television seems to be making derogatory remarks about them, and every footfall in the stairwell is expected to knock at the door.

Sometimes dysphoria comes on suddenly, but at other times the dysphoric terror whispers its name only to be dispersed by another episode of hypersexuality, either coming on spontaneously or being triggered by a readministration of the drug. It is also possible for the user to exhibit paranoia-like symptoms while the hypersexual state continues, as if the subject feared to be caught in so undefended and helpless a state of ecstasy. Even an unintoxicated person is quite vulnerable during orgasm, and full-body orgasm horizontalized over hours of time is necessarily a long period of vulnerability. What if a parent or a cop or even an unintoxicated friend were to barge in and discover the user's humiliating frenzy? What if they were to find the user engaged in the sexual fury that hypersexuality requires? What if they were to discover the array of objects the user gathers around like children's toys, the pornography, the drug gear, the sexual devices?

If the user tries to ignore putative threats from the external environment, and lies down to go to sleep, he or she finds the mind still racing even when the entire mechanism of desire has been disconnected. One of the commonly reported features of stimulant withdrawal is the sound of an accusatory voice that the hearer cannot silence, going on and on about the stupidity of yielding to the drug and all its attendant desires. It is as if some "little voice of conscience," quieted by the drug, were suddenly amplified on an internal public address system. The voice excoriates the user for financial profligacy in purchasing and using up the drug, and for every social lapse she or he has just made while in the enthusiasms of intoxication. It may generalize about the user's overall bad character and personal failure. It is a parental voice, to be sure, and its charges often penetrate deeply into the psyche and cause great pain. It is one of the weaknesses of reason that its arguments are stronger after the fact of yielding to desire than they are beforehand. This is because ordinary (nonstimulant) desire can be at least momentarily satiated when its specific interest is obtained, whereas reason cannot be satisfied as long as the brain is sentient. These post facto remonstrations are aggravated by the interdiction of sleep, and the fact that the physical effects usually outlast the euphoria. But there is also the possibility that the mental reaction to hypersexuality becomes even more insatiable to match the insatiability of stimulant desire.

The result is a giant letdown, disappointment inflated to a kind of absolute. The realization comes that hypersexual desire cannot be satisfied, that the death orgasm that would be its only fitting conclusion is not going to occur. With intranasal cocaine use, the onset of dysphoria cannot be reversed by readministration after a certain point. But any stimulant introduced by any administration will confront the user with the same deadly situation once the supply has simply run out with no possibility of obtaining any more. The advent of dysphoria is said to be the worst with crack and freebasing. The understanding that nothing the user does can restore the hypersexual state leads to a despair as intense as the previous frenzy. The withdrawing user tosses and turns, and often begins to sweat as the body tries to discharge the drug more rapidly than the liver and bladder allow. The despair is made even more inescapable and frustrating as momentary flashes of the high return. This can be the direct result of physiological events, such as the belated dissolving of clumps of the drug in the respiratory system, or by the moving around of residues as the sinuses begin to clean themselves out. The user may think that hypersexuality is returning, and be more than willing to accede to it instead of letting the crash take its course. Out of drugs, a user may drip or force water into the nostrils as a way of squeezing the last potency out of earlier administrations. These activities may actually restore the high, but never for very long, even though they (or the anticipation of them, as some users in order to keep desire and anticipation alive postpone these final measures as long as bearable) may interrupt, if not finally mitigate, the misery of the high's end. Amphetamine crash, while often said to be as noxious as cocaine's, is more prone to spontaneous and sometimes relatively sustained reassertions of hypersexuality. Some amphetamine takers report being able to go to bed still high and rest in a kind of vampire sleep until the next wave comes on, at which time they "awaken" and resume the frenzy of desire.

The quintessential crash comes in the period when a return to hypersexuality is out of the question, but sleep will not come. This condition can last for hours. Sometimes the withdrawing user will get up, shower, try to eat or even to go to work rather than submit to passive misery. Eventually every stimulant user falls headlong into this void, where all values save one—self-hate—are shaken or destroyed. The interior rhetoric of this particular kind of self-hate is remarkable for its savage candor. It speaks as both prosecutor and judge with the undisguised loathing of a prison guard. It may become autonomous and refer to the user in the second person rather than the first. This is a mind voice whose findings the exhausted hypersexualist is compelled not only to hear but to respect and accept. It brooks no counterarguments or cross-examinations, because it is right. It can scan the user's memory from earliest childhood to the time of the now-dying high and discover patterns of fault and corruption at the core of character itself. When it is finished, however long this may take, an uncomfortable sleep comes; and the next day the user moves in the gray untransformation of a world without desire, a world without anything worth dying in ecstasy for.

The most recent wave of cocaine use in the United States began immediately after the fall of Saigon. At first it appeared (and in its early stage may still appear) to confirm Consumerism's new union of intellect and desire. It blurred the boundaries between labor and pleasure, bringing libidinous enthusiasm to work, and the urgency of work to recreation. It was a powerful antidote to the despair that followed the countercultural era, where in effect both sides lost—one its utopian dreams, the other its war. One of cocaine's mottoes is "Tomorrow's Energy Today." And so the borrowing of energy from tomorrow presaged the economic basis of the Reaganite boom. Both of them were more about mood elevation than any real change.

Where the one has left the country more or less permanent recession, the other has left us crack. And this is why cocaine has become the most demonized of drugs. In its evolution from snorting to smoking, it has changed from a harmonious confirmation of America's slow resurgence after Vietnam to a ghastly parody of Consumerism's metaphysics of desire. Its second-stage emptying of language into groundless hopes and promises parallels the deterioration of public rhetoric during the 1980s. And the unfortunate hypersexualist is the reductio ad absurdum of the consumer, compelled into a frenzy of desire that can never be satisfied. The War on Drugs forced the consolidation of small cocaine-producing and -importing operations into giant cartels, just as junk bonds spawned huge and ungainly conglomerates that swallowed up middle-sized companies. Cocaine has been Consumerism's mirror on the wall, showing its physiognomy in the coldest and most unflattering light, and so it is no wonder that the official response has been to smash the mirror, especially when this can be done in the name of morality.

To be sure, the crack-smoking skel is not the same kind of person as the ordinary mall walker.[18] The crackhead has only one consumer choice, where the storehead has millions. A shopper is less likely to sicken or die as a direct result of his or her purchases, so long as alcohol and tobacco don't figure too prominently among them. A heavy credit-card user, however, may meet the same financial fate as a freebaser. Stimulants at their higher doses are drugs of intense focus and almost no peripheral vision. Unlike marijuana and LSD, they do not transform the phenomenal world so much as transcend it. Shopping, though, is also a process of narrowing the field of vision, from the dazzling array of things for sale to the unitary consummation of the purchase itself. It too excludes the disinterested, aesthetic, and contemplative ways of being in the world. It is not so much the comparability of the speed freak and the shopper that is telling; it is, instead, the identity of the weltanschauung that creates them both. So long as there can be an economics and metaphysics powered by desire, there will always be some of their subjects who are carried away by "lust as pure abstraction."

Stimulants can accomplish with one stroke what Nietzsche calls a "revaluation of all values," sub- and inverting the hierarchies of motivation by which people conduct their daily lives. A person who has found the hypersexual stage may very well never be the same again; the memory of it may change the rest of life. It is also true that anyone who has used stimulants may learn from the experience, although this knowledge may be distressing. A kind of wisdom can be gained from witnessing the voracity of human desire at its uttermost, and from understanding one's own fundamental corruptibility in the face of it. As King Pentheus discovered in Euripides' play *The Bacchae,* ungoverned will can bring down palace walls, and tear apart both family and community. Moreover, it brings down with it all the models of consciousness from which traditional morals are derived. This is why the rhetoric and policies of war were unleashed on cocaine in the 1980s. But no matter how many more billions are appropriated to law enforcement, no matter whether the user or the producer is attacked, this war will meet with no success so long as it is a war against desire fought by an agency of desire. The use of stimulants will decline when there is a different motivation for life and work than the desire for acquisition without end, when there is room in the world for satisfaction, for sitting still.

Mystery
10 Drugs I:
Alcohol

Alcohol is so much a part of the
fabric of Western life that it has become
an element of the landscape. From the density of
cities to the isolation of dirt roads, the neon iconogra-
phy of beer and spirits illuminates every corner of the American
universe. Bar and lounge find their place in every architectural gesture, from corporate obelisks to bayou lean-tos to blocks of converted factories. Billboard images of bottles and their venerable
marks—Old Grand-Dad, Hiram Walker, Johnny Walker, Jim Beam,
Jack Daniels—give patriarchal comfort. Wherever you go in the
West, alcohol is offered like the grasp of a hand—or in place of it. Yet
beneath alcohol's icons and institutions lie its familiar wastes: broken
glass, a body in the gutter, the wreckage of cars, promises, families,
and dreams.

As alcohol affects every cell in the body, so it touches every
moment of our history from Homer and Plato to the beery home-
comings from a dry Iraqi war. Wherever the cultivation of grapes,
hops, or grain is known, the transmutation of those nutrients into
that alternative diet has also been practiced. How deeply alcohol is
woven into our history can be seen most clearly in those moments of
the drug's negation, when its afterimage proves as strong as its presence. In those times of its denial, alcohol merely vacates the surface
of the landscape and crawls into the secretive holds of those same
buildings and streets: the fluorescent church basement of an AA
meeting; bootleggers building and tending stills in dry counties of
the South; or the reassertion of the socially metamorphosed drug in
Prohibition's backdoor speakeasies.

Like the cannabis drugs, alcohol can be described only in a web of
contradictions. It is a depressant, but also a stimulant; it encourages
sexual behavior, but depresses sexual performance; it promotes an
atmosphere of relaxation and friendliness but leads to tension and
violence; it makes people gregarious but at its extremes finds them
reclusive and alone; its imagery is masculine but its subscribers are

more than equally women. To some degree, again as with cannabis, these are constructions put upon it by its opponents. The character imputed to alcohol varies according to the agenda of the adversary. If the concept of user construction is tenable, every individual drinker should behave differently, and this would explain the plethora of contradictory interpretations of alcohol. But at the same time, the psychoanalytic position is that all drinkers, while drinking, are diseased in the same way: "Diagnosing a psychiatric illness in a person who is drinking heavily is impossible. Heavy drinking produces insomnia, depression, anxiety attacks, delusions, and hallucinations."[1] Not only does an inquiry into alcohol stumble across these contradictions, it also stumbles over itself on the way to them.

Even if alcohol is one thing to all drinkers, even if it is a rare fixed element in the polymorphous world of drugs, its very ubiquity means that there simply are too many places from which to look at it. To investigate crack there is really nowhere to go but the crackhouse, which provides only a single angle of vantage. To study pot one may go any number of places, but always to their back alleys or curtained rooms. To study heroin one must go specifically to junkies. But for alcohol there is no right place to begin. Because it is inescapable it becomes impossible to find.

Like every manifestation of the ineffable, alcohol is often anthropomorphized, usually as a man. It walked the agora of Greek antiquity in a mask of Bacchus. Jack London called it John Barleycorn, incarnate on whiskey labels as a grandfather or a gentleman. This personification is a response to alcohol's penchant for evasion, since it can also be characterized in the palest abstractions: as the "cause" of the car wrapped around a tree, the "reason" for teenage pregnancy, the "explanation" for the dissolution of a marriage. It is protean, the perfect example of a drug whose effects are intertwined with the personality of the user, and the social arena where that user's character is exercised.

Alcohol absorbs equal amounts of praise and blame in the world, since no one can find the last argument against it. It evades its attackers by changing itself into something else. Yet whatever it becomes, it is still entirely itself—whatever that is. It is universally held to be guilty, but no one can say exactly what it is guilty of. You can make specific grievances against it—it killed someone I love, it makes me be someone else, I get dyspepsia from it—but at last it has no characteristics apart from the person who drinks it.

Alcohol is the familiar stranger. The familiar stranger is counted on to reduce the heterogeneity of wedding guests to the lowest denominator that is still sufficiently common. Suddenly what *is* simply *is*. And in this *is*-ness there is a faint aroma of promise: that if the night were driven far enough, at its ulterior side would be some paradise. It turns old bawds of city streets, where too much has happened, into innocent lanes of possibility. It lets things be what they pretend to be. Filth becomes romantic and elegance becomes the backdrop for tawdry scenes. Alcohol is the theater of appearances; it is the willing suspension of disbelief; but in just the right amount it plays on the pulses, for a short time, a world that is not exhausted, a night that is forever young.

My discussion could end at this moment, since I have apparently left myself nothing to say on the subject. But one additional thought presents itself. If alcohol is so empty a signifier, in this it resembles nothing more than sobriety, which as I argued earlier is a null set defined only by adjacent regions of intoxication. Alcohol is bounded on three sides by its own absence, but on the fourth it opens into a morass of half-recognized chimeras: disinhibited mixtures with other drugs; violence, unprotected sex, accidents, amnesia, and death. These outgrowths of alcohol intoxication are more permanent than the high itself, and remain to be contended with after the drug wears off. By contrast, sobriety leaves no such legacy to intoxication. As a mirroring myth, sobriety's greatest drawback (besides its virtual nonexistence) is its insistence on the status quo, even though that is an impossible demand. Alcohol is an agent of transformation both physiological and psychological, and many of the changes it potentiates are irreversible even if the user never touches the drug again.

How to characterize these changes? Alcohol is ordinarily the drug that introduces neophytes to the essential permissiveness of being high on something. It is therefore regressive and progressive at the same time. Against the background of childhood's regulation it suggests that breaking rules, particularly with respect to what used to be called "manners," is possible after all. But it also brings the user back to an earlier point in childhood when the rules were not yet fully codified. It is a return to the game called Dark Fun where children shut out the lights and play hide-and-seek in an attic two floors above the adults, and on discovering each other linger to touch and explore. In the adult disorder of a drinking party there are chance encounters on the way to and from the bathroom, unscheduled

embraces, and whispered surprises. Inappropriate attractions are disinhibited and their tropisms followed without regard for the consequences. In this respect alcohol is not so different from cocaine.
Once in the thrall of either one (or both) the user uses more and
more, and follows the urgency of arbitrary desires with little internal
policing.

So the issue is not progression or regression so much as transgression, the crossing of boundaries interdicted by some social authority.
But what authority? Here there is no answer apart from the individual
user. If all acculturation is born of restriction, there is still no universal
code even of manners, let alone ethics in the grand sense. The authority in question is quite simply whatever the user accepts as such. But
why would anyone establish authority only to transgress against it?
The only possible conclusion is that the user does not choose the
authority, but has it forced on her or him. Transgression is thus the
"crossing of a boundary" that the user accepts as valid but unjust.
Alcohol cannot overthrow the authority; it can only taunt it. If there
is an explanation for this mystery, it lies in alcohol's self-contradictory
capacity to heighten and deaden feeling at the same time. It is an anesthetic as much as heroin and cocaine, and because it dampens pain it
seems capable of promoting joy—joy that ought to occupy a greater
space in consciousness, or so the user thinks. Alcohol's famous disinhibiting is really only the elation born of a momentary respite from
restriction and suffering. And again as with cocaine, the pain is only
deferred and not escaped, as the ambiguities of feeling finally self-
destruct and leave authority unscathed.

The elation arising from relaxation of suffering can take on a life of
its own. When experienced as joy, it is a sensation achieved by deadening other sensations. Liberation from pain can be felt as liberation
pure and simple, and this feeling can create the illusion that anything
is possible regardless of laws, odds, or ethics. A user who experiences
alcohol in this way is likely to seek that which is most inhibited, and
so some drinkers turn to violence or sexual misconduct while others
only dance, masturbate, or get facile in conversation. The aftermath
of the high is therefore more than a physiological reaction, more than
headache and nausea. It is also the vengeful rebuilding of all those
barriers the drug was able momentarily to dissolve. Because alcohol
anesthetizes some feelings and heightens others, it effects a schism in
the brain, a sorting out of its own boozy purviews of consciousness, a
staking of its own terrain.

Drugs like alcohol, marijuana, and nicotine—for which all generalizing descriptions are self-contradictory—can only be understood contextually. To understand an alcohol high, a whole string of questions is necessary: Who is the drinker? What is she or he drinking, how much, and for how long? Who is the drinker with? Who are those others? What are *they* doing? What are their values? Where are they? What time is it? What has the drinker always dreamt of doing that makes him or her excited and afraid? What have the others always dreamt of doing that makes *them* excited and afraid? As Jack London wrote, "The desire for alcohol is quite peculiarly mental in its origin. It is a matter of mental training and growth, and it is cultivated in a social soil. Not one drinker in a million began drinking alone. . . . The part that alcohol itself plays is inconsiderable, when compared with the part played by the social atmosphere in which it is drunk."[2] And that, of course, can be nearly any set of social circumstances, at least in the West.

What *about* the social backboard off which alcohol must be bounced? It would be an absurdity to speak of the effects of cocaine in the absence of a user, but it is equally senseless to speak of the effects of alcohol in the absence of the user *and someone else*. Who is this perennial other? Is it there when the drinker drinks alone? If so, then it is not the social circumstance alone that counts, but the drinker's application of that setting as a possible locus for the appearance of the other. Alcoholism would then recapitulate the search for love or sex. Perhaps "to drink with" is a relationship of greater intimacy than we imagine. The "one-I-am-drinking with" may be the only constant in a life of infidelity and death, uncontrollable change and reversals. It is because this other isn't there that we drink.

This sort of rhetoric is reminiscent of the old view, common in the 1960s, that drug use is an expression of mystical impulses.[3] Quick administrations of drugs serve the same purpose as years of *zazen* on hardwood floors. Alcohol's legality is then the crucial fact of its difference. Westerners are advised that this is the only acceptable way to seek transcendence. The incorporation of liquor and beer icons into the landscape is therefore a phenomenon not so different from the placement of churches around town commons in New England, or the central location of cathedrals in Western cities, except that alcohol's shrines are more numerous and ubiquitous. All through human settlements are signposts of worlds beyond: the muezzin calling from a minaret, the virgin in the side yard of a three-decker, the wink of Johnny Walker over the passing lane of an expressway. Transcendence must be immanent, and never at odds with the warp and woof of the avenue.

If the charges brought against alcohol are true, let it be remembered that nonchemical religions have also led to violence, breach of trust, and the erosion of families by devices like war and celibacy. Again, this is where alcohol's legality is so important. Practices with true religious content tend to seek acceptance, as was the case with the Dionysian religion in the outlands of ancient Athens. Although the cults of hemp and LSD may seek legalization, the cultures of heroin and stimulants do not. Prohibition is now a cautionary tale like *The Bacchae*, a parable of violent disruptions when the god is denied. The notion of a legal high is not really an anomaly if we understand its social construction in congregational terms. Drinking bonds millions of otherwise dissimilar people together, just as Catholicism does. No wonder the only successful antidote, twelve-step programs, maintain many of the social and religious structures of alcoholism and Catholicism while replacing the sacrament with black coffee.

With this in mind, the "ism" in alcoholism is revealed in a different light and a heightened significance. It is not only the medical "ism" found in botulism but also the ism of creed like Catholicism or Stalinism. The medical "ism" denotes a physical malady: the complex of medical problems associated with chronic consumption of alcohol. But the wider "ism" suggests a coherent view of the universe. What beliefs, however, could this system contain, if every utterance about it is only as true as its opposite? Is alcoholism like the systems of Hegel and Marx, where opposites are equally true and give way to a higher truth as they approach the Absolute, the classless society? Is it about resolving class contradiction when there is only one class left—the drinkers? No, there is nothing systematic about it. The drinker's involuted rationale for continuing to drink is what passes for its logic. But the refusal to press the dialectic to synthesis has an element of tolerance about it, a pessimistic shrug and another draft. Alcohol-related violence may be the nastiest sort precisely because it has no basis in any real difference, hence has no reason either to start or to cease. It is the form of contradiction only. And so the contradictory nature of statements about alcohol despairs of any better resolution than a bar fight.

To be able to resist solving contradictions is sometimes seen as a state of grace. Whitman, Emerson, and Nietzsche thought so, and Keats seemed to like holding contraries in an eternal balance called "negative capability." What characterizes drinkers is a postponement, if not a cancellation, of the resolution of any dialectic. If Hegel's logic progresses through concatenating predications of the Absolute, alcologic *fails* to progress because of the futility of *any* predication of alcohol. Where Hegelian or Marxist dialectics is generative, alcohol's is *de*generative. Opposite predications simply coexist in defiance of any means of resolution. Here is the heart, then, of the problem: alcohol feels like a state of grace in that the drinker escapes the Western obsession with dialectical thought and the resolution of contradictions, but in fact the same old polarities keep snarling at each in a perpetual stalemate without either changing or vanishing.

Drinkers and ex-drinkers alike keep searching for a god or an Absolute because it is a way of reestablishing an eschatology for a universe that seems to have ground to a halt. Because alcohol is legal, this search can be carried out in open social fields. If all drugs were legal they would come to resemble alcohol in this respect. But they aren't. And so alcohol is a drug of unending quest, whose principal affect is a longing too divine to be satisfied. This longing survives the habit in those who quit—but for those who haven't, tonight is always The Night.

Mystery
Drugs II:
Acid Metaphysics

The first problem in thinking
about LSD and the other psychedelics[1]
arises from the Easternizing language initiated
by Aldous Huxley in *The Doors of Perception, Heaven and
Hell,* and *Island,* and then by Timothy Leary and his associates
in *The Psychedelic Experience,* where, as one contemporary complained, "their insistence on forcing their insights into a framework
which is essentially Tibetan produces a strained, somewhat artificial
effect like the efforts of early astronomers to force the movements of
planets to fit into the Ptolemaean system."[2] Because these texts determined the popular reception of the family of psychedelics, it is now
difficult to guess how else these drugs might have been welcomed in
Europe and America. What would have happened if psychedelics had
entered directly into the West without a prejudice generated from
the scripture of a distant religion? There is a chance that they might
have led to that rarest of moments, a purely Western mysticism. But
the question also has the pointlessness of "What if the South won the
Civil War?" Huxley's first interpretation still influences, and sometimes even determines, not only discussion of the subject but the
drugs' effects themselves.

The persistence of this gloss on psychedelics is all the more
remarkable considering the diminution of Western interest in Buddhism since the 1960s and 1970s, and that LSD use, despite mythol-
ogy to the contrary, seems not diminished significantly since that
supposed heyday. Although purists may dismiss later party-use of the
drug as "just another high,"[3] users are still prone to prevision their
trips as journeys to illumination, whether explicitly mystical or otherwise. And still this illumination can often be found only by a purported escape from the West, that is, to a place where the tripper is
always a foreigner, always an Other. With this much alienation for
the user to look forward to, it is a wonder that the drug ever gained
popularity in Europe and America. Why did it, then? One possible
explanation is that this voluntary otherness is felt by some as the

delightful estrangement requisite to the experience of beauty. But these are only the good trips. What about the bummers, when there is a kind of tourist's panic, wondering if you've gone too far into otherness and whether you'll ever get back?

But why is this otherness "Oriental"? It is possible to wonder whether Huxley and his successors weren't unconsciously recuperating the old chinoiserie of opium, the whiff of China contained in that drug's cultural construction. It was this Easternism that had Coleridge seeing Kubla Khan and Baudelaire hymning "l'Orient de l'Occident, la Chine de l'Europe."[4] Subsequently this Orientalism was transferred to another drug, as Baudelaire and Nerval associated their use of hashish with their real or imaginary journeys to the East. But in both of these cases, opium and hashish, the use of the drugs in question actually originated in the Orient, and the supplies that the European writers obtained were always, of course, imported. But psilocybin and peyote are thoroughly Occidental, and LSD was synthesized in Basel. There is no family of drugs that is so thoroughly Western in its origins, despite speculations about prehistoric hallucinogen use in Asia Minor, or reveries of an African genesis of consciousness on the grasslands.[5] Was the Easternization of psychedelics simply force of habit? Are "China" and Tibet just Western metaphors for the right brain? Is there an assumption in the West that transcendence and euphoria can come only from outside sources?

If so, this provides further evidence of the hegemony of neo-empiricist metaphysics in the West. Any experience that has its origins in something other than sensory downloading, any experience that cannot be experimentally reproduced, any complex that appears full-blown in the mind without external correlative is simply beyond the reach of Occidental comprehension, and therefore must be referred to the East. After all, even drugs indigenous to the Western hemisphere must still be referred to a local "other": peyote to Native Americans, cocaine to South Americans or African-Americans, marijuana to Mexicans, and so on. Perhaps this is just another instance of our *pudeur* about getting high. "Real civilization" does not offer us drug experiences. We need to go slumming in other cultures to get them if we must.

A more charitable explanation might be that the Eastern reading of the trip is simply preferable to experiencing acid's psychological anarchy with no interpretive frame at all. The West is accustomed to maps, instructions, guidebooks, primers, and scripture. Maybe it's

not an accident that Leary's "manual," *The Psychedelic Experience,* is
bound in authoritative biblical black. LSD is slippery terrain, and any
sort of cartography might relieve the anxiety. The trouble is that we
Westerners assume that the map has been drawn up to conform to
some "real" geosphere. We are not receptive to the idea that the terrain might conform to the map. If this is true, then Leary and his colleagues were trying, through the appropriation of a Tibetan sacred
text, to propel the user's encounter with the drug in a particular
direction. In the "General Introduction" to *The Psychedelic Experience*
we read: "Different explorers draw different maps. Other manuals
are to be written based on different models—scientific, aesthetic,
therapeutic. The Tibetan model, on which this manual is based, is
designed to teach the person to direct and control awareness in such
a way as to reach that level of understanding variously called liberation, illumination, or enlightenment."⁶ The key phrase in this passage
is "teach the person to direct and control awareness," suggesting that
without the charts drawn up by previous explorers the tyro tripper
would simply be lost, incapable of superimposing her or his own
order on the experience. Instead of LSD having inherently Oriental
properties, then, it may be that its early proponents were only seeking to superimpose upon it a template that is at once earthly and
wholly other.

There is another aspect to the question, a more social one. The
United States, during the first era of LSD's popularization, was at
war with an Asian and largely Buddhist nation. Vehement opposition to that war on the part of young Americans may have led some
of them to think that all things Eastern were good and all things
Western bad, so that if acid were good it must be of the East. In this
context, acid could confer a sense of political redemption on the
user, or at any rate permit a momentary escape from the imperialist
nightmare. It would not, of course, have been the first time that a
misty view of Eastern superiority entered the West. In America
alone, Emerson and Thoreau referred frequently to Hindu scrip-
tures, and later Ezra Pound fashioned a modernist heterodoxy out of
his idiosyncratic theories about the Chinese language. But in the
1960s these visions were made concrete by political turmoil and division. Even the fundamentally apolitical Leary must have been
touched by this historical setting. Dropping acid was endowed with
the intrigue of going behind enemy lines. It was glamorized in this
way as a treason of consciousness, analogous to the political treach-

ery of Jane Fonda or Susan Sontag going to Hanoi and returning to tell about it.

Whatever the reason—one, all, or none of the above—it is a tribute to the power of interpretation as an art that the Easternization of psychedelics is apparently irreversible, even for users too young to remember the acid Orientalism of the 1960s. At the same time, there have been efforts to place the use of these drugs within the historical matrix of the West. There are some records of psychedelic dosing before Huxley.[7] One is the memoir (written many years later) of Dr. Albert Hofmann, who synthesized LSD-25 in 1938 and then put it aside until April 16, 1943.[8] Although his text was written after he had tripped on several other (post-Huxleyan) occasions, Hofmann connects his drug's effects not with the Far East but with the Eleusinian mysteries as he understood them from the work of Karl Kerényi. Since Demeter, in whose honor the mysteries were performed, was a goddess of agriculture in general and grain in particular, a grass fungus like ergot might have provided the appropriate sacrament for the goddess's autumn celebration. Whatever the merits of this speculation, it testifies to the lengths Europeans will go in order to locate their mystical traditions. On the other side of the Atlantic, Native American peyote cults have sometimes provided a nearer analog. In her memoir *Movers and Shakers: Intimate Memories,* Mabel Dodge Luhan recounts a full-blown peyote bummer at her apartment in New York in 1914 (!), but the only connection of her stoned guests with actual Native American practice is parodic and even blasphemous.[9] R. Gordon Wasson ate mushrooms with Oaxacan Indians in June of 1955 (and several times thereafter), and published an essay about it in *Life*.[10] He too made a connection with "the ancient mysteries."

These accounts provide clues for what the interpretation of psychedelics would have been like without the Orientalizing of Huxley, Leary, Alpert, Ginsberg, and so many other acid pioneers. But, the question of whether or not Easternization prevented Europeans and Americans from receiving acid on its own terms may really be beside the point after all. Those who avoid Buddhist or Hindu terminology invariably grope for some other transcendental language within their own cultural matrix. The real question is a much more intractable one: Why is the association of acid with some kind of mysticism so inescapable? Why must LSD be "like" enlightenment or illumination? Why must it be "like" meditation or a religious experience?

Why must it be "like" anything? There is no other class of drugs for which this is the case. Cocaine is not "like" some other human activity, nor is heroin or marijuana. Why is acid, whose users always declare its insights in some sense inexpressible, incomplete without an analogy?

Perhaps it is the Western intolerance for the unspeakable that makes an exterior interpretation of psychedelics necessary. And perhaps this is also the reason why indigenous mysticism is relatively rare in the West. If, as postmodern philosophy has asserted, all of reality is located in language, then how can we speak of alternative realities without new languages? Sensing this, perhaps, the acid pioneers reached for their exotic terminologies, or went out of their way to spell peyote *peyotl* so as to make it as heterolinguistic as possible. But insofar as they were forced to labor with the crude functionalities of English, German, or French, the things they sought to convey could only be languaged obliquely in cumbersome terms like Huxley's "Is-ness" or "Mind at Large." What are those things? What do the psychedelics reveal that cannot be expressed, and that drives users to arcane vocabularies in order to create verbal analogies?

"Objectively, what can we say of the status and effects of LSD? . . . The physiological effects of its ingestion are lowering of thresholds; acute distortions of time, space, color and depth perceptions; and modifications and sharpening in figure-ground relations and in body image."[11] So goes Nathan Adler's symptomatic survey. According to Leary and his associates, there are three principal effects: "its characteristic features are the transcendence of verbal concept, of space-time dimensions, and of the ego or identity."[12] Here I would like to go out of order and begin by considering the alteration of time and space under the influence of these agents.

It is difficult to generalize about how this realignment takes place. Not only does it vary from user to user and trip to trip, it can also vary from moment to moment during the same trip. If it is impossible to generalize, there is still one statement that can be accurately made: quantitative chronometry and measurable spatial extension are superseded by more fluid and provisional matrices. The fact that it is three o'clock is so irrelevant that it can make the user laugh. It is not that time stops, but that consciousness moves *with* and not *through* it. Rather than conforming to the invariable metronomic rhythm of *chronos,* time follows the movement of consciousness. This is *kairos,* or "occasion," the ascendancy of vertical over horizontal temporality. It is as if time were liquid rather than solid, forming itself around the interaction between mind and objects rather than enforcing or scheduling the form of that relationship.

A similar relativity governs spatial relations, as if in a dramatization of Einsteinian rather than Newtonian physics. Although in a superficial sense acid's visual tricks may seem to be little more than a display of funhouse mirrors,[13] in fact there is something far more interesting going on. Adler touches on this with what he calls "modifications and sharpening in figure-ground relations." It is not only that space is perceived as bendable, then, but that the object that comes into focus is not positioned within its field in the ordinary way. Our vision is integrative in that it situates the focal point within a periphery so that we can locate objects and move safely among them. But with psychedelics, the object in focus can sometimes seem to reformulate its own background, or the background can make it stand out in a more than purely visual way. It is this latter event that Huxley tried to designate by the term "Is-ness." The object's focus becomes more than a spatial matter. The arbitrary nature of what is focused on at any given moment assumes the proportions of a miracle. The object becomes a marvel by virtue of its being singled out from such an enormous field of possibilities. Stripped of all function, revealed in the most minute details of its surfaces, it can seem to be lit not by lamps or the sun but by an interior luminescence. Its existence is no longer contingent upon its background, its social usages, or the interest of the viewer. It necessarily occasions, then, a contemplative experience. Space is no longer a matrix of fixities, inches, miles, and furlongs, but (as Einstein conceived it) a kind of liquid that bends around objects. Attributes like texture and color become more important than size. And so the universe can be seen in a grain of sand. Acid vision is for these reasons very much at odds with the consumerist "interestedness" of perception. As Huxley put it, "It would seem that, for the Mind at Large, the so-called secondary characters of things are primary. Unlike Locke, it evidently feels that colors are more important, better worth attending to, than masses, positions and dimensions."[14]

Users tend to interpret objects endowed with this "suchness" in a variety of ways, depending on their own values and systems of belief. Many believe that they are (however paradoxically) seeing directly into a noumenal realm. The objects they are perceiving are certainly no ordinary phenomena, and their reception cannot be the result of the quotidian operations of cognition. How each user interprets this characteristic acid spatiality is a very individual matter. In the 1960s friends jokingly asked each other after trips whether they "saw God." This might be the construction put upon it by those who believe in God, or who desire to. But a Hegelian might believe she has seen the Absolute, or a Platonist the Idea. A mystic might believe that he has communicated for a trice with the Mind at Large. Anyone who believes in any transcendental realm, whether expressed religiously, metaphysically, or aesthetically, seems to feel that that realm has been accessed under acid.

At this point these privileged perceptions apparently cease to be purely cognitive. The firm consumerist divide between subject and object dissolves, and the effect is felt in every activity of the mind. It becomes a question of language. "Our subject-predicate language builds dualism directly into the realities that we construe and is not inevitable or in the nature of things. Other cultures and other languages construe and organize experience in different ways and slice reality into different categories."[15] This is one of the reasons why taking these drugs relocates the user from the Western tradition to "other cultures and other languages" (or some ad hoc version of them, at any rate). Here Leary speaks of "transcendence of verbal concept." To anyone who has done a modicum of research in this field, it may seem perplexing that an experience that supposedly escapes the verbal realm has triggered so many thousands of pages of verbiage. The language distortions notable in attempts to describe psychedelic consciousness suggest that this is another instance of "speaking about the unspeakable," which is of course just about as possible as rubbing your eyes and seeing the invisible, or eating the inedible. All the great exponents of the literature of psychedelics come face to face with this dilemma: they require language to talk about the inadequacy of words.

An underlying factor is the change in views of the relationship between language and thought since the 1960s. Although some LSD research continued after the interdiction in 1966, there is certainly a long hiatus between the works of the pioneers and contemporary reconsiderations. Leary and his colleagues are part of the countercultural worldview of their era, and it is difficult not to see this as a Romantic revival—possibly the last. The idea of transcendence had a renewed currency then, as visionary and epiphanic experience were thought to come from beyond the perceptual veil, from a noumenal or supernatural realm. Poetry, momentarily privileged in the resurgence of expressive art theories, was thought to have some relationship to this realm, principally because it is in some ways illogical and nonrational. But it was normal to think of oneself as having inexpressible "deep" thoughts and sensations. The notorious breakdown of pedagogy during this time, when traditionalists complained bitterly that students were no longer being taught to write syntactic English, was the result of an assumption that the student always "knew what s/he meant" even if what came out on the page was unintelligible. Teaching writing was seen as a commitment to helping students express their thoughts and feelings in a more powerful way, rather than as the technical task of training them to write within the regulations of grammar whether they had anything to say or not. There was, in those days, an equation of peace and silence. Someone who said or wrote nothing was thought to be in a state of grace. The idea of escaping language was tied to the hope of direct noumenal perception, and Leary no doubt believed that going beyond words was one of the great benefits of the drug for which he was proselytizing.

When LSD was still available for research in the 1960s, it was generally thought that it decreased language ability.[16] But it is surprising how little work was actually done on this problem. This may reflect the lesser preoccupation with language a quarter century ago, or it may suggest that the problem was too commonsensical to attract much grant money. *Of course* LSD makes it hard to speak and write. An experience common to many users of psychedelics is the sensation of having some tremendously important insight that needs to be written down at once. Paper and pencil are procured, but the choice of each word seems so onerous that the hand cannot keep up with the racing flow of urgent information. Finally, with great labor, a sentence is completed, then placed on a side table till the next day, when it is found to be gobbledygook. This archetypal acid occurrence seems to indicate a rich and overflowing universe of preverbal thought, whose capture is simply beyond the crude mechanisms of syntax and semantics. But this question, like all the others, was abandoned when the psychedelics were made illegal, and all research ceased in the ensuing silence of "Just Say No."

It may therefore come as a surprise that Terence McKenna, the foremost contemporary proponent of psychedelic experience, differs from his predecessors in accepting the idea of "a world made of language," as he puts it. His psychedelic champion, the shaman, understands the totality of language even as he guides the user toward the Transcendent Other:

> For the shaman, the cosmos is a tale that becomes true as it is told and as it tells itself. . . . This is why the shaman is the remote ancestor of the poet and artist. Our need to feel part of the world seems to demand that we express ourselves through creative activity. The ultimate wellsprings of this creativity are hidden in the mystery of language. . . . Only by gaining access to the Transcendent Other can those patterns of time and space and our role in them be glimpsed. Shamanism strives for this higher point of view, which is achieved through a feat of linguistic prowess. A shaman is one who has attained a vision of the beginnings and the endings of all things *and who can communicate that vision.*[17]

At other times McKenna goes even farther: "DMT . . . conveys one into wild, zany, elf-infested places. It's as though there were an alternative reality, linguistically as well as dimensionally. One tunes to a different language channel and then, with this language pouring through one's head, one can observe the other place."[18]

If McKenna has adapted psychedelic transcendentalism to the age of language philosophy, we need to ask how it is that his view differs so drastically from the "beyond words" position of his acid forebears. One answer is that McKenna is not talking about the same drugs. He is an advocate for the tryptamine family, and regards ergot and morning glory drugs like LSD mainly as dissolvers of social habit, and not as gateways to the Transcendent Other. But his notion of language is wider than the common usage of the term. The Transcendent Other he identifies with the Logos, but Logos made visible: "We are going to go from a linguistic mode that is heard to a linguistic mode that is beheld. When this transition is complete, the ambiguity, the uncertainty, and the subterfuge that haunt our efforts at communication will be obsolete. And it will be in the environment of beheld communication that the new world of the Logos will be realized."[19]

This Language-Other is attuned to digital technology, and has a message for the information age: "Within the mushroom trance, I was informed that once a culture has complete understanding of its genetic information, it reengineers itself for survival."[20] Like Leary and Ginsberg, McKenna believes that psychedelic drugs hold the promise of "bootstrapping" (to use one of McKenna's favorite locutions) the human species to its next evolutionary level. To create an etiological basis for this proposition, he argues that it is the symbiosis of humans and the psilocybin mushroom that brought about consciousness in the first place. The mushroom contains and has always contained information, along with the capacity for processing it. It is we who have lost touch with this data source by anathematizing the use of the plant and replacing its sacraments with the emptiness of organized religion. Taking "heroic doses" (as he calls them) of these plants can enable us to regain touch with this symbiote, and resume the evolutionary process that historical Western civilization has interrupted and delayed.

McKenna has adapted the idea of a psychedelic evolutionary leap to the postmodern, antiromantic world, and in so doing has preserved and retooled the work of Leary, Wasson, and the others. Yet despite his narrow choice of drugs and his widened view of language, he is perhaps not so far from his mystical ancestors. Like Leary, he uses the Jungian notion of synchronicity to plot psychedelic time. And like the Easternizers he ties the action of his drug to the dissolution of the ego, that phallic and dominating self of the Western patriarchies. He sees in these drugs a potentially radical political opposition—not in the sense of an opposing politics so much as an opposition to politics. Like Huxley, and in distinct contrast to Leary and Ginsberg, he believes in the creation of a latter-day shaman class who may use these drugs and then convey their information to the general population. Their growth into a mass movement of the kind seen in the 1960s would be too dangerous. Despite the electrifying apocalyptic fervor of his work, however, his ideal scenario of psychedelic redemption seems out of touch with the actual situation, which is this: acid and mushroom use are once again increasing, but without as much metaphysical verbiage.

Take the gospel about the psychedelic dissolution of the ego. Users in the 1990s don't find this an inevitable component of their trips. I'm not talking about Rave and Acid House party users, the "desecraters" that acid and mushroom proponents are always condemning for recuperating the drug for dancing. I'm thinking of people who drop and stay home, read, talk, and listen to music. They are using these drugs as media for introspection, for exploring the self's folds and wrinkles.

They wouldn't think of preprogramming overlays of Buddhism or Frazerian anthropology. Why should they? Leary and his colleagues, insisting on a trip through the Tibetan afterlife, knew all along that the outcome depended on the character of the user and the circumstances of the administration: "The nature of the experience depends almost entirely on set and setting. Set denotes the preparation of the individual, including his personality structure and his mood at the time. Setting is physical—the weather, the room's atmosphere; social—feelings of persons present towards one another; and cultural—prevailing views as to what is real." One would suppose that this proposition, which has gained acceptance for the study of many other drugs besides psychedelics, would mean that the user should be left alone to construct the experience according to his or her own needs and predilections. Yet the next sentence reads: "It is for this reason that manuals or guide-books are necessary."[21]

What would it mean to leave users alone to construct their own trips? A terrifying prospect, this, implying the existence of an individual imagination with supernatural properties, another vestige of Romanticism. What if the menace of acid in the 1960s was nothing more or less than the old menace of American individualism—that rhetorical icon, that template, to which politicians pay homage, then nullify with laws and fees and paperwork? What if these drugs, instead of "freeing Westerners from their slavery to the ego," enabled them to master that ego, to become truly themselves? Could this explain the psychedelics' sudden illegality? What if the enlightened self is the supreme revolutionary? LSD became illegal only after the CIA gave up on it as a chemical weapon. As long as it was a potential armament, research could continue, but as a substance with therapeutic (or "spiritual") potential it was interdicted even to academic empiricists. As soon as it was wanted in the street, it was relegated to the street forever.

Dr. Leary and his drug were expelled together, and east of Eden they have wandered ever since. Among his many subsequent books is one with the telltale title *High Priest*. Unlike R. Gordon Wasson and Terence McKenna, Leary chose a priestly rather than a shamanistic model for his advocacy of psychedelics.[22] He was committed to a doctrinal interpretation of their psychoactivity, evident in his desire to produce an accompanying scripture. At the same time, anyone who has read Leary knows that dissolution of the ego is a trick not in his repertory. In later times he became the Hugh Hefner of drug culture, interviewed in *Playboy* and dwelling as much upon his sexual conquests as his spiritual prowess. What acid needed was a model of self-creation, not a hastily constructed Tibetan orthodoxy. It needed an exemplary ego, not a dissolved one. It is both Leary's success and failure that he understood that. He combined the model of organized religion with pseudo-Oriental cant, where what was needed was an avatar of personal revelation comprehensible within the individualist rhetoric of Europe and America. This, even more than the rhetoric of Easternization, compromised LSD's potential for bringing about the mass societal change of which its proponents dreamed. Similar objections could be brought against Allen Ginsberg, whose persona is grounded in Whitman's individualism but attenuated by the peppering of Oriental lingo that dislodges it from the America it is always driving across.

But this was long ago. What's remarkable is that mushrooms and acid are still around in the postideological age. If psychedelics were done a disservice by both CIA and Buddhist preconstructions, the question then becomes more difficult and interesting: how are these drugs constructed now, in the welter of competing interpretive structures known as postmodernism?

Here McKenna, who is well aware of postmodern schismatics, is not much help. He knows that things fall apart, but he sees this as a fall from a tryptamine paradise that will someday be regained. He believes that ego-driven dominator culture has run its course, and that some great revelation is at hand—an upheaval that will propel the species back into the archaic age of partnership culture and psychedelic shamanism. He has given a date—2012—for this apocalypse. In so doing, he is replacing one template with another. He foresees an eschatology that will rebundle all the loose cultural and intellectual sheaves. This will come when the Others encountered in the mushroom trance succeed in conveying their species-saving information to us. The approaching unification of technologies seems to play a role in this, as do—perhaps unfortunately for McKenna's argument—the appearance of UFOs and the heightened public interest in near-death experiences. As someone raised, along with McKenna, in the twilight of Modernism, these speculations appeal to me. But the more realistic problem concerns the survival of psychedelic use in this age of unraveling centers and universal abandon, and here all the ethnopharmacological learning in the world is of no use to us.

A contemporary user approaching an administration of a psyche-delic drug may or may not be aware of all the history that is attached to these substances—not only the lore of the 1960s, but the archaic past, the Eleusinian mysteries, Soma of the *Rig Veda,* peyote cults, ergot grain goddesses, and all the arcana exhumed by the acid pio-neers to invent a tradition for their discoveries. If he or she knows all this, it may flavor the experience, but more than likely this knowl-edge will be sketchy at best. The psychedelics are among the most pronouncedly user-constructed of drugs. Almost every writer on the subject, including Leary, agrees that this is the case. This is an age when historical knowledge does not usually congeal into coherent narratives. History is far more likely to be viewed as a clearinghouse of tropes and images, just as recorded music is viewed by rap artists as a warehouse of potential samplings. And history is only one of the multitude of frequencies that a tripper is equipped to receive.

Because of the temporal transformations prompted by the use of these drugs, it is unlikely that a historical narrative would be experi-enced as such in any case. Just as objects "open up" spatially, so too their historical trappings are shaken away, leaving them momentarily isolated in time, just as they are more vividly set off against their spa-tial backgrounds. The postmodern "recuperation" of the past is accentuated as context is threshed away. "The trip" comes to be a process of reassembly, of bringing diverse elements together under the aegis of the drug itself, as their only unifying field. These ele-ments can be objects, ideas, language, sexual acts, or social inter-actions. It is up to the user to arrange these things. The result is an improvised performance piece of consciousness, a dramatization of the choices made by the undrugged mind every day, as it grapples with a world in fragments. Although this process of assembly is cer-tainly provisional, in that it lasts only for the duration of the drug, it is likely to have a long-range effect. It becomes a privileged moment, like a religious or an aesthetic experience, bracketed off from straight chrono-metry. Afterward it can be contemplated and forgotten, or seen as a paradigm for the process of self-assembly that ordinary life has become. How a user goes about orchestrating the trip, then, can teach her or him about the orchestration of a Tuesday afternoon.

For all its temporal distortions, the trip, as its (spatial) name sug-gests, has a beginning, middle, and end. It is a *surrogate narrative* for a world that has become an endless and beginningless middle. Yet it is only the most general Aristotelian template. Unlike a session of cocaine sniffing where, whatever the beginning and middle are like, the end is always bad, for psychedelics no part of the narrative is written by anyone but the user and the company he or she is keeping. Unlike injected or smoked drugs, which skip the beginning and move directly to the middle, these drugs come on slowly, giving the user time to adjust to them before they intensify into their greatest strength, before "peaking." The process of coming down is also gradual, unlike the sudden crash of the stimulants. The curve of getting high and coming down is smooth enough that the various parts of the trip are closely related to one another, thus conferring on them a sense of narrative unity. "Straight" time in the age of television is so fragmented that it takes a psychotropic possessed with great powers to open up a coherent narrative space.

Again, the content of this narrative—the setting, characters, plot, tone, atmosphere—is not predetermined by the drug. It is ad-libbed by the drugged. With closed eyes the user can see opening as if high above the great interior space I once nicknamed the "cathedral of the self" for its expression of pure promise, of an infinite capacity for growth, thought, and experience. Under these circumstances the disintegration of ideological Modernism can be felt as a relief. There is no ruling tale to tell; there is only the story that I am improvising.

Obviously this is not to say that all such tales are equanimous and sweet. Because the content is not predetermined, it is certainly possible that it will be as violent as a television detective show or as terrifying as a trip to hell. There is wide agreement among those who write about psychedelics that the causes of bum trips almost always have to do with set and setting; that is, they have to do with circumstances that exist apart from the so-called effects of the drug itself. If we asked a person to leap up and improvise a performance piece without prior notice, the things that were already in her mind would interact with the situation in which we made the request. It is hard to predict what would come out. But even in this hypothetical scenario, there would be a moment of self-preparation in which the performer would prevision what sort of piece to play. The tripper may also have this sense of preparation. Improvisation has its own limits and formal devices.

Why, then, don't people who are going to bum out refrain from taking the drug? The answer is painfully simple. No one knows the self that well—never mind the brain under LSD. We do not know in advance what is going to provoke our anger or give us satisfaction on an ordinary afternoon. We may secretly rehearse speeches for the great moments of our lives, but somehow they never happen as we anticipate. Neither the Peruvian shaman nor the neophyte sophomore can preimprovise. There is danger in all of it, danger in having to contrive a series of events under the narratizing influence of a powerful drug. But living is dangerous, too. Birth is the leading cause of death; it is fatal every time.

Squares and Cubes:

1 2 Combinations of Drugs

It is a rare person whose first experience of a psychotropic is with cocaine or heroin. The easy availability of legal substances makes it far more likely that a user's career will begin with tea or coffee, cigarettes or alcohol. There is a tendency to think of these as "base" drugs upon which other experiences are constructed at a later time. But watching children in line at the supermarket or at the candy counter of a convenience store suggests that sugar may be the primordial drug for neophytes. Children's famous avidity for sweets clearly resembles drug hunger at its most urgent. Terence McKenna argues that "Sugar abuse is the world's least discussed and most widespread addiction. . . . Sugar abuse is often involved in the development of serious alcohol abuse; an absolute correlation has been shown between high sugar consumption and high alcohol intake outside meals. After alcohol and tobacco, sugar is the most damaging addictive substance consumed by human beings."[1] Andrew Weil finds the origin of getting high in even earlier childhood behavior: "Anyone who watches very young children without revealing his presence will find them regularly practicing techniques that induce striking changes in mental states. Three- and four-year-olds, for example, commonly whirl themselves into vertiginous stupors. They hyperventilate and have other children squeeze them around the chest until they faint. They also choke each other to produce loss of consciousness."[2]

Whichever custom has the privilege of origin, it seems probable that the legal drugs offer the essential permissiveness for the use of others, if only because such use is easily visible to children. Teenagers are acutely aware of adults' drinking and smoking habits (as well as their more outré ones, of course), and often these practices become associated with adulthood itself. The difficulty antismoking activists are presently having with adolescent nicotine use suggests that the practice has a powerful symbolic value, something that has not been lost on tobacco companies in their advertising strategies. Besides, whatever the public rhetoric on the subject, it becomes clear to children sooner or later that our culture is so permeated by a myriad of drugs that there is no such thing as freedom from them. The acquisition of early drug experience is a part of adolescence on a par with sexual experimentation.

The fact that most users begin as they do has led to the development of what is sometimes called "the domino theory" of drug acquisition. Modeled on the Cold War hypothesis of the same name, this conjecture holds that using "soft" drugs like nicotine, alcohol, and cannabis leads inexorably to taking "hard" drugs like LSD, heroin, and cocaine. The best rationale for this theory is gained by reading backwards from the "hard" drugs, since most smack-, blow-, and acidheads have used marijuana, and most marijuana smokers have drunk alcohol or smoked cigarettes.[3] Of course this is a case of *post hoc, ergo propter hoc.* Run forward, the model is less persuasive. There are many drinkers who never try marijuana, and many pot smokers who never try any "hard" drugs. The theory is also undermined by the sloppiness of its taxonomy, since the substances classified as "soft" or "hard" have little in common with others in their class. But the hypothesis is valuable for the conduct of the drug war, since it suggests rapid and irreversible escalation: a city controlled by Communists leads to a red continent unless there is swift, forceful intervention.

This theory is easily adapted to the new therapeutic regime. "Drug addiction" is now understood as a "progressive disease" that moves through its list of substances in the same way that a malady produces one symptom after another during its course. "Drugs" are once again undifferentiated. This adds a strange emphasis to the hypothesis: the notion that a user doesn't want one drug or another, but seeks "drugs" in some general way, as if all highs were the same, as if the addict were really addicted to the condition of addiction itself. So the problem is *getting high.* The existence of a vast variety of drugs on which to get high has provided plenty of counters to be moved up and down into some semblance of order, stacked hierarchically from bad to badder to baddest. Getting high, no matter on what, when, or in what circumstances, is now regarded as a disorder. And the progression of the illness is demarcated by the user's successive drugs of choice.

What is hard to refute in this argument is its apt if oblique reference to the acquisitive collecting of vices. It is a rare Westerner who takes no drugs, but almost as rare is the taker of only one. Vices are like pets; they are the cats and dogs of our houses, and once we have one of them we are likely to end up with more. As with a kitten, a momentary burst of affection can lead to years of commitment. Every day the animals must be fed: coffee brewed, ice-cube trays filled, stocks of cigarettes and booze and rolling papers checked and replenished. A vice unslaked for even a day yowls like a hungry quadruped. Those who work their way up to cocaine often have quite a menagerie of older specimens to care for. Still, the sequence that the domino theory insists on is just as silly as the notion that a couple must first buy a cat, and then a dog, before having a baby.

Some drugs appear to have a strong mutual affinity. Sometimes this can be ascertained only in the absence of one of them. The fact that a cigarette smoker trying to quit finds temptation increased when drinking coffee or alcohol is the commonest case in point. There are many people who think that cigarettes and alcohol together are in effect one drug. It is easy to chalk this up to habit: the user is simply accustomed to taking both of these substances at the same time. But this is another empiricist dodge. The potency of the combination must have a basis in the consciousness potentiated by the two together. Since both alcohol and nicotine are self-contradictory in their biochemical impact—each is simultaneously a stimulant and a tranquilizer—the combination serves to square the ambiguity. Perhaps they both work as relaxants when the user first sits down at the cocktail hour. Perhaps nicotine goes into its stimulant mode when enough alcohol has been consumed to make the user groggy or inattentive. Or perhaps the two together increase the outer limits of stimulation and relaxation beyond the range offered by either one alone.

It is also possible that nicotine, in its ability to punctuate the passage of time, can be used as a kicker to "officialize" the effects of almost any other drug. A smoker is almost certain to have a cigarette after finishing a joint, snorting a line of cocaine, or taking a shot of heroin. This is reminiscent of the proverbial punctuational practice of smoking after sex. It is a celebration and confirmation of a moment of pleasure. It also intensifies the sensation of the other drug administration. Only a "transparent" drug like nicotine could serve this purpose. Smoking is the perennial accomplice, an uncritical yes-man that throws in its lot with substances of more obvious powers.

If nicotine metamorphoses itself according to the presence of other drugs, at the other end of the spectrum there are drugs that turn all the others into themselves. This is a particular characteristic of the stimulants, as was noted in chapter 9. Someone in the third stage of cocaine or amphetamine intoxication is apt to interpret any drug as just more coke or speed. It is sometimes a puzzle to first- and second-stage users why someone in stage three would smoke marijuana or drink alcohol, since it seems as if they have been "going up" all this time only to use the secondary drugs to "come down." Yet the stimulants turn all the others into accomplices, not only natural side-kicks like nicotine but substances as different in nature as cannabis. The ultimate manifestation of this puzzle is the "speedball," an injected mixture of heroin and cocaine. This shot allows the stimulant to blow out not only the ceiling but the floor of consciousness, asserting the drug not only in its usual speedy purviews but also in the regions of peace and contemplation that it usually disdains.

Between these two extremes, drug combinations are likely to have individual and situational constructions. Drinking alcohol and smoking pot at the same time can work out in a number of different ways. "Many marijuana smokers use alcohol while smoking, but there is no predictable result of this combination. Some people find themselves more stoned, others less stoned, others sleepy or headachy."[4] For some users the order in which the two are taken is important. A person who starts smoking hemp late on a night when he or she is already very drunk is liable to become nauseous and vomit. But smoking first and drinking later rarely has that effect. Very heavy and habituated drinkers are likely to find the effects of pot subsumed under the dominance of the alcohol. People who give up drinking but continue to smoke cannabis often report that it works more pronouncedly in the absence of alcohol. But these are generalizations, and the combination may develop differently with different users and in different conditions.

What emerges as a pattern from these common examples of drug mixing is that any particular high is more "about" one drug than another. The others then come to play secondary roles. A kind of momentary hierarchy is formed. The domino theory holds that the "harder" drugs always supersede the "softer" ones, but that model wants to put them in a quasi-chronological sequence of replacement. In fact it is not a question of superseding so much as changing and appropriating. These changes are not wrung by any predetermined taxonomy. Liquor in large quantities can swamp pot's psychoactivity, but there are also pot smokers who savor a glass of wine as a gustatory sensation to be enhanced by the hemp. Even in polydrug administration, there tends to be a substance of choice, whether by long habituation or the whim of the evening. The character of that drug then tends to impose subservient positions upon the rest, causing them to abet its action.

This is not to say that the central drug cannot change during the course of a multidrug high. It is not unusual to see people who are already very drunk snort a couple of lines of cocaine and suddenly wake up. This is usually ascribed to the stimulant intervening to prolong and enhance the alcohol high, but it can also precipitate a shift of the central drug. Some cocaine users are quite uninterested in that drug's character, employing it only to sustain drinking binges. But there are others who, perhaps having scruples about using coke, get drunk only to lower their inhibitions against sniffing it. External circumstances such as availability may also affect the balance. Sometimes a blowhead will drink heavily as a consolation when the white powder is not around; but then it may suddenly appear as the night goes on, pushing alcohol onto the back burner.

Beyond these internal adjustments and refinements, there is also an indiscriminate kind of mixing that tends to obscure the nature of the individual components. Weil and Rosen lament: "These days it is not unusual to see groups of people drinking alcohol, snorting coke, and smoking pot, as well as using tobacco, drinking coffee, and eating chocolate—all at the same time and in large doses. Such polydrug consumption tends to promote immoderation and lack of awareness about the nature of the substances being consumed."[5] But what awareness is being promoted, then? It is possible that just as children play with the oxygen supply to their brains in order to experience a prototypical high, at the far end of intoxication's vast varieties there is a return to that simplest of imperatives: to get as high as possible regardless of the means. To speak of getting high in this way is perhaps misleading, since the general desire to attain that condition is evidently a normal part of our cultural existence. Very heavy and indiscriminate drug consumption aims at a kind of getting high that seeks, in some paradoxical way, to transcend the means of doing so. As such it can be seen as a regression to the most infantile practices. And like the whirling and choking, it can be dangerous as it loses discriminations. Many overdoses can be attributed to a simple loss of interest in the specific substances that are taken to get high. What does this look like to the multidrug user in the throes of extreme toxicity? Perhaps it is the clear light that is always reported as the center of a near-death experience, those tales so close in tone and imagery to drug narratives. Perhaps the experience of *getting* high is always relative, always positioned somewhere in relation to the absolute condition of *being* high. And perhaps being absolutely high, as a condition that allows no change, is the end of becoming, and therefore the end of life.

Between a relatively uncomplicated high using a small number of substances and the indiscriminate employment of *anything* to further the high there lies a kaleidoscope of shifting shades and emphases, reaffirming the potential infinity of the inquiry. If drug combinations could be considered with all their variables—which drugs, in what quantity and purity, over how much time, in what sequences and frequency—we would find ourselves wandering once again in the garden of forking paths. Such an undertaking would have greater validity than studies of isolated drugs since it would reflect the way drugs are actually administered, and the highs achieved. But it would be beyond the reach of a single lifetime.

PART IV

*Problems
with
Drugs*

Drugs
1 3 and
Violence

In the early 1990s consternation
about violent crime in American cities,
and even exurban areas, escalated to the point
where by 1994 it was ranked first in importance among
political issues in the public opinion polls. What *is* all this violence anyhow? It is the fighting of the War on Drugs, which (like any
other civil war) has turned streets and even private homes into battlefields. The conventional war rhetoric has it that drugs *cause* all this
violence by disinhibiting aggression among users. Proponents of
legalization argue that the prohibition has driven the cost of drugs so
high, and made availability so problematical, that users must resort
to criminal means in order to obtain the substances they want or
need. These positions contradict at this point: one believes drugs
incite violence, while the other holds that lack of drugs does so.

Exploring the relationship of drugs and violence leads to a string
of questions. What is violence? What different kinds are there?
Which drugs are commonly involved, and under what circumstances? Would the present level of savagery be diminished if all the
drugs in the world disappeared, or does it have a life of its own? A
case-by-case study would lead only to anecdotes or empirical induc-
tions, and would reveal more differences than similarities — generalization is all too often the product of a preexisting article of social or
political belief. Yet one thing is certain: there is no such thing as violence without a context. Just as aspirin cannot alleviate my pain in
my absence, so no drug can perpetrate a crime in the absence of a
criminal. Still, it is common to hear people talk as if a vial of crack
could leap up out of the sidewalk and strike a victim down.

Violence is the equal and opposite reaction to the forces of human
coherence. This definition has the virtue of applying to many different kinds. Domestic violence is the equal and opposite reaction to
the unifying power of the family. Random violence, including public
acts of rage or money-motivated crimes directed against any target
that comes into view, represent the equal and opposite reaction to

the unifying power of the community. Gang violence is the equal and opposite reaction to the unifying power of a common demographic of age, ethnicity, and geography. Acts of terrorist sabotage and acts of war represent the equal and opposite reaction to the unifying power of species identity. Every one of these is a figure for the rending asunder of something that seems to want to cohere. It is assumed that these micro- and macrocosmic coherences are "good," and hence that violence is bad.

Is there any such thing as good violence? Marxist theory used to think so, dividing it into three kinds: revolutionary, reactionary, and criminal. The first was armed uprising intended to further the revolution, the second was counterrevolutionary reprisal against the first, and the third was apolitical, individualistic, and purely self-serving. Only the first of these was "good." Does Consumerism have a meta-narrative worth killing and dying for, that could create a category of "good violence"? Of course it does. The police reaction to "bad" violence is always held to be "good," and is endlessly, ritually celebrated in our teleparables. And there is another sort of violence that is always held to be good: the activities of U.S. military forces in conquering and securing consumer markets around the world.

By the end of the Cold War, America had become every bit as much of a garrison state as the Soviet Union. The militarization of the economy, coming at the same time as the collapse of the industrial age, caused thousands of people to enlist in the armed services because there was no hope of any other employment. As a result the United States has an unusually large number of citizens who have undergone basic and sometimes specialized military training. These are often the only skills a veteran has to offer an employer after he or she is discharged. Since the War on Drugs is one of the rare occasions when the U.S. military has been deployed against American citizens, there would appear to be nothing out of the ordinary in applying military training to the civilian world. Although some veterans enter the field of law enforcement or private security, others make their services available to gangs or the organizations that ship and market contraband. And of course still others apply their skills in the pursuit of private rage or vendetta. The fact that American factories produced more military hardware than anything else during the 1980s also means that there is no shortage of weaponry to implement any of these purposes. Just as guns and tanks left over from World War II and the Korean War were available for use in Vietnam, so too the armaments manufactured for use in the Cold War have been carried over into its successor, the War on Drugs. The large number of trained and armed citizens means that all of the "equal and opposite reactions" against cohesive social powers not only possess the power of military force, but also retain some of the aura of "good violence" that its original context supplied for it.

It is natural that the state and its corporate sponsors wish to avoid this sort of analysis, which suggests that having sown the wind, they are now reaping the whirlwind. In order to displace responsibility for arming and training every schismatic impulse in the private and public worlds, some external force must be found and blamed: Communism, while it lasted, then terrorism, then "drugs." There is a civil war in progress between those who benefit from the consumerist paradigm, and those who for economic or existential reasons are enslaved by it. Rather than acknowledge a real basis for this rebellion, the state wants to portray this last heterodoxy as insane, as intoxicated. Since Consumerism, as a neo-empiricism, is inherently inconsistent, it is not past believing that the state could be supplying the same drugs it spends fortunes combating. Is it a coincidence that drugs are the most abundant in poor communities, the ones that can least afford them?

By tagging this antagonistic army with the name "drugs," Consumerism not only gains simplicity and exonerates itself, it also implies that the enemy is high and crazy, as if there could be no sane reason for the latter's hostility. Now the state wants to disarm that enemy. Gun-control legislation, however appealing to humanistic sentiment and liberal pacifism, is really a belated recognition of the fact that the state has inadvertently supplied and trained the other side in a civil war. As in all military conflicts—and both international drug traffickers and local street gangs are organized according to military models—neither side is likely to agree to unilateral disarmament.

Although the official narrative expressing this madness is always the same—user gets high, pulls a weapon, kills innocents—there are disparate parables for specific substances, in which each drug is accused of precipitating a slightly different chain of events. With heroin, the scenario is this: the user, profoundly addicted, runs out of the drug and has no money to purchase more. He or she is therefore left no choice but to knock over a liquor store before the painful and devastating withdrawal begins in earnest. In this archetypal narrative the advent of violence is clearly due to lack of drugs rather than to drugs, since users of heroin and the other opiates are ordinarily quiescent as long as the high lasts. Of course, lack of drugs would not be a problem were there no habituation to begin with. But this will never be the case. For as long as opiates have been available, a certain percentage of the population has always chosen to use them. The question is only how and where they will acquire the drug. In many ways, the problem of heroin and violence appears to be the easiest to solve: simply provide the stuff free of charge to anyone willing to register as an addict, or take a chance by deregulating and decriminalizing the trade in the hope that market competition will result in lower prices.

One of the difficulties in considering this question emanates from the fact that we are being asked to do so on the basis of a template, a repeated parable, a recurrent image. The fact is that heroin use has undergone a transformation in recent years, one that calls into doubt the utility of the paradigm of addiction implicit in the boilerplate narrative. The greater purity of the drug has enabled users to administer it by means other than injection. The normal visceral terror of needles, combined with wide dissemination of information about AIDS, drove users away from heroin for much of the 1980s. Now, however, it is possible to sniff it, or mix it with tobacco or marijuana for smoking, and still get appreciably high. There is some evidence that those who snort or smoke it do not fall into the same kind of tyrannical habituation that intravenous users do; or at any rate the process is more gradual. It also appears that this new breed of user can go without the drug for long or short periods of time without becoming withdrawal-sick. This new situation makes a realistic appraisal of heroin's relationship to violence trickier, since any judgment made on the basis of the older needle paradigm no longer applies.[1]

Cannabis drugs aestheticize whatever is going on, including violence. Hemp makes it distant and balletic, somehow unbelievable, as if it were happening on video or celluloid. The original assassins were given hashish to facilitate the act of killing, and to reward and embellish it with visions of Paradise. But if violence is not on the agenda, a marijuana smoker wouldn't put it there unless he would have done so anyway, without the drug. Similarly, it was Charles Manson and his cohorts, and not LSD, that killed Sharon Tate. If MDMA (Ecstasy), marijuana, and the psychedelics vanished this instant from the face of the earth, there would be no discernible change in the rate of violent crime. If there are drugs that contribute to the present brutality, they would need to meet the following criteria: (1) they would have to accentuate both rage and the self-confidence needed to act upon it; (2) they would need to be of a class or classes of substances that cause users to become active rather than pacific; and (3) they would have to be substances capable of creating an escalating or rolling high, so that at high toxicity the stuff would act differently than at lower doses, and create an immediate and urgent need for itself.

The drugs that fit these criteria—alcohol and cocaine—are the ones most commonly found on-site when the guns come out, and it is on them that the crux of the problem rests. The fact that one of them is legal and the other isn't suggests that changing the law is unlikely to change the violence. This contrasts with the case of heroin, where the law is nine-tenths of the problem. Alcohol and stimulant highs endow users with inflated confidence, at least at the lower and middle levels of toxicity. At the highest levels it is likely that the physical ability to inflict physical harm diminishes—who do you fire at when you're seeing double? Alcohol, or cocaine in the dysphoric phases of withdrawal, can certainly give anger enough righteousness and drive to promote its strong expression. Even though alcohol is a central nervous system depressant, while cocaine is a stimulant, depending on the context either one can work either way. A cocaine user in stage-three toxicity can appear very quiet to an onlooker, as he or she sits and pulses with full-body orgasms. A drinker, too, can sit peacefully by a fire with a bottle of wine or drive into a tree at great rates of speed.

What a user actually does when high is always a function of social circumstance, and if that "setting" is military or paramilitary then it is likely that violent action will ensue. The Persian Gulf War was the first and only conflict in American history in which troops were denied alcohol. Drinking has always been part of war for Western soldiers, and sometimes other drugs have been available on the battlefield. Military action and the action of a drug can merge into a single and consistent state of consciousness.[2] Alcohol, nicotine, and cocaine are the most suitable drugs for this merger, since they encourage action rather than contemplation. But marijuana will always "go along."

The narratives that conjoin drugs and violence tend to insulate their parabolic events from any specific context. They are usually situated in the inner city, a code suggesting that their characters are members of ethnic minorities. Despite the fact that *all* recreational substances are used principally by Caucasians, these narratives have the effect of drawing the fronts in the civil war along racial lines. The collapse of Marxism, and the consequent isolation of Marxist analysis, has made the real divide less visible. It is finally an old-fashioned class war that is in progress, since people with less money are less likely to participate fully in the standard consumerist worldview. They are excluded from the narrative of information, desire, and purchase because they cannot complete it, lacking the wherewithal for its consummation. They are not, however, likely to be excused from the motive force of desire, which achieves heterodox expression in behaviors of drug desire and acquisition. If the enforcement of the consumer paradigm is constantly celebrated in cultural imagery of the police and the military, it is not surprising that those kinds of power are mimicked in heterodox social organizations.

Heightened public concern about violence is a form of war weariness. If the Cold War ended, and if Israel can settle with the PLO, and if Northern Irish Protestants can make peace with Catholics (maybe), then why can't the armies withdraw from *our* cities too? It is unfortunate that the state's response, under the Clinton administration as under its predecessors, is only to commit more troops to battle.

Blow Money:
1 4 Cocaine, Currency,
and Consumerism

Of all heterodox moneys, drugs
are among the most complex and subversive. Where drug currency can be safely contained—for example, in the hermetic use of cigarettes as
prison money—it can be ignored. But during the past fifteen
years or so, when the drug business has passed from the hands of
amateurs into the workings of international cartels, cocaine has
become not only a world-class commodity in and of itself, but a
medium of exchange as well.[1] Politicians and radio program directors
have taken it as bribes, musicians, strippers, and prostitutes have
accepted it as payment, and American government agencies have
employed it as tender in illegal arms transactions. On a national
scale, the economies and politics of several Central and South American countries have been superheated but also mutated by the manufacture and shipping of it (as they were centuries before by refined
sugar). Among individual users—and this is true for users of heroin
and other drugs as well—a cocaine habit profoundly changes the
scale and use of expenditure, and alters the personal economy, usually for the worse. From an Olympian perspective, it would appear
that the international cocaine trade differs from conventional consumer markets only in that its extralegality exempts it from taxes,
fees, and the necessity of presenting public books. It is arguable that
in an age when "free trade" and the "free market" have been the twin
pillars of public money policy, the cocaine trade represents an ideal,
unfettered as it is by any regulation other than the perennially useless
efforts of police and the military to eradicate it.[2] Why, then, is it
anathematized? Why are alcohol and tobacco heavily regulated but
juridically tolerated? What is the point of the endless War on Drugs
when that business seems to exemplify the virtues consumerist economics claims for its own?

In a politics that seeks above all else to protect and augment the
property of the wealthiest citizens, money is assigned a particularly
wide range of significations. When President Reagan was shot in an

assassination attempt, he advised the press as he entered the hospital that he had been told that the gunman "came from a good family." By "good" he meant wealthy. This telltale locution indicates that a positive *moral* value is assigned to the possession of large amounts of capital. This conflation of virtue with the ability to implement desire seems at first glance to be at odds with some varieties of Christianity, which at the beginning considered wealth to be a liability as far as salvation is concerned. But there is a Protestant tradition that holds that an abundance of worldly goods is a sign of divine favor, and many denominations, along with Islam, Catholicism, and Judaism, have never been averse to accumulation. A similar conflation takes place in the arts, where the only "good" record or book is one that makes money, and where there is no dissident critical framework able to contradict the overriding criterion of financial success. One by one all the traditional Western measures of value have been conflated, and calibrated to cash flow. The dynamic of profit and desire has subsumed all other relationships. Although there is still a constant chorus of remonstrances from the defenders of old values, the 1980s nonetheless cheered the First World assertion of financial hegemony. You know who you are, and how good or bad you are, if you know your net worth. This, so late in our overpopulated history, is what passes for stability.

Now the trouble with cocaine, from the consumerist vantage point, is that it resembles money as closely as it does, the way a cancer cell mimics a normal or ordinary one. Cocaine trafficking accumulates excess value at a wildly faster rate than most "legitimate" enterprises. This is not solely a matter of the volume of business, though blow money moves and grows faster, and generally achieves a greater rate of profit, than ordinary capital. Instead, what sets this business apart is not so much the nature of its activity, which is only buying and selling, after all, but the nature of the commodity itself. The important analogy between cocaine and cash is that both derive their value from a relationship to desire. Conventional money is a reservoir of general desire that permits the implementation of specific ones. It also spawns a reflexive metadesire: the desire for money itself. The more money, the more desire; the more desire, the more vitality in private life and public enterprise; the more money, the more ability to make money—or so the conservative argument goes. There is no such thing as "enough money," and so desire lives and grows without horizon. So too there is no such thing as "enough cocaine" from either the user's or the seller's point of view. Cocaine is also about reflexive metadesire, but it is about the eclipsing of all other desires rather than their potentiation. If cocaine were a commodity like coffee, simply a psychoactive substance to be exchanged for cash, it would present no problems for the global monetary system, and would not be outlawed. The problem is that there is a reciprocity of excessive desire between the seller and the user of the drug, so that they come to mirror each other. Each becomes party to a radical enhancement of desire that threatens conventional money in its limiting function while promoting its aspirations to infinity.

Money comes in many forms nowadays: physical but symbolic metal and paper cash; credit, charge, debit, and ATM cards; electronic entries in the spreadsheets of banks and businesses, and so on. Although money is protean, and can no longer be correlated to any one form or any one class of commodities, cocaine is a repository of great value where a denomination of a hundred dollars is as small as a piece of pocket change. But, unlike any form of conventional money, it is a physical substance *consumable in and of itself,* without the need of translation into any other good or form. Yet the act of consuming it—and here is where cocaine is both unique and closest to money itself—permits no satisfaction. In fact, one of the principal symptoms of cocaine intoxication is an overwhelming desire to consume more cocaine. Instead of money's measuring power, which both limits and suggests limitlessness, cocaine represents desire that at least temporarily overrides money's limiting aspect and permits the illusion of infinite consumption, infinite profit, or infinite expenditure. This is why the confessional literature about cocaine is full of cautionary tales about "snorting the house" and ending up in the streets. The dream of an eternal high is like a capitalist's reverie of an economy without cycles, where the booms last forever and recessions never occur. In point of fact, the high/crash cocaine dynamic is just like capitalism's boom/bust, but a user in the throes of the drug cannot recognize this, like a financial player in prosperity unable to prepare for the inevitable crash.

Cocaine cannot be accepted as a conventional medium of exchange because it is more like money than money itself is. It is money as absolute value internalized not only through consumerist epistemological "downloading," but directly through the respiratory system or epidermis into the bloodstream. It is mainlined money.

"Riches . . . ," Schopenhauer says, "are like sea-water; the more you drink the thirstier you become."[3] But with cocaine one would skip freshwater forever, and keep drinking the sea. The dazzling panoply of conventional consumer goods has meaning and attraction no longer. In the full flush of a cocaine habit, the user invariably curtails or eliminates all other expenditures in order to maximize the funds available for the drug. Since cocaine kills the appetite for food, it is possible to limit even that, the last expense to be cut in ordinary conditions of deprivation. It is as if there were a world where people struggled as they do in ours to accumulate capital, but where they never spend or invest, somehow vaporizing it without returning a cent to the macroeconomy. Although it is true that money paid for cocaine circulates thereafter, cocaine at the end of the cash cycle simply disappears, leaving in its wake only an overwhelming desire for more of itself. Cocaine as money thus removes the consumer from the macrocosm of consumption into a one-expenditure microcosm whose laws are nonetheless the same, and whose resemblance to the larger markets makes it a dangerous simulacrum.

Where capital accumulations can be invested and made to grow, an accumulation of cocaine can only diminish. The sole way to reverse the diminution of supply is to exchange some kind of conventional money for more of the drug. There is, in this repetitive act, an implicit contempt for ordinary currency, whose supposedly abstract universalism is reduced to one concrete and endlessly repeated transaction. If money in the era of Consumerism is the arbiter of all virtue, moral, aesthetic, and social, to negate money in this way is to negate "the good" in all its manifestations. In other words, cocaine exposes in its skeletal simplicity the very paradigm of Consumerism: spend, get, and feel throughout the process the most exquisite euphoria. Cocaine is therefore not as abstract as money, and yet at the same time it is more so. Worse still, it is an embarrassing parody of the free-market economy.

A level of income may be compared to a heroin habit in that one becomes accustomed to a certain daily dosage, which, if reduced, causes panic and symptoms of withdrawal. But with cocaine the preferred dosage is infinite: the user keeps going until the supply runs out or the body simply cannot remain conscious (or alive) any longer. It is, in other words, impossible to lose interest in cocaine just because you've had enough of it. So too money often remains one of life's most enduring interests. Accumulating money is something we would gladly do until our final breath on earth. The co-terminousness of desire and life is comparable for both money and blow. Cocaine asks us to contemplate the absurdity of a world powered by desire alone. It began as a drug of the rich because it felt as though it confirmed their paradigm—with passion, in the veins and the loins. It is now a drug of the poor, the substitute both affective and intellectual for an opportunity to engage in the broader fiduciary and cultural world from which those without money are excluded. Every time money is exchanged for cocaine, money's claim to be identical with value itself is called into question. But the basic monetary principal of desire is affirmed too lasciviously to sustain the pieties of the free market.

Perhaps the crowning metaphor for the relationship between money and cocaine can be found in the practice, universal before the advent of freebasing and crack, of nasally inhaling the alkaloid through a rolled-up bill. In this act there is a significance attached to the denomination of the bill so utilized. Never mind that a user confronted with a line of the drug would certainly find a way to snort it if even a single were unavailable, twenty is usually the lowest acceptable size to offer around. A hundred or anything larger is a statement of great authority. This custom may go back to the days when cocaine was a drug for the wealthy, or at any rate for the profligate or for those pretending to be rich, but it has carried over into the time of the drug's vulgarization. There is perhaps a tacit assumption that the larger denominations are cleaner, since they (may) change hands less frequently and more ceremoniously. Cleanliness is desirable not only because of the fear of disease—herpes, for example, can be transmitted by sharing snorters—but also because the purity of the drug is valued.

So money retains its hierarchical prestige, but only to be rolled into a cylinder too narrow to read the denomination of the bill anyway. The banknote is then subjected to a strange debasement. It is sniffed through, leaving residues of drugs and snot at the respective ends, then unrolled, licked inside and backrolled, repocketed, and recirculated as if it had never undergone such a subjugation. Money thus becomes a medium for drug consumption in a degradingly literal sense, but it retains its value after the act, whereas the drugs involved are gone. Still, the money has been for an instant parodied in its governing role over drug exchange. It has been forced to enact its symbolic function physically, as if an "ass-licker" or sycophant were abruptly called upon to perform the literal act that provides that appellation.

The problem may be restated as follows: money is supposed to be the universal medium of desire. It is supposed to be exchangeable for anything whose price falls below the amount of money (or money and credit) available. Money is therefore supposed to approximate desire itself. And yet a person already high on cocaine would always choose more of the drug rather than a greater value-amount of money if that money could not be immediately exchanged for more cocaine. The element of deferred or retained desire that usually characterizes money is tantamount to no desire at all under the influence of the cocaine high. If the money cannot be transmuted at once into the drug needed to sustain the high, then that money is valueless. In this way cocaine short-circuits the very mechanism by which money and desire achieve identity, displacing the mantle of "pure desire" onto itself. "Blow money," or money convertible immediately into cocaine, along with the capital accumulations resulting from such transactions, is therefore a continuing global threat to all the conventional national currencies, which are rolled into little tubes to facilitate the infinite high.

Sex, Drugs, Technology, and the Body

Without the paternal metaphor [God]
holding things together, one became the arti-
san of one's own body, fiddling around, experiment-
ing, creating new parts or treating the psyche like an organ, a
sick organ. One became a maniacal bricoleur of one's own body.
AVITAL RONELL   Crack Wars

The mystique of self-administration makes every user his or her own doctor and pharmacist. This means that heretical medical rationales are available for almost all illicit substances, even as their therapeutic potential (marijuana for glaucoma or multiple sclerosis, or to ease chemotherapy; LSD for the dying; heroin for pain) is denied by a health-care establishment that is committed to selling the "legitimate" products of pharmaceutical companies.

All sorts of tales are told by users about therapeutic side effects. Some think that snorting cocaine or drinking whiskey can cure a cold, or that scotch or heroin can profit the lower intestine, or that red wine can help anemia. These are vestiges of folk medicine, and are laughed at by allopaths. Questions of efficacy aside, however, users of forbidden drugs tend to believe that they are in control of their bodies, and that their tinkering enhances their understanding of the way their bodies work. This kind of bricolage, to echo Avital Ronell, can be self-delusory, but it can also be perceived as dangerous, since it removes potential patients from the offices of physicians and the databases of chain pharmacies. Its greatest blasphemy is not so much its refusal of allopathic theories and techniques, although this may be the case, but its throwback to an old individualistic self-reliance. There is a casting off of the moral overtones of conventional medicine. The approach of mainstream medicine—pitting a curative substance against a disease, or, more precisely, against the *symptoms* of a disease—is reminiscent of all Western dramas of good versus evil, and as such admits of no gray areas or separate peaces.[1] It interprets the body as a battlefield, neutral and passive, on which

Armageddon is played out over and over again: will you be cured and join the saints, or die and be stricken from the Book of Life? It is for this reason that the disease metaphor of drug use has now replaced the old rhetoric of criminality and moral failure. The medical lexicon has become allegorical. It is a way of preserving moral strictures against drugs in the absence of any common ethical discourse. The penalty for many drug violations is now a remanding to compulsory treatment, which brings the user back into the purview of conventional medicine, and the oppositional morality of the West.[2] The association of treatment and punishment is a savory one, bringing, as it does, several forms of authority to bear at the same time. The doctor and drug dealer, the judge and jailer, the priest and confessor, are all rolled into one.

Drug users' attempts to gain dominion over their own bodies are therefore blasphemous in a multitude of ways. One thing that most instances of this bricolage have in common is that they try to thresh away the moral resonances of allopathy. Let's consider a low point, the moment when drugs and the body seem to be most at odds with each other: the hangover. The word itself asserts a causal connection between last night's administration of drugs and a feeling of physical and psychological illness the following morning. No one seems to question this case of *post hoc, ergo propter hoc*. There is a moral precept embedded in the term, to the effect that after every pleasure there must be a correlative pain, and that the punishment of a hangover is therefore perfectly attuned to its crime, like chopping off the right hand of a thief. It is assumed that it is a chemical confirmation of guilt, and an incentive to repentance. In fact many people experience it this way, even if they have no general scruples about getting high. The tacit assumption is that if the sufferer had not indulged on the previous evening he or she would feel perfectly well the next day. But of course there is no way of proving this.

Is a hangover really retributive? Must it be thought of as punishment, or can it be considered a sequential development of the high? The narrator in Alan Hollinghurst's novel *The Swimming-Pool Library* professes an increase in sexual desire the day after drinking too much.[3] This would be *pleasure* hanging over, a happier gloss on the term. A strong speed high can reassert itself uninvited the following day. It might be as delightful as the original dose if it were allowed to be, if it weren't smothered in the proper regret. In LSD hangovers, stationary objects appear to be smoking, and moving objects leave visual trails behind them. There would be some interest in all this, if we let there be. Perhaps the aftermath of a high is every bit as user-constructed as the primary high itself.

It might be instructive to think of instances where hangovers do not occur, or are not severe. People who drink large quantities of alcohol every night usually claim that they never experience any ill effects on the mornings after. The sober interpretation of these statements is usually that the heavy drinker is so accustomed to being hungover that he or she simply doesn't notice it anymore, having nothing to compare it to. A physiologist might explain it in terms of increased tolerance, or pathologically higher levels of the liver enzymes that metabolize alcohol. But a third and less popular thesis is that heavy drinkers *learn* how to manage the effects of toxicity. Instead of triggering fusillades of guilt and self-loathing, they make themselves aware of what the stomach wants or doesn't, or how to relax the neck and temples *before* a headache begins. They rely on baths and showers, not only to cleanse the toxins that collect in the hair and on the skin, but also for rehydration. They may take a potion of some sort— Gatorade, tomato juice, or the bartender's favorite, soda water and bitters. The point is that the most experienced users of alcohol (and other drugs that produce difficult aftereffects) know that the illness (if that is what it is) is at least partly voluntary. They escape most hangovers because consciously or unconsciously they do not accept the moral dynamic that insists on them.

Of course this thesis has a limitation, since for any ingested substance there are levels of toxicity that inevitably produce physical illnesses. There are also differences among hangovers from various drugs. With cocaine, for example, there is an interim stage between euphoria and hangover—the crash, which takes place before sleep. The true cocaine hangover is complicated by a consequence of the euphoria itself, namely that it arouses hypersexual desire without encouraging the closure of orgasm. While the crash is anerotic, the hangover can provide an occasion for the user to discharge the sexual tension built up during the euphoric portion of the high. There is an element of relief in it, along with the dehydration, exhaustion, nausea, and headache.

Still, the construction of hangovers always has renunciation at its core. The sufferer is expected to repent sincerely of the supposed cause, take the blame upon the self, and look for treatment and forgiveness. Hangover's principal rhetoric is vomiting, an objectifying narrative at its finest. It is a rite of purification, reversing the flow of time as surely as that of the peristalsis, and undoing what was done some hours before. It turns things inside out, and it revises history. It confesses, and in confessing reveals itself while concealing another whole set of things, like what "really happened" as opposed to what just "came up." If punishment is expected for doing drugs, then punishment will be dispensed. If hangovers are to be believed, then every drug contains its own antidote, as if there were some hypothetical midpoint from which every deviation is subsequently matched by an equal and opposite deviation in the other direction. Yet even if there were such a point, why should it reassert itself by yet another deviation from itself?

I would like to suggest that hangovers are *not* the referencing of the high to a criterion outside the consciousness of the user, but instead are simply a continuation of the high in a more or less dysphoric phase. If given a moral gloss, they alienate the user from her or his body. The body is felt to have been wronged by the prior night's indulgence, and its pain is accentuated by the user's feeling that it is justified in its complaint. This is why hangovers seem tinged with moral retribution: the sense that the body is right, that it has been a victim and now has a good case against the consciousness that abused it for short-term gratification. This is reinforced in a culture where medicine, law, and morality have become conflated as they are today. The notion of drug use as a victimless crime has been replaced by a model in which the user's body is the user's victim. Sometimes these arguments are framed in economic terms, citing the cost to employers of sickness, absenteeism, and poor performance by users, or calculating the cost to the gross national product of hospital expenses incurred by drug takers. Sometimes, as in the case of the secondhand tobacco smoke controversy, the victimized body is pluralized. But in every instance the effect is to schism a user into multiple parts, each of which is assigned a part in the newest staging of the battle against evil.

The hangover is a good illustration of the submission of pain to a moral template. In the case of pleasure, however, there is no escaping this predetermination of experience. A good measure of the vehemence of the War on Drugs has come from its harnessing of traditional American puritanism and the attendant suspicion about pleasure. The worry is that drug use is capable of removing pleasure from an ethical matrix. This danger is perceived as greater than in the case of pain, since the medical establishment has chosen never explicitly to concern itself with pleasure. There is, to be sure, a conscious preoccupation with it in the legal taxonomies of interdiction, where a substance's ability to cause euphoria is often an important criterion in the decision to prohibit it. Erich Goode notes the resemblance of heroin and morphine as follows:

> These two drugs are not very different pharmacologically and biochemically, except that pure heroin is several times as potent as morphine. . . . An experienced drug addict would probably not be able to discern the difference between comparable doses of heroin and morphine, and a pharmacologist would have to look very, very closely to distinguish the laboratory effects of the two drugs. . . . Nonetheless, heroin is declared to have no medical uses whatsoever. It is considered a menace, a killer. Morphine, on the other hand, is regarded as a boon to mankind.[4]

The tacit distinguishing element can only be this: morphine is used to avoid pain, and heroin is used to induce pleasure. Medicine excludes substances that potentiate euphoria not, of course, by legislating against them, but by not mentioning them. The augmentation of pleasure is not a subject treated in the curricula of medical schools. But why not? Because there is still a prevalent belief that it is morally wrong to do anything to increase physical pleasure, or at any rate that it is not in the Hippocratic oath, the physician's job description.

There is a brute psychology that applies to this. It reads: our own pleasures are harmless, but the things that give pleasure to others are either frivolous or morally reprehensible. There is almost nothing on earth so hard to endure as the spectacle of others enjoying themselves by way of an activity in which we do not engage. Because I do not ski, for example, I am convinced that skiers are either silly or downright crazy for wanting to risk life and limb sliding down mountains on sticks in the dead of winter. The abstinent always shrink from the indulgent. And when the subject turns from amusements to sexual activity, the resistance becomes even greater, since to allow others their preference in this area is always to cast doubt on one's own accommodation with this ineluctable appetite. Every person's sexuality has been constructed with painstaking care, balancing physical and metaphysical needs, desire and character, pleasure and self-image. The last thing one needs to see is a representation of someone else's very different accommodation. Because one has not chosen that pathway oneself, what is presented is always a picture of what one has rejected, or never dared to consider. And that picture is almost always repugnant.

Part of the demonization of drugs has been accomplished by associating the use of psychoactive substances with outré sexual practices. This association hinges on an implicit causality: the use of drugs *makes* people act sexually in "abnormal" ways, that is, in ways other than one's own. In my discussion of stimulant "hypersexuality," I tried to show how cocaine and amphetamines can in fact permit a wider array of sexual behaviors in individual users, but I argued that this is a result of the apotheosis of desire itself rather than a change in the object of desire. Stimulant use has given grist to the mill of those who link drugs and sex, since the indiscriminate nature of hypersexuality cannot help but create images of whatever it is one fears most in the sexual universe. There is no question that at the highest degrees of their potency stimulants can do just what puritans dread: they can harness the intellect utterly to the service of powerful erotic impulses. They can also do more than alcohol, which is usually thought to disinhibit only what's already there; for stimulants can really introduce new sexual acts into the user's repertory. Given, however, the highly idiosyncratic nature of sex practices, it is possible to see a wider variety of behaviors as a beneficial thing that might outlast a particular intoxication to enrich the user's sexuality afterward, with or without the readministration of a drug.

Having been concerned up to this point primarily with the impact of various drugs on consciousness, and ceding to biochemists the catalogue of pharmaceutical effects on the body, I want now to turn to the question of how certain drugs may or may not affect *consciousness of the body*. Needless to say, generalization is again disingenuous here, since (putting drugs aside altogether) people have very different relationships with their bodies. How a particular drug affects body consciousness assumes that we have some knowledge of how the user has previously constructed this kind of awareness, and of what potential for change and development is present within an individual character. Some researchers, though, have made broad statements:

If we . . . question the operational consequences of drug
ingestion, we find an intensified awareness of the body
and a shift in its focus and orientation. General feelings
of conscious existence, as it is normally sensed in the
functioning of the body, are either amplified or tuned
down; attention shifts and there are distortions in the
experience of the body and the surrounding field.[5]

Most of the time the body is perceived as a quiescent landscape peri-
odically dotted with points of pain or zones of pleasure. When it is
called upon to perform a physical act, the body is expected to execute
it without a great deal of unusual sensation. Medical pathology is
indicated when too much pain or dysfunction accompanies a resting
or active body. Putting aside the advent of pain from long-term
effects of drug administration—lung congestion, gastritis, inflamed
mucous membranes, collapsing veins—the difference between body
consciousness in pathology and in intoxication is that in the latter
case the landscape changes when it is demarcated with more "land-
marks" of pleasure. A stimulant high can give an action as simple as
walking a little of the excitement of orgasm, while an opiate can
cause a stripe of blissful relaxation to roll down the ventral side. The
famous enhancement of taste buds under the influence of hemp
drugs is an accentuation of an already existing zone of pleasure, but
on that model sexual sensations can also be savored and intensified.
In their different ways, various substances can and do change the
configuration of the body's internal landscape so that nodes of pleasure stand out more saliently. It is possible to conceive of drug use in
general as (among all those other things) a set of technologies for
making these happy changes in the somatic terrain.

Pharmacology is not the only technology that seeks to enhance
the body's capacity for registering physical euphoria. Telephone sex
has been available for many years now, and there are all sorts of on-
line cyberspace "rooms" where participants play out their interactive
fantasies. But this is only the beginning. As virtual-reality technology
becomes more widely available, it is expected that there will be even
more sophisticated erotic technologies. There is even a field called
teledildonics that is developing a full-body suit equipped with a multitude of sensors that will enable the user to engage in sexual contact
with other users in a VR network.[6] Probably those who regard computers as electronic bookkeepers or typewriters will see this as a per-

version of a utilitarian device. The emergence of these applications, however, suggests that technology is inherently neutral until it is put to some use or other. Similarly, there are a myriad of reasons why people use psychoactive substances. They may be in search of relaxation, enlightenment, energy, or escape. Sexual enhancement, or at any rate the accentuation of the body's ability to convey pleasure to consciousness, is only one other reason. But it is a significant one. Of all forms of somatic bricolage, those concerned with accentuating physical delight are among the most universal. Drugs or no drugs, computers or no computers, every sexual act, whether solitary or interpersonal, tends to be orchestrated to a greater or lesser degree. Onanism is particularly prone to this sort of staging, since the accompanying internal narrative is subject to instantaneous recall and revision without giving any consideration to another player. The narrator creates a situation, summons a virtual partner or partners, and begins a discourse whose aim in the achievement of orgasm. Yet if the narrative is not proceeding satisfactorily toward that end, or is lacking in interim gratifications, it may be reversed or suspended and modified. These imaginative tinkerings are accompanied by physical adjustments intended to stimulate one or more of the participant's repertory of erogenous zones.

The superaddition of drugs or computers may enhance the technological complexity of erotic bricolage, but it does not change its fundamental nature. A twosome sipping champagne before going to bed are not really doing anything different from an on-line couple five thousand miles apart smoking joints before donning their teledildonic body suits. Drugs of all sorts are deployed to alter the situational field in which sex takes place. Those who find fault with drugs because they lead to sexual activity are laboring under the delusion that without drugs no sex would take place. Because both drug use and sex involve manipulation of the body in the interests of pleasure, they are easy to amalgamate in a puritanical agenda. This much they have in common: neither one will cease (nor has ever ceased) because of legislation or theological restriction. And because both are unavoidable elements of human existence, they are certain to intersect, as they do.

All of this takes place in a medical environment where bricolage is already taking place on a scale unimaginable only a short time ago. The mechanistic character of allopathy has made organ transplanting common, and it is easy to foresee an increasing variety of prosthetic devices available for those with money enough to buy them. The advent of drugs like Prozac and Rogaine suggests that medical technology is deeply involved in somatic enhancements that make full-body VR suits seem like mere toys. Government regulation has, after all, removed from the prescription rolls almost all the drugs that customers actually wanted for euphoric effects. Amphetamines are the clearest example. Restricted to the point where they could no longer be scripted by doctors, these drugs quickly metamorphosed into street commodities, changing their form from the pills favored by pharmacists to powder or the smokable "ice." The competition between MDMA (Ecstasy) and Prozac also illustrates the new competition between pharmaceutical corporations and illegal chemists. There is no doubt that these drugs are trying to reach the same clientele, even though the former is sold as a sex and love drug and the latter as a preparation for almost any psychiatric diagnosis. As William Gibson prophesied in his *Neuromancer* trilogy, modifications and extensions of the body are becoming a commercial enterprise with a limitless potential for innovation and profit. It is difficult to deny that the present-day computer and medical industries are modeling themselves on the paradigms of body intervention created by the world of illegal drug use.

This is why it continues to be convenient and plausible to blame "drugs" for the side effects of this brave new world of body manipulation. Transsexual surgery and its hormonal supports, breast implants, penile implants for permanent erections, aphrodisiac backlash from Prozac and L-Dopa—are these so different from illicit parodies of medical practice like the cocaine enema or a popper popped just when the orgasm (instead of the angina) begins? Body bricolage now seems destined to continue even after death, as the science of cryogenics shows. The current fascination with near-death experiences hints at a time when visions of the "clear light" will be available as inhalants for the affluent.

Seen from this angle, psychoactive drugs can be revisioned as simply another technology for change, as citizens of the postmodern universe reject one of life's "givens" after another. It is no longer reasonable to claim that "drugs destroy the mind" and turn users into carnal wolverines. Drugs do whatever chemistry, circumstances, and specific user application propel them to do. The same can be said for computers. Just as the boundaries that separated the various communications and data-processing media have already broken down, so too the body technologies are all merging with each other, and with other electronic frequencies. The ancient art of acupuncture is now enhanced with a battery and alligator clips.

No wonder drug users show so little hesitation about tinkering with their bodies. The notion that an organic creature should be left alone merely to exist with all its inherent powers and limitations seems utterly quaint. We have entered into the world of codes that determine the fact and nature of being, and whether the entity in question grew from a single cell or was manufactured in a shop is now an irrelevant bit of ancient history. If even personality is susceptible to modification by Prozac and related medications, it is difficult to defend misgivings about physical tinkerings and ameliorations. Surgical, pharmacological, and cybernetic prosthesis will gradually merge into a single technology where the body is concerned, and not all of its manifestations will be curative and anesthetic. Some will be about pleasure, and some will be about getting high.

Toward a
Diversity of
Consciousness

A number of templates have been
superimposed upon the inevitable human
practice of getting high. The dominant model
ever since Homer's *Odyssey* has been the criminal one,
but today it is being seriously challenged by a medical schematic. The growing identification of drug use with sickness has created a movement to reassign the responsibility for combating drugs
from the police and the military to the medical establishment. Most
liberal drug reformers subscribe to some variant of this theory, and
certainly their argument is a strong one from a humanitarian point of
view. Alcohol and nicotine cessation programs have been test cases for
this proposed transfer of authority, since these drugs are legal, and not
completely monopolized by law enforcement. Users are therefore up
for grabs by doctors and hospitals competing for business. Dan Waldorf, Craig Reinarman, and Sheigla Murphy refer to this position as
"the presumption of pathology. By this we mean that virtually every
politician, journalist, drug warrior, and moral entrepreneur speaks of
our nation's drug problems as if no rational human being would want
to get high. . . . It is a rare, perhaps foolhardy, soul who speaks of
drug users as people making rational choices."[1]

Thomas Szasz argues that people want drugs, not treatment, and
he cautions against compulsory drug-abuse therapy as a manifestation of the growing tyranny of the health-care establishment.[2] We
cringed at accounts of Soviet incarceration of homosexuals, artists,
and political dissidents in mental institutions, but as our prisons
become overcrowded we are being escorted step-by-step to the same
practice with respect to drug users. The debate at this moment
echoes discussions of homosexuality twenty or thirty years ago, when
it was argued that treating it as a disease was somehow kinder and
gentler than criminalizing it. The grueling political battle to gain full
citizenship for homosexuals, while far from over, can provide an
example and an inspiration for those who want to change the way
drug users live in our society. It is remarkable that gay and lesbian

activists were finally able to fight free of the disease model at the very time when a deadly epidemic had just made its beachhead in the male homosexual community. Today they are debating a variant of the disease model that claims that homosexuality is genetically determined. The issue of whether or not a certain behavior is voluntary or involuntary is really a red herring, since it wants to assert that the identification of a behavior's *cause* can explain (and by extension "cure") it. At its strongest moments, the crusade for homosexual rights has been based on pure realism. Love and sex between people of the same gender has existed from the dawn of time, and all efforts to eradicate it are based on an incomplete understanding of human nature.

This sentence can be rewritten about the use of drugs: the practice of getting high has existed from the dawn of time, and all efforts to eradicate it are based on an incomplete understanding of human nature. We have already seen that the full power of law, the police, and the military has been unable to stop it. I believe that we should learn from the past and avoid going through an equally futile stage of medical explanation and repression. Progressive forces in America have been fighting since the 1960s to broaden the platform of democracy to include all races, ethnicities, sexual orientations, religions, and physical and mental challenges. It is time now to add another diversity to that list: diversity of consciousness.

What sense does it make to condemn millions of Americans to lives of concealment, danger, and discredit? If the aim is to enable them to contribute productively to society to the greatest extent they can, then it is obviously wrong to imprison and hospitalize them. The question should be: how can we allow people to get high safely, without imperiling their capacity for work, love, and citizenship? What is at stake here is the drawing of a borderline between public and private life. Despite the individualist and antigovernment rhetoric of the Republican Party, private life now finds itself caught in an ever-narrowing circle. Once we thought that owning property gave us the right to be left alone on it. Now the home-as-castle has become the locked bedroom door, but up against parabolic microphones, heat sensors, and enormous databases that door cannot stand on its jambs much longer. The implications of the War on Drugs for traditional relationships of corporation, state, and individual in the West are far-reaching. Not only because of drugs but also because of AIDS, the state has entered into the confines of the human mind and body as never before. George Orwell in *1984* has his character Julia say, "It's the one thing they can't do. They can make you say anything—*anything*—but they can't make you believe it. They can't get inside you."[3] Winston Smith agrees; but by the end of the novel both are proven wrong.

This destruction of privacy has come about only partly as a result of ideology and premeditated policy. Presumably, few politicians and executives have set meddling in the homes and bloodstreams of others as deliberate goals in their careers—at least I hope this is the case. Rather, these intrusive practices have burgeoned simply *because they are possible*. So many changes in technology have happened so rapidly that their development and marketing have come without adequate consideration of the social and political consequences. It is another instance where the humanities and social sciences have moved much more slowly than engineering. This circumstance is now irreversible, and we must learn to live with a diminished sphere of physical and psychological privacy. What crosses the blood-brain barrier is now open to the same surveillance as what crosses international borders. There is a customs in the cranium, a Checkpoint Consciousness.

But predator/prey is only one of many possible relationships between technology and drug users. As swiftly as techniques of interdiction have blossomed, chemists with the same new information have created "designer drugs," some of them from corporate laboratories with "legitimate" medical and commercial intentions, but others synthesized in covert facilities and meant from the first for the black market. Like all technologies, pharmacology is essentially ambivalent. It can promote health, or it can be employed to tame and control populations, as the CIA hoped when it began to experiment with LSD. But pharmacology can also generate new ways to get high. There is a parallel with computer science, which appears to be a tool for the curtailment of privacy and individualism, but which by dint of its frenzied growth has created an enormous cyberspace full of dark corners in which every sort of heterodoxy flourishes. The current sympathy and overlap between drug takers and hackers (both groups are called "users") are based on their common perception that the reprogramming of consciousness, whether human or electronic, promises a quasi-evolutionary leap. It is significant, perhaps, that Timothy Leary, one of the first to suggest Darwinian possibilities for a drug, moved into the field of software design after his release from prison. Drug and computer outlaws think of themselves as constituting a political resistance to Consumerism. The underground economy depicted in William Gibson's novels, where trade in pharmaceuticals and software is one and the same, appears to have become a reality.

A third component of this underground is medical technology itself, where the so-called "health-care crisis" is precipitating great changes in the roles played by drug companies, doctors, and patients (if that is the right word for them). A cursory study of history shows that until early in the twentieth century doctors, shamans and quacks, makers and dispensers of snake oil, herbal preparations, and patent medicines were all pretty much in the same business, with the principal differences among them found in their marketing strategies. In the gathering shadows of World War I, the traditional division of trade among these various agencies and practitioners began to disintegrate, and they commenced to invade each other's territories. As Szasz points out, "Before 1907, all drugs could be sold and bought like any other consumer good."[4] Subsequent legislation and regulation have had the effect of privileging doctors and large corporate drug makers by creating the prescription system, which separates big manufacturers from small and individual drug preparers, and physicians from drug dealers. None of these functions actually changed, of course, but an artificial system of human and pharmacological classes resulted. This may account in part for the utterly arbitrary nature of drug taxonomies. At the moment, this system appears in turn to have reached the point of dissolution. With many drugs available that have no medical addresses—that is, they do not treat specific ailments—the initiative for prescribing has now shifted from the doctor to the consumer. As Szasz, again, has it, "The advertising of prescription drugs encourages people to pressure their physicians to prescribe the drugs they *want,* rather than the drugs the physicians believe they *need.*"[5] Now doctors are finding themselves in the role of drug dealers, or worse, mere accomplices to pharmacists. No doubt health-care reform, if it does transpire, will contain provisions to enable doctors and druggists to maintain their image of difference from street dealers and synthesizers. But this distinction is becoming even more arbitrary and tenuous as biochemical information becomes easier and easier to obtain (partly through the labyrinths of on-line cyberspace) and act upon.

What is likely to happen, then, is not the collapse of the distinction, but a reconfiguration of it. As the concept of "private practice" is replaced by a corporate health maintenance organization model, physicians will lose the status of mediators between patients and drug companies. The decision to prescribe a medicine, product of one corporate entity, will be made by a doctor who is now little more than an employee of another corporate entity. Presumably HMOs will have, or already have, house policies about what gets prescribed to whom under what circumstances. Having no middle ground, medical practice will be divided between the administration of corporate policies, on the one hand, and the direct treatment of patients on the other, with the latter becoming virtually illegal. One can envision, as William Burroughs did in *Blade Runner, A Movie,* a medical world schismed completely in half.[6] Corporate and underground drugs and practitioners will compete for patients, though of course the deck will be stacked in favor of the aboveground institutions.

Clearly, the advent of AIDS hastened this divide, as medications with the potential to help sick and dying people were subjected to cumbersome testing, or in some cases were banned outright. An earlier instance is the laetrile controversy, which looms larger and larger retrospectively as a symptom of change. The consignment of some therapeutic drugs to the fugitive status of street intoxicants suggests that the fiction of the prescription is finally coming to an end. The distinction between scripted and back-alley medicaments will be based more than ever on marketing and profit rather than efficacy. The addition of products like Rogaine and Prozac to the prescription lists reinforces the notion that the pharmaceutical companies are trying to invade the markets previously served by quacks and outlaw dealers. Soon everyone may be engaging in the same bricolage of the body that the illicit user always has. But the new and expanded medical corporations are calling on the state to help them get their share of the interdicted markets. This would be the effect of "legalization," which is little more than a recognition that there is a lot of money to be made in euphorics and herbal remedies, and that the "legitimate" health-care establishment wants its share.

Most of the recent condemnations of the War on Drugs have partaken of the rhetoric of medicine. Drives to legitimate the therapeutic applications of marijuana and heroin can be mounted on commonsensical grounds, skirting the whole question of getting high. At a rally for the legalization of marijuana at my university, I heard a speaker refer to pot as "the number one remedy for stress, which is the world's number one disease." These developments foreshadow the "medicalization" of all drug use, legal and illegal. They suggest that any user could make a medical (rather then hedonistic) case for her or his drug of choice. In other words, one reaction to the "presumption of pathology" is to assert that the use of psychoactive substances is not the disease, but the cure. This of course assumes that undoctored consciousness is, because of stress or materialistic values or some other infection, sick. Although this reaction to the disease model is redolent with poetic justice, it still casts the problem within medical discourse. And worse, its negative assumptions about the nature of "straight" consciousness are no more justifiable than the positive ones on which the rhetoric of the war depends.

It is possible to harbor suspicions that these reformers are unintentionally (or intentionally?) serving the interests of the drug companies who want to enter the euphoria market by whatever means they can find, even by appeals to emotionally charged libertarian buzzwords like "choice," "freedom," and "individualism." The pharmaceutical companies have a vested interest in medicalization. Criminalization forced these multinational corporations to stop selling anything with euphoric value, most notably LSD and the amphetamines. They have had to give up millions of customers who want drugs that will get them high. Medicalization will force these users back into the drug companies' market, and will artificially escalate "demand" for all sorts of new products, which, on the model of methadone, will be prescribed as part of "treatment."

And so the next stage of the War on Drugs, the time of medicalization, will abandon the reign of enforcement terror for a vocabulary of inclusion, beckoning the user to surrender to "care," to trade in his or her street drugs for straight drugs, to stop seeing the dealer and see the doctor instead. Heroin can be swapped for methadone, booze for Antabuse, Camels for Habitrol, even cocaine for Prozac. Perhaps THC (cannabis that can't be grown in the backyard) will be scripted for stress, glaucoma, and nausea. After all, the great pharmaceutical houses can rightly say that they (and not street labs) invented LSD and amphetamines. They can call implicitly on this background in producing euphorics as they try to put the rogue drug sellers out of business by means more effective than guns and surveillance—by entering their markets and beating them at their own game. And they can also offer, in lieu of the paranoia of meeting somebody in an alley, the comfort of crossing the well-lit threshold of a health maintenance organization.

Szasz, Milton Friedman, and other upper-case Libertarians believe that their alternative—an unregulated free market in drugs—is a way to end the war without exchanging the legal and police tyranny for a medical one. But I suspect that the outcome would be the same, since tearing down the whole edifice of law, policy, and enforcement would only speed the entry of drug and health corporations into the previously prohibited markets. There would, however, be advantages for users, since they would not be criminalized any longer, or compelled to turn themselves in to institutions in order to obtain intoxicants. The problem with the Libertarian position is that it believes that there really *is* such a thing as a free market—as if corporations cannot collude and conspire just as easily as governments can. Authority is authority, whether it flies the American flag or the logo of Bristol-Myers or Kaiser Permanente. The assumption that citizens would be freer under direct corporate rule than under the present arrangement—corporate rule halfheartedly mediated by the state—seems dubious to me.

Reform is doubly difficult because of the suppression of discourse about drugs during a dozen years of recent history. The rhetoric that lumped diverse substances together makes it seem as if there has to be a blanket solution that will cover all drugs in all situations. But this may not be possible. I believe that cannabis is something of a special case that can be disposed of almost as a side issue. Despite the best efforts of drug warriors and their contract scientists, none of the deleterious consequences attributed to pot and hashish have been made to stick. To be sure, if potheads inhaled the same volume of smoke that tobacco users do, they would suffer respiratory consequences. But they usually do not. It is also true that chronic use can reduce men's testosterone levels. But is this such a problem in an overpopulated world? None of the medical prophecies of disaster lavished upon the spread of pot during the 1960s have come true, even though use has not declined. Compared with alcohol, marijuana seems utterly harmless. Whatever violence attends it is a product of the law and not the substance. Pot doesn't break up families (unless somebody's busted). It doesn't rot livers. It doesn't promote overconfidence. It doesn't make the user want some other drug, or in fact do anything the user wouldn't do anyway. All it does is play a descant over the phenomena of ordinary life.

Marijuana, despite its interdiction, remains one of the top cash crops grown by American farms. Legal cultivation would be a boon to agriculture, especially if the tobacco market declines in the years to come.[7] Despite the portrayal of drugs as foreign, were pot legal not one cent spent on it would need to leave the country, and not one cent would have to go to organized crime, since users can easily grow their own supply.[8] The trouble is, of course, that the plant is so easy to cultivate that no one would need the synthetic alternatives that the drug companies would like to sell. The doctrine of "free herb," elaborated widely in the 1960s and still alive in Rastafarian culture, disallows profiting from the weed, and this, along with the disinterested and contemplative nature of the cannabis high itself, places the pot smoker outside the matrix of consumer appetite and exchange. Nor would it be possible to collect taxes on this trade; it would be like trying to tax crabgrass or dandelions. It is this escape from the macroeconomy that makes legal cannabis too subversive to be considered seriously, and which apparently justifies enforcement measures that rely on procedures that not long ago would have been unthinkable: the deployment of the United States military against American citizens.

The tendency of Consumerism to totalize itself, to enter every market and reinterpret every action according to its empiricist world outlook, could militate either for or against deregulation, depending on how one envisions the future of the hemp market. If cannabis use is thought to erode the metaphysics of appetite, with no compensatory opportunities for profit, it will remain illegal forever. But if it is seen as too profitable a commodity to leave to the black market, then there will probably be a struggle for control between pharmaceutical companies and agricultural interests that foresee a wider variety of uses for the crop. What is least likely to happen is laissez-faire reform that will unfetter the user and small grower.

No matter which of these readings is right, the first step should be to repair the damages caused by the War on Drugs. Two immediate measures should be taken: (1) All inmates held in federal, state, or local prisons on cannabis sales or possession convictions should be released in an immediate general amnesty, provided the crimes for which they are serving time did not involve weapons. Although this would reduce prison overcrowding only slightly, it would at least be a step in the right direction. All property seized in forfeiture actions should be restored to the owners; (2) Prohibition of possession, cultivation, and sales should be repealed at the federal level, and states should be permitted to repeal or amend their laws as they see fit. By ending the hypocrisy and irrationality of the present situation, not only hemp itself but millions of users would be personally decriminalized. This would permit a public debate that is presently impossible because of the legal repercussions that proponents of change fear they may incur by exercising free speech.

It is impossible to predict the outcome of that debate, but it is doubtful that the specter of increased use raised by the prohibitionists would materialize. The flat reality of the situation today is that anyone with money who wants to buy a drug can do so at will, regardless of the law and its enforcement. Complete deregulation would answer the easy part of the question of what to do about the presence of drugs in the social world, since cannabis causes so little disruption compared to alcohol, tobacco, crack, and heroin. The culture of marijuana is also traditionally less insular than those of other drugs. A pot smoker does not limit his or her associations to other pot smokers, so that there would be no need to "reintegrate users into society" following deregulation. This proposal has the virtue of realism, but probably has little chance of adoption, since there is no money and power to be accrued by police, National Guard, hospitals, or drug companies if people are allowed to grow a weed and do what they please with it.

The empirical sciences must always narrow their circumference to suit the needs of a particular study. They must produce "results," so that their process of measurement inevitably forms and limits the very things they are measuring. When trying to discuss drugs, I have constantly come up against a near infinity of variables—the garden of forking paths—which intimates that there are aspects of consciousness that cannot be explained by physiology, genetics, behaviorism, psychoanalysis, or demography. This confrontation with boundlessness suggests that the problem has what Alcoholics Anonymous calls a "spiritual" dimension. As Thomas B. Gilmore summarizes it, "Alcoholics Anonymous regards alcoholism as a threefold illness, physical, mental and spiritual."[9] In the interests of making a fresh approach to the problem, I have tried to avoid employing illness as a metaphor for drug use, working instead from the assumption that the impulse to get high is an inevitable component of human nature. But the anguish and controversy that mark most discourse on this subject suggest that we are not comfortable with this constituent of our spirit. The guns and prisons, the suspensions of civil liberties, the surveillance and betrayals—besides their concrete reality they are also symptoms of some malaise almost too great and too deep to be articulated.

The trouble with AA's approach lies in the assumption that it is the drug user who is afflicted with a spiritual illness. If spiritual health would be the slight ascendancy of the affirmative over the negative, then Consumerism's New World Order—and not some poor drug user—is the locus of this "illness." Consumerist metaphysics, which cannot allow the gratification of desire, relies on dissatisfaction to keep its parishioners conscious and purchasing. There is always something missing, something that must be *owned* to bring about positive feelings. But once the next object is bought and possessed, giving a brief moment of satisfaction, hunger must be stimulated again. It is a losing battle.

Spiritual institutions like churches and museums have been commercialized during the consumerist age. The worship of gods and artworks may have begun as anticommercial, since neither God nor the permanent collection is a marketable commodity per se. But Consumerism has both mutated the old institutions and spawned new ones—TV "religions" whose main function is to solicit money from viewers, or mail-order catalogues from great museums offering reproductions or lesser artifacts. Consumerism, by turning these old spiritual institutions into mercenaries, has replaced transcendental values by monetary ones. The most important religions are the richest ones. The greatest novel is the one that sells the most copies. There is a market in spirit as there is a market in everything else, and as a result any sort of disinterested spirituality, or any noncommercial art like poetry, is nearly invisible.

The commercialization of drugs is a manifestation of the same phenomenon. Sacramental use of peyote by Native Americans or of ganga by Rastafarians may once have existed outside the flow of profitable traffic, but all psychoactive substances since the death of the counterculture have been subsumed into it. The pitfall with drug use as it is practiced today lies in the assumption that a dose can produce a spiritual event on demand, so that this ineffable realm becomes as manipulable by technical means as a pulse rate or a database. This notion is as repugnant as the idea that a sinner can gain redemption by purchasing a papal dispensation.

If there is a spiritual disease reaching epidemic proportions, it touches everyone, users and straights alike. Some drug users at least hope to modify Consumerism's fatal dynamic, even if their chances of success are slight. And who is worse off in a pandemic? Those who try, however lucklessly, to fight it, or those who trudge day after day to the mall in search of the curative purchase, the object that will turn the rhythm of their spirits positive, only to return again and again on the same hopeless mission? The fact that a tab of LSD is bought and paid for does not necessarily preclude the possibility that the drug could have the effect of clarifying the movements of spirit outside of any of the interpretive mechanisms. So too it is possible that an adherent of an established religion might have a mystical experience, or that a visitor to the Louvre might really be moved by one of the paintings on the wall. Perhaps it is in the nature of spiritual experience that it takes place in spite of its worldly surroundings. Maybe spiritual events are always unexpected, even (or especially?) to the meditator who sits for years in anticipation of one.

Consumerism no longer has any significant opposition in the political and economic realms. But this does not mean that time has stopped. It only means that whatever change eventuates will have to come from *within* the metaphysical universe that Consumerism has created. And this is so variable and uncontrolled that it can unleash all sorts of unexpected backflows and inconsistencies. The counterculture of the 1960s can in retrospect be seen as a symptom of the transition from industrial to information capitalism. In the aperture created by this change a brief window of spiritual activity opened with the assertion of transcendental values like love and peace, however naive it seems to say so today. With this came a spasm of scorn for an acquisitive metaphysics driven by money and appetite. Perhaps another window is opening today. Perhaps the cyberculture's claim that it is a new counterculture is not so frivolous.

It may be, as Terence McKenna believes, that it is precisely the *information* aspect of Consumerism that will cause it to evolve or even mutate. In his explorations he has encountered entities that seem wholly other, and who offer the possibility of a renewal of spirit through a symbiotic relationship between humanity and themselves. They are creatures of pure data, and as we gain knowledge about DNA and the digital nature of the universe, we can utilize their teachings to end temporal conflicts and make a spiritual and evolutionary advance. True, the *present* applications of digital technology seem unlikely to bring about any such rebirth. The bar code on product packaging only lubricates the moment of purchase, while data processing seems likely to supercharge marketing research and other forms of corporate surveillance. Just because information can be accrued and manipulated more effectively does not mean that the information is of any interest or value. But as technologies merge, and telephones, computers, cinema, audiotape, televisions, and radios become part of the same network, it seems only a matter of time before human genetic structure and brain function are interfaced with the rest. When a single underlying structure of both mind and matter is known, sooner or later something besides profit and loss is likely to come on-line.

There is no question that drugs will be one of these interacting technologies. They are just as likely to play a role in curing a "spiritual disease" as they are to exacerbate or to *be* it. It all depends on what drugs we are talking about, who makes them, who takes them, who administers them, and under what circumstances. Technologies are tools, and tools can be used for constructive or destructive purposes. I can drive a nail with a hammer, or break someone's skull. But the ambivalent nature of tools does not mean that they won't be used.

What I see in drug use is a series of reactions to a spiritual disease, the way quail fly in all directions if you toss a stone at them. And this disease is the result of living too long in a world ruled by desire. Seeing no opportunity for political dissent, a certain percentage of the population is seeking change through dissent of consciousness. America's three hundred thousand drug inmates are *prisoners of consciousness*. Whatever solution is found to "the drug problem" must offer reconciliation and reintegration to these dissenters. Diversities, including diversity of consciousness, are valuable only if the diverse parties are eventually to be included in the same community. Otherwise the celebration of difference becomes a new segregation.

We must understand that the War on Drugs is a real war, one in which neither side will ever be able to bring the other to unconditional surrender. No lasting peace can ever come from the will of one side alone. This war will end as all intractable wars do, when the parties are sick of bloodshed. There must be a formal cease-fire, to be followed by peace talks. Let all the diplomatic protocols apply, just as if the enemy were not ourselves. The silence wrought by the "Just Say No" campaign must be replaced by words, many, many words. And these words must come not only from police, doctors, sociologists, criminologists, and the usual experts, but from gang members, drug users, drug dealers, and underground manufacturers.

This book has been an attempt to "throw words" at the subject, as if it were opening some of the issues that will be broached at that peace conference. It is a terribly partial effort, since it has concentrated primarily on self-administered drugs of pleasure and desire. But in the long run these substances will be seen as part of a continuum with the drugs of healing, and with altogether new classes of substances. Once this totality is reunited after its forced division by antiquated laws and prejudices, and once it is integrated with the other technological systems that are developing and changing so swiftly, then the weapons will be laid down.

Is this a utopian reverie? Very likely. Peace always is.

NOTES

PREFACE:
WRITING ABOUT DRUGS

1. Andrew Weil, *The Natural Mind* (Boston: Houghton Mifflin, 1972), p. 70. I think of Weil's book as an ancestor of the present one. He was hoping to avoid the disciplinary boxes that limited inquiry even then. His book is a landmark of independence and toleration, but its very virtues make it seem quaint today: he is able to confess his own drug history without discrediting himself, or falling into the trap that he describes. Even as he bravely struggles to escape the various professional discourses, he cannot help reminding his readers that he is a Harvard man and a medical doctor. In other words, he is still "qualified" to discuss the subject.

2. "The confession is a ritual of discourse in which the speaking subject is also the subject of the statement; it is also a ritual that enfolds within a power relationship, for one does not confess without the presence (or virtual presence) of a partner who is not simply the interlocutor but the authority who requires the confession, prescribes and appreciates it, and intervenes in order to judge, punish, forgive, console, and reconcile; a ritual in which the truth is corroborated by the obstacles and resistances it has had to surmount in order to be formulated; and finally, a ritual in which the expression alone, independently of its external consequences, produces intrinsic modifications in the person who articulates it" (Michel Foucault, *The History of Sexuality,* vol. 1, *An Introduction,* trans. Robert Hurley [New York: Vintage Books, 1980], pp. 61–62).

3. Allen S. Weiss, *The Aesthetics of Excess* (Albany: State University of New York Press, 1989), p. ix.

4. As Solomon Snyder writes, "Let us say that a researcher wishes to understand events in the brain that give rise to the subjective feeling of joy. Laboratory researchers often scrutinize the behavior of animals in order to elucidate the general mechanisms by which the human brain functions, but when the subject of inquiry is an emotion, this approach has obvious limitations" (*Drugs and the Brain* [New York: Scientific American Books, 1986], p. 3).

5. I'm borrowing this term from criticism of cyberculture. "I really have no objection to someone who has come into our community, lived here and

participated, analyzing [his] experience and trying to put it into perspective. I think the objection to the 'critics' who are now fawning over cyberthis and cyberthat is that they are perceived as intellectual carpetbaggers who don't bother to learn the terrain before they create the map" (Mark Dery, "Flame Wars," in *Flame Wars,* ed. Mark Dery, special issue, *South Atlantic Quarterly* 92, no. 4 [fall 1993], p. 567).

INTRODUCTION TO PART I:
THE VERY SHORT HISTORY OF SOBRIETY

1. Determining a state of consciousness even from the *presence* of a substance is difficult enough. See, for example, George E. Vaillant's review of criteria for diagnosing alcoholism, in *The Natural History of Alcoholism* (Cambridge, Mass., and London: Harvard University Press, 1983). Vaillant finds that "Indeed, the diagnosis of alcoholism depends so much upon definition that some individuals believe that all dimensions are meaningless and suggest that there are as many alcoholisms as there are drinkers" (p. 22).

2. Erich Goode, *Drugs in American Society* (New York: Alfred A. Knopf, 1972); Andrew Weil and Winifred Rosen, *From Chocolate to Morphine,* rev. ed. (Boston: Houghton Mifflin, 1993).

3. Weil and Rosen, *From Chocolate to Morphine,* p. 9.

4. David F. Musto, *The American Disease: Origins of Narcotic Control,* expanded ed. (Oxford and New York: Oxford University Press, 1987), p. 261. Throughout this section I am indebted to the summary in the added chapter of Musto's new edition.

1. *PHARMAKA* AND *PHARMAKOS*

1. *The Odyssey,* book 9, lines 91–102. Translated by Robert Fagles (New York: Viking/Penguin, 1995).

2. The Cuban missile crisis of October 1962 first dramatized this complete internalization of the Other, and later became the determining moment of the counterculture. That week our teachers had no heart to conduct classes, but asked us to be quiet while we stared at the siren on the firehouse roof and waited for the world to end. Our reaction was no ordinary adolescent rebellion: our parents offered us not only boredom but death and extinction. Against this backdrop, Freudian paradigms pale to academic puzzles and games. We fell asleep on those nights with eros pitted against thanatos, refusing to believe that the end of the species would happen before we had sex, imagining fucking for the twenty minutes we would have before history ended. When Kennedy died, or Martin Luther King or

Malcolm X or another Kennedy, or when the green bags began to come back from Vietnam, everything followed like a syllogism from the nuclear premise: the fate of the Other was identical with the fate of the Self.

3. It is surprising that the racial ambiguity about the Iranians was not exploited more dexterously by government public relations aides and the press. These sources were content to let the Iranians be seen as Arabs by the American public, whereas Iranians are in fact Caucasians who might more effectively have been portrayed as whites perversely and voluntarily adopting a "nonwhite" ideology in order to make a mockery of Euro-American values. During the Cold War, the particular animus reserved for Cuba stemmed from the fact that its people are denizens of our own hemisphere perversely and voluntarily adopting an alien ideology in order to make a mockery of U.S. civilization.

4. Thomas Szasz, *Ceremonial Chemistry* (Holmes Beach, Fla.: Learning Publications, 1985), pp. 19–27. Szasz argues that *pharmakos* originally alluded to human sacrifice, the ultimate purging of an individual from the social body. But there is no hard evidence of this practice in Greek antiquity, even among interdicted religions like the cult of Dionysus. He runs the etymology as follows: "The root of modern terms such as pharmacology and pharma-copoeia is therefore not 'medicine,' 'drug,' and 'poison,' as most dictionaries erroneously state, but 'scapegoat'!" The real etymological connection, I believe, is simpler. There must be a primordial word that holds at its semantic core the notion of purgation, since the drugs referred to by this term purge the body, where the scapegoat is the thing purged from the body politic. I don't think, in order words, that Szasz's case for a religious basis of this verbal confluence is persuasive. The intersection is probably a result of the evolution of medical terminology.

5. Northrop Frye, *The Anatomy of Criticism* (Princeton, N.J.: Princeton University Press, 1957), p. 148.

6. Ibid., p. 45.

7. For a complete account of the presentation of the cocaine narrative on television news, see Jimmie L. Reeves and Richard Campbell, *Cracked Coverage* (Durham, N.C., and London: Duke University Press, 1994).

8. If this speculation seems like mere paranoia, consider the following headline in the *New York Times* of September 26, 1993: "Data Show Drunken Walking Is Deadly Walking." The article announces a $370,000 study to be conducted in Baltimore, along with new training programs for bartenders and waiters. The article quotes National Highway Traffic Safety Administrator Jim Hedlund as saying, "This is a bigger problem than we had thought previously" (p. 31).

9. I have tried the following experiment on my classes, and also on groups of older adults. I ask how many present, within the last twenty-four hours, have *not* ingested an iota of caffeine, nicotine, alcohol, or any illegal or prescription drug. The response gives an indication of the populousness of a "Drug-free America."

10. See Erich Goode, *Drugs in American Society* (New York: Alfred A. Knopf, 1972): "Most of us believe that all drugs have some intrinsic property that automatically classifies them as drugs. . . . The classic definition of a drug to be found in nearly every introduction to pharmacology is 'any chemical substance that affects living protoplasm.' Unfortunately, this widely adopted definition is far too broad to be of real use—a glass of water fits the definition, as does a bullet fired from a gun, a cold shower, a meal, a cup of coffee, aspirin tablets, or even this book. When we turn to the social definition, we find that the concept 'drug' is a cultural artifact, a social fabrication. *A drug is something that has been arbitrarily defined by certain segments of society as a drug*" (pp. 17–18; emphasis in original).

11. In *Land of Desire* (New York: Pantheon, 1993), William Leach chronicles the fantastic measures early department stores took to charm and entertain their customers. It is interesting to note that this is no longer the case, as enormous undecorated warehouses have replaced magnificent emporia like Macy's and Wannamaker's. Wal-Mart is the crackhouse of Consumerism.

12. "Most of the people in the drug culture are profoundly disconnected from the rest of the country. They live in places where it is harder to answer the question 'Why not?' The issue is, how do you reconnect them? How do you give them some reason to live the life you're calling them to live?" (from a preelection interview with Bill Clinton in *Rolling Stone*, September 17, 1992, p. 44).

13. Frye, *The Anatomy of Criticism*, pp. 41–42.

2. WHAT IS "STRAIGHT" CONSCIOUSNESS?

1. As I wrote the preceding sentence, the telephone rang: "Hello! I'm Darryl, a telecommunications program calling for The Village Green at Stowe, Vermont." Every frequency and format of every communications and information-storage medium is now somehow engaged in sales or the transfer of money. William Leiss, Stephen Kline, and Sut Jhally, in *Social Communication in Advertising* (Toronto: Methuen, 1986), put it this way: "Advertising is not just a business expenditure undertaken in the hope of moving some merchandise off the store shelves, but is rather an integral part of modern culture" (p. 7).

2. "Most consumer items today are combinations of two types of characteristics, physical and imputed" (ibid., p. 59).

3. "Common ordinary speech" is not the only kind of discourse formed by the consumerist paradigm. Leiss, Kline, and Jhally define a "privileged form of discourse" as speech that has "a place of special prominence in our lives. A century ago in North America and western Europe the forms of privileged discourse that touched the lives of ordinary persons were church sermons, political oratory, and the words and precepts of family elders. . . . The space left as these influences have diminished has been filled largely by 'the discourse through and about objects.' We intend this phrase to convey the idea that communications among persons, in which individuals send 'signals' to others about their attitudes, expectations, and sense of identity, are strongly associated with—and expressed through— patterns of preferences for consumer goods. . . . A significant portion of our daily public 'talk' and action is about objects (consumer goods), and about what they can do or should mean for us" (ibid., p. 3).

4. A similar association of drugs and work is evident in the history of Prohibition. See, for example, Sean Dennis Cashman, *Prohibition: The Lie of the Land* (New York and London: Free Press, 1981): "It is, moreover, not mere coincidence that the prohibition movement and the Industrial Revolution originated, developed, and culminated in the same periods. In the nineteenth and early twentieth centuries accidents arising from drunkenness at work were more dangerous than before. Mistakes with mechanical drill, loader, and conveyor belt had more damaging consequences than those with pickax, shovel, and wheelbarrow operated by hand. Abstinence was an absolute prerequisite of employment for many an industrial boss obliged to protect his workers and, more important, his machines and production. . . . Some companies discriminated against drinkers in matters of promotion and dismissal. Others denied benefit payments to workers whose sickness or injury was in any way caused by their drinking" (pp. 5–6).

3. A PHENOMENOLOGY OF ADDICTION

1. Nathan Adler, *The Underground Stream: New Life Styles and the Antinomian Personality* (New York: Harper and Row, 1972), p. xi.

2. It is interesting to note that in the 1990s a new term for marijuana, "the chronic," has been popularized in the work of the rap artists Dr. Dre and Snoop Doggy Dogg.

3. William Burroughs in *Naked Lunch* (New York: Grove Press, 1959) has Dr. Benway say: "Some of my learned colleagues (nameless assholes) have suggested that junk derives its euphoric effect from direct stimulation

of the orgasm center. It seems more probable that junk suspends the whole cycle of tension, discharge and rest. The orgasm has no function in the junky. Boredom, which always indicates an undischarged tension, never troubles the addict. He can look at his shoe for eight hours. He is only roused to action when the hourglass of junk runs out" (p. 35).

4. Ibid., p. 57.

5. Nicotine is physiologically and psychologically self-contradictory. "Tobacco can be either a relaxant or a stimulant depending on the needs of the person, and depending how the drug is ingested—it seems that short puffs increase stimulation, while deep ones relax" (Robert Ornstein, *The Psychology of Consciousness*, 2d rev. ed. [New York: Viking/Penguin, 1986],p. 164).

6. In the United States, an additional fragmentation of *spatial* consciousness among nicotine addicts has resulted from the redivision of social space into smoking and nonsmoking areas. In the awareness of a smoker, the world is now divided into zones where smoking is and is not permitted. This changes patterns of movement and social association, and reinforces the smoker's self-perception as a member of a "minority of consciousness" that must plead for its "rights" under the same principles of diversity that other spatially limited subgroups invoke to preserve their cohesion. As for the comma metaphor, it is interesting that Richard Klein uses the parenthesis: "The moment of taking a cigarette allows one to open a parenthesis in the time of ordinary experience, a space and a time of heightened attention that give rise to a feeling of transcendence" (*Cigarettes Are Sublime* [Durham, N.C.: Duke University Press, 1993], p. 16). Klein is interested in what is contained within the parentheses, where my figure of the comma emphasizes the fragmenting effect of smoking on the surrounding temporal extension.

7. Oscar Wilde, *The Picture of Dorian Gray* (Harmondsworth, England: Penguin Books, 1949), p. 91.

8. There is, however, always *some* rhythm. This is what makes it possible to discuss addiction in general as well as addictions to specific drugs. Solomon H. Snyder has remarked: "Whatever the source of drug craving, everyone agrees that the triad of tolerance, withdrawal, and drug-seeking behavior characterizes all the major addictions. Because of this formal similarity of the addictive processes for different drugs, perhaps the same or closely related fundamental mechanisms underlie all addiction" (*Brainstorming* [Cambridge, Mass.: Harvard University Press, 1989], p. 66).

9. Adler, *The Underground Stream*, p. 9.

10. "Within forty-eight hours of the Celtics' decision [to draft him], Len Bias died of heart failure believed to be triggered by cocaine intoxication.

Tragic and stunning, the timing and circumstances of Bias' death would have dire symbolic consequences—consequences that would make the fatality, without a doubt, the single most important kernel event in the cocaine narrative during the 1980s" (Jimmie L. Reeves and Richard Campbell, *Cracked Coverage* [Durham, N.C., and London: Duke University Press, 1994], p. 138).

11. Snyder quotes a young New York junkie as saying: "The thing about heroin is that it gives a human being a purpose in life. It gives him an occupation, an identity, friends, a chance to be better at something and above all it takes up time" (*Brainstorming*, p. 42).

12. Jack London, *John Barleycorn; or, Alcoholic Memoirs* (New York: Signet, 1990), pp. 185–210 passim.

13. Ibid., 196.

14. Robert S. de Ropp gives the origin of the term "cold turkey." During withdrawal, "the hair on the skin stands up and the skin itself is cold and shows that typical goose flesh which in the parlance of the addict is called 'cold turkey'. . . ." He also has an origin for another familiar withdrawal term: "His whole body is shaken by twitchings and his feet kick involuntarily, the origin of the addict's term 'kicking the habit'" (*Drugs and the Mind* [New York: Grove Press, 1957], pp. 152–53).

15. "'A heart-warming sight,' says Benway, 'those junkies standing around and waiting for the Man. Six months ago they were all schizophrenic. Some of them hadn't been out of bed for years. Now look at them. In all the course of my practices, I have never seen a schizophrenic junky, and junkies are mostly of the schizo physical type. Want to cure anybody of anything, find out who doesn't have it. So who don't got it? Junkies don't got it'" (Burroughs, *Naked Lunch*, p. 33).

16. Burroughs apparently had a spontaneous resolve to seek help. He says of himself that "I awoke from The Sickness at the age of forty-five" (ibid., p. xxxvi).

17. Snyder, *Brainstorming*, p. 65.

18. I do not mean to minimize the medical dangers of tobacco. Legalization has done nothing to diminish them. But this would not be the same for heroin, where the means and circumstances of acquisition and administration are more dangerous by far than would be the case if the drug were injected safely, and its quantity and quality monitored. The thesis that the *lack* of drugs causes social problems is less true for crack, whose excitable users, unlike heroin addicts, are not necessarily seeking peace and privacy.

INTRODUCTION TO PART II:
WHAT DRUGS DO AND DON'T

1. The case currently made by proponents of nootropic drugs resembles claims made for cocaine and amphetamines in the naive years of their early popularity. "The word nootropics was coined to describe substances that improve learning, memory consolidation, and memory retrieval without other central nervous system effects and with low toxicity, even at extremely high doses" (Ward Dean and John Morgenthaler, *Smart Drugs & Nutrients* [Santa Cruz, Calif.: B and J Publications, 1990], p. 37).

4. USER CONSTRUCTION

1. See book 1, chapter 2 of John Locke, *An Essay concerning Human Understanding*, ed. Peter H. Nidditch (Oxford: Oxford University Press, 1975), pp. 48–65.

2. See William Leach, *Land of Desire* (New York: Pantheon, 1993), p. 4. Leach gives an account of the historical development of this cult, relating it to traditions of American Edenism and the myth of beginning anew.

3. Nathan Adler, *The Underground Stream: New Life Styles and the Antinomian Personality* (New York: Harper and Row, 1972), p. 5.

4. Norman E. Zinberg, *Drug, Set, and Setting* (New Haven: Yale University Press, 1984).

5. Andrew Weil, *The Natural Mind* (Boston: Houghton Mifflin, 1972), p. 29.

6. "What can a sociologist tell us about drug use that we do not already know? If there is anything particularly distinctive about the sociologist's view, it is his emphasis on *social context*. . . . The sociological perspective stands in direct opposition to what might be called the chemicalistic fallacy—the view that drug A causes behavior X, that what we see as behavior and effects associated with a given drug are solely (or even mainly) a function of the biochemical properties of that drug, of the drug plus the human animal, or even of the drug plus a human organism with a certain character structure" (Erich Goode, *Drugs in American Society* [New York: Alfred A. Knopf, 1972], pp. 3–4).

7. "In spite of the dissimilarity of . . . drugs, most drug taking follows a general pattern, largely one of expectation" (Robert Ornstein, *The Psychology of Consciousness*, 2d rev. ed. [New York: Viking/Penguin, 1986], p. 163).

8. Adler, *The Underground Stream*, p. 7. Solomon H. Snyder concurs with this finding: "Indeed, the whole history of opiates through the ages teaches us that what matters is not so much the drug itself as how people use

it and how society views this use" (*Brainstorming* [Cambridge, Mass.: Harvard University Press, 1989], p. 43).

9. Weil, *The Natural Mind*, p. 194.

5. "HIGH": DRUGS, PERCEPTION, AND PLEASURE

1. Solomon H. Snyder argues that other drugs under certain social conditions can also be transparent: "At the turn of the [twentieth] century the typical opiate addict was a middle-aged woman living an essentially normal life, married and raising a family. She purchased opium legally in the form of patent medicine and used it orally. Since she was fairly tolerant to the effects of the drug, her day-to-day activities could proceed much like her neighbors', with no evidence of physical or emotional disturbance. She was rarely worse off than being drowsy about midday and tending toward constipation. Because the effects of opium last longer when taken by mouth than when injected intravenously, she did not have sudden rushes of euphoria. By the same token, she rarely would experience withdrawal symptoms" (*Brainstorming* [Cambridge, Mass.: Harvard University Press, 1989], pp. 37–38).

2. Erich Goode, *Drugs in American Society* (New York: Alfred A. Knopf, 1972), p. 7. Goode's other two invariable effects: "A person with a .2 percent blood-alcohol concentration will not be able to operate a complex piece of machinery as well as he could when sober. Nearly everyone will go through some sort of withdrawal distress after long-term administration of a gram a day of barbiturates. But drug effects with such narrow variability are themselves limited in number; drug effects that are highly sensitive to external conditions and about which interpretations vary enormously are far more common" (ibid.).

3. Belladonna may be another exception, since it disables the eye's ability to distinguish between light and darkness. A belladonna user can light a large room with a single candle, and read by it.

4. Examples include DTs and amphetamine psychosis. See Solomon H. Snyder, *Drugs and the Brain* (New York: Scientific American Books, 1986), pp. 138–39.

5. Kant calls this "Imagination." Unlike the modern word, Kant's term designates not a creative but a regulatory function that orchestrates sensory information prior to the mind's higher and more complex evaluations of it. It is a "gatherer of images" that mediates between perception and the judging of it. Snyder believes there is a physical location in the brain stem that performs just this function.

6. Aldous Huxley, *The Doors of Perception* (New York: Harper and Row, 1963).

7. This term, too, is a specialized one, designating the submission of ordered sensory inputs to the inherent structures of consciousness itself. Imagination's matrix is only preliminary to this stage. Any perception, however garbled by a drug's effect on imaginative ordering, must still reach the point of judgment in every instance.

8. In view of this near infinity, consider the silliness of an antidrug television commercial run in the United States beginning in 1989 that shows an egg with the voice-over "This is your brain." The egg is then dropped into hot oil on a grill, and the voice says "This is your brain on drugs" as the egg cooks. The outline is "Any questions?" In fact this metaphor raises nothing *but* questions, about its strange and dubious identifications of the brain with an egg, of cooking with destruction, of drugs with cooking oil. If the metaphor can be disentangled (it is presumably intended to be a visual rendition of the term "fried," which means "high"), it is probably saying that (undifferentiated) drugs cause the destruction of the mind, and that this is the only possible outcome. This lack of differentiation is particularly disconcerting since the ad was produced by the Partnership for a Drug-Free America, which was funded almost entirely by tobacco and alcohol companies.

9. There are transitive and intransitive feelings. The former are relational, but the latter have no object at all, as in "I am sad," an affective statement that doesn't answer the questions "Why?" or "Because of what object?" But neither sort of feeling, transitive or intransitive, can rationalize itself; in both cases the intellect answers questions later. Or: feelings can express but not explain themselves. Psychoanalysis is based on the proposition that feelings can be understood only if they are verbalized, and causally tied to memory and desire. The problem is that feelings, if they are to be understood in this way, must be referred outside themselves to allegedly objective causes. This referencing dislodges feelings from the present, in order to give them a history. But is this necessary? The vocabulary of affective life is a rich and subtle one, capable of making minute distinctions among kinds and degrees of feeling. A survey of this syntax would be a life's work; but not for *this* life. It is enough to say that it would be a study of self-consciousness above all; for even if a cognitive awareness of someone or something else is extraneous to intransitive feelings, *self*-awareness is nonetheless entailed in *any* affect. Feeling requires that the subject become, at least provisionally, its own object. This must be the case, or no feeling could be known at all.

10. A figure for this kairotic isolation of pleasure can be found as early as *The Odyssey*, where Apollo causes the sun to slow its progress through the

heavens so that Odysseus's reunion with Penelope, after their twenty-year separation, can be extended beyond the limitations of *chronos*.

11. Cited in Robert Ornstein, *The Psychology of Consciousness*, 2d rev. ed. (New York: Viking/Penguin, 1986), p. 167.

7. DRUGS, REGRESSION, AND MEMORY

1. Philip K. Dick, *A Scanner Darkly* (New York: Vintage Books, 1991), pp. 276–78. The novel was originally published in 1977.

2. Vladimir Nabokov, *Ada* (New York: McGraw-Hill, 1969), p. 545.

INTRODUCTION TO PART III: DISCLAIMERS

1. A remarkably moving testimony to heroin and its contradictions in its posthypodermic era is "Listening to Heroin" by "Ann M." in the *Village Voice* of August 23, 1994.

2. See Alethea Hayter, *Opium and the Romantic Imagination* (London: Faber and Faber, 1968).

3. William S. Burroughs, *Naked Lunch* (New York: Grove Press, 1959), p. 224.

4. Ibid.

8. CANNABIS AND THE WAR AGAINST DREAMS

1. For an extensive account of reinterpretations of marijuana's effects, see Jerome Himmelstein, *The Strange Career of Marihuana* (Westport, Conn.: Greenwood Press, 1983).

2. Lester Grinspoon, *Marihuana Reconsidered* (Cambridge, Mass.: Harvard University Press, 1971), p. 123. Grinspoon's remarkable volume, written at the height of a period of toleration, mixes clinical and belletristic sources into an extended (and at times overwhelming and contradictory) account of the effects of cannabis intoxication. The text he is citing in this passage is R. P. Walton, *Marihuana, America's New Drug Problem* (Philadelphia: J. B. Lippincott, 1938), pp. 104–5.

3. In those instances where a marijuana user "freaks out" and experiences panic after administering the drug, the problem usually lies with a failure to make this reconciliation, leaving the user in a frightening condition of estrangement from her or his own senses.

4. Those who believe that there could be such a thing as "beauty of argumentation" or an "aesthetics of ideas" will not be shocked by this suggestion. A text is a complex object that can be evaluated by formal as well as

semantic criteria. Ralph Waldo Emerson's idea of an argument creating "spires of form" appears to have influenced Nietzsche in some of his assertions that intellectual belief is only a manifestation of aesthetic preference or taste.

5. For a survey, see Grinspoon, *Marihuana Reconsidered,* pp. 148–50.

6. Nathan Adler, *The Underground Stream: New Life Styles and the Antinomian Personality* (New York: Harper and Row, 1972), p. 82.

7. The retail cost of an ounce of marijuana in 1980 ranged from $60 to $80. By 1994, city dwellers were paying $350-$500 an ounce, and rural prices were about $200–$250.

8. Leo E. Hollister, "The Mystique of Social Drugs and Sex," in *Sexual Behavior: Pharmacology and Biochemistry,* ed. M. Sandler and G. L. Gessa (New York: Raven Press, 1975), pp. 89–90.

9. For example, see R. C. Kolodny, W. H. Masters, R. M. Kolodner, and G. Toro, "Depression of Plasma Testosterone Levels after Chronic Intensive Marihuana Use," *New England Journal of Medicine* 290 (1974): 872–74.

10. Grinspoon quotes a Federal Bureau of Investigation report from the late 1930s: "He [the marijuana user] really becomes a fiend with savage or 'cave man' tendencies. His sex desires are aroused and some of the most horrible crimes result" (p. 17). For a summary of the contradictory literature on the subject of cannabis as an aphrodisiac, see Grinspoon, *Marihuana Reconsidered,* pp. 312–22.

9. RUNAWAY ENGINES OF DESIRE

1. "When one pill at breakfast makes you a new person, or makes your patient, or relative, or neighbor a new person, it is difficult to resist the suggestion, the visceral certainty, that who people are is largely biologically determined. . . . Drug responses provide hard-to-ignore evidence for certain beliefs—concerning the influence of biology on personality, intellectual performance, and social success—that heretofore we as a society have resisted" (Peter D. Kramer, *Listening to Prozac* [New York: Viking, 1993], p. 18).

2. "Crack was a parody of Reaganism, I concluded, a brief high with a bad aftertaste and untold bodily damage" (Jefferson Morley, quoted in Jimmie L. Reeves and Richard Campbell, *Cracked Coverage* [Durham, N.C., and London: Duke University Press, 1994], p. 218).

3. The conflation of cocaine, amphetamines, ephedrine, phenmetrazine, methylphenidate, and related drugs in this discussion is supported by clinical literature. The following is a typical assertion: "Although differences in some

pharmacological properties of various CNS [central nervous system] stimulants do exist . . . their clinical similarities and common actions as indirect dopaminergic and noradrenergic agonists make it not surprising that they can cause quite similar psychotic syndromes" (Burton Angrist, "Psychoses Induced by Central Nervous System Stimulants and Related Drugs," in *Stimulants: Neurochemical, Behavioral, and Clinical Perspectives*, ed. I. Creese [New York: Raven Press, 1983], p. 19). Solomon H. Snyder corroborates this: "In terms of their effects on the brain, cocaine and the amphetamines are virtually indistinguishable. Any differences in effects reported by people using the two drugs only reflect differences in rate of entry into the brain related to the mode of use. For example, inhaled cocaine acts more rapidly than orally ingested amphetamine. . . . We usually think of cocaine and amphetamines as being quite distinct, but that is largely because of the very different ways they entered our culture. Cocaine is primarily regarded as a recreational agent, in spite of the fact that it has definite therapeutic utility as a local anesthetic. Conversely, amphetamines were originally synthesized as therapeutic agents, and only subsequently were they discovered to have mood-altering abilities that made them attractive candidates for abuse" (*Drugs and the Brain* [New York: Scientific American Books, 1986], pp. 121–22). Subjective and anecdotal testimony supports this neurochemical evidence. Clinical literature describes the advent of what is usually called "stimulant psychosis" as a function of a variety of factors: amount of dosage over time, amount of any single dosage, and the user's prior experience with stimulants. But it makes no distinctions based on which of the stimulants is in use. It is universally attested that a kind of "reverse tolerance" develops in long-term or very heavy users, where even a small readministration can catapult the user into a "psychotic" mode. But which particular stimulant is used to attain that level of toxicity does not seem to matter.

4. Ernest L. Abel, *Psychoactive Drugs and Sex* (New York and London: Plenum Press, 1985), p. 100. Literature on first-stage amphetamine consciousness is thin, since most studies employ intravenous injectors as principal subjects, and these users, like freebasers and crack smokers, move directly to the third stage of intoxication, skipping the first and second. See also Lester Grinspoon and Peter Hedbloom, *The Speed Culture* (Cambridge, Mass., and London: Harvard University Press, 1975), pp. 96–103.

5. Abel, *Psychoactive Drugs and Sex*, p. 63.

6. Quoted in R. M. Post and N. R. Contel, "Human and Animal Studies of Cocaine: Implications for Development of Behavioral Pathology," in Creese, ed., *Stimulants*, p. 177.

7. Jean-Paul Sartre's *Being and Nothingness* is an excellent example of second-stage stimulant consciousness.

8. Abel, *Psychoactive Drugs and Sex,* p. 63.

9. "Several investigators have indicated that prior exposure to CNS [central nervous system] stimulants alters the response to subsequent challenges in various fashions that suggest 'potentiation' of effects—i.e., response may be augmented or prolonged or the dose threshold for, or latency to the appearance of the behavior may be diminished" (Angrist, "Psychoses Induced by Central Nervous System Stimulants and Related Drugs," p. 10).

10. Richard Smart, *The Snow Papers: A Memoir of Illusion, Power-Lust, and Cocaine* (Boston and New York: Atlantic Monthly Press, 1985), p. 318.

11. Nathan Adler, *The Underground Stream: New Life Styles and the Antinomian Personality* (Harper and Row, New York, 1972), pp. 85–88.

12. Abel, *Psychoactive Drugs and Sex,* p. 63. One of ethnographer Terry Williams's informants describes a favorite sexual activity of crack smokers: "A master blaster is nothing more than a big rock of crack. But a double master blaster is something altogether different. That's when a man is being buffed by a girl while he's smoking on the pipe with crack in it and he comes. He gets a blast from the pipe and from the girl sucking him. A girl gets a double when she has the pipe and the dick in her mouth at the same time" (*Crackhouse* [New York: Penguin Books, 1993], pp. 120–21).

13. Angrist, "Psychoses Induced by Central Nervous System Stimulants and Related Drugs," p. 9.

14. Smart, *The Snow Papers,* p. 107.

15. Abel, *Psychoactive Drugs and Sex,* p. 63.

16. Adler, *The Underground Stream,* p. 88.

17. Ibid., p. 3.

18. In New York City in the late 1980s the slang term "skel" cropped up to designate a crack addict. What the drug does to the embellishments of Consumerism it also does to the user's body, eventually.

10. MYSTERY DRUGS I: ALCOHOL

1. Donald W. Goodwin, *Alcohol and the Writer* (New York: Penguin Books, 1988), p. 196.

2. Jack London, *John Barleycorn; or, Alcoholic Memoirs* (New York: Signet, 1990), p. 235.

3. See, for example, Robert S. de Ropp, *The Master Game* (New York:

Delacorte Press, 1968). Here the author of *Drugs and the Mind* argues that drug use is in essence a misdirection of mysticism, although psychedelics like LSD and cannabis can be valuable in at least *suggesting the existence* of an ego-less state of transcendence.

11. MYSTERY DRUGS II: ACID METAPHYSICS

1. LSD, DMT, STP, mescaline, psilocybin, peyote, and magic mushrooms can be differentiated chemically and etiologically, and many users believe them to be quite discrete. But given the enormous range of experiences reported by the users of each one, it is difficult to class them according to their effects on consciousness. Terence McKenna makes a good case for the difference between tryptamine drugs (DMT, psilocybin, and amanita mushrooms, along with preparations like yagé and ayahuasca) and the peyote and ergot families. His view is that "All psychedelics appear to be the same psychedelic at low doses, doses just over the threshold. But as larger doses that are still pharmacologically safe are taken, differences appear" (*The Archaic Revival* [San Francisco: HarperCollins, 1992], p. 53).

2. Robert S. de Ropp, *The Master Game* (New York: Delacorte Press, 1968), p. 41. See Aldous Huxley, *The Doors of Perception* and *Heaven and Hell* (New York: Harper and Row, 1963); *Island* (New York: Bantam Books, 1971); and T. Leary, R. Metzner, and R. Alpert, *The Psychedelic Experience* (New Hyde Park, N.Y.: University Books, 1964).

3. Martin Lee and Bruce Shlain, *Acid Dreams* (New York: Grove Press, 1985), p. 289. This volume provides a panorama of the history of psychedelics, particularly in its account of military and CIA research. About the persistence of LSD use, the authors offer the following numbers: "According to the National Institute of Drug Abuse, 8% of today's high school seniors are using LSD, and 25% of people from eighteen to twenty-six years of age have experimented with hallucinogens." I have taken informal surveys in my classes since I began teaching in 1971, and have found that the frequency of acid use has not changed appreciably at any point during that time.

4. Charles Baudelaire, "L'Invitation au Voyage," *OEuvres complètes* (Paris: Bibliothèque de La Pléiade, 1961), p. 253.

5. See, for example, Terence McKenna, *Food of the Gods* (New York: Bantam Books, 1992); or R. Gordon Wasson, Albert Hofmann, and Carl A. P. Ruck, *The Road to Eleusis* (New York: Harcourt Brace Jovanovich, 1978); or R. Gordon Wasson, Stella Kramrisch, Jonathan Ott, and Carl A. P. Ruck, *Persephone's Quest: Entheogens and the Origins of Religion* (New Haven: Yale University Press, 1986).

6. Leary, Metzner, and Alpert, *The Psychedelic Experience,* pp. 11–12.

7. Huxley first tried mescaline under the supervision of Dr. Humphrey Osmond in May of 1953 (Lee and Shlain, *Acid Dreams,* p. 46).

8. Albert Hofmann, *LSD: My Problem Child,* trans. Jonathan Ott (New York: McGraw-Hill, 1980).

9. Reprinted in John Strausbaugh and Donald Blaise, eds., *The Drug User: Documents 1840-1960* (New York: Blast Books, 1991), pp. 115–25. The earliness of Luhan's experience is remarkable, since the Native American Church was not established until 1918.

10. Reprinted in Strausbaugh and Blaise, *The Drug User,* pp. 70–79.

11. Nathan Adler, *The Underground Stream: New Life Styles and the Antinomian Personality* (New York: Harper and Row, 1972), p. 5.

12. Leary, Metzner, and Alpert, *The Psychedelic Experience,* p. 11.

13. In an interview on National Public Radio's program *Fresh Air* on March 5, 1990, Ken Kesey was asked about LSD. He said, "It's a lens through which I look at the world, but it's hard on the eyes."

14. Huxley, *The Doors of Perception,* p. 27.

15. Adler, *The Underground Stream,* p. 74.

16. D. V. Siva Sankar, Harold Abramson, Ronald Bradley, Steven Eagle, Roland Fischer, Leonide Goldstein, Jack Peter Green, Albert Hoffman, Carl Johnson, Sungzong Kang, John R. Smythies, and Peter N. Witt, *LSD—A Total Study* (Westbury, N.Y.: PJD Publications, 1975), p. 348.

17. McKenna, *Food of the Gods,* pp. 6–7.

18. McKenna, *The Archaic Revival,* p. 62.

19. Ibid., p. 22.

20. Ibid., p. 39.

21. Leary, Metzner, and Alpert, *The Psychedelic Experience,* p. 11.

22. For the priest-shaman distinction, see McKenna, *Food of the Gods,* pp. 62-64, and Brian Inglis, *The Forbidden Game* (London: Hodder and Stoughton, 1975), pp. 25–28.

12. SQUARES AND CUBES: COMBINATIONS OF DRUGS

1. Terence McKenna, *Food of the Gods* (New York: Bantam Books, 1992), p. 175.

2. Andrew Weil, *The Natural Mind* (Boston: Houghton Mifflin, 1972), p. 19.

3. A 1987 survey of 111 cocaine users revealed that "all had used cannabis; 95% had used hallucinogens other than LSD or PCP; 86% had used LSD; 61% had used narcotics other than heroin; and 29% had used heroin. . . . A large number reported concurrent use of these substances, that is, use within a couple of hours of each other" (Patricia G. Erickson, E. M. Adlaf, G. F. Murray, and Reginald G. Smart, *The Steel Drug: Cocaine in Perspective* [Lexington, Mass.: Lexington Books, 1987], p. 75).

4. Andrew Weil and Winifred Rosen, *From Chocolate to Morphine*, rev. ed. (Boston: Houghton Mifflin, 1993), pp. 162–63.

5. Ibid., p. 163.

13. DRUGS AND VIOLENCE

1. The new heroin user also roils the debate over legalization options. If registered "addicts" were given free or cheap heroin, what would become of the second tier of the market—the uncommitted snorter or smoker? Would they try to have themselves declared "addicts"? Would there be reprisals in their jobs or public lives? What would happen to the price of their heroin? Would the supply given to "addicts" remain confined to the prescribees, or would some of it end up in the wider market? If the latter, would the transfer come about without violence?

2. I have a friend who fought in World War II and Korea who reenlisted in his mid-forties in order to fight in Vietnam. This man, who describes himself as an alcoholic and is a deeply committed member of Alcoholics Anonymous, explains his participation in three great wars as a quest for a kind of battlefield high. He believes his drinking was an attempt to recapture this euphoria in peacetime.

14. BLOW MONEY: COCAINE, CURRENCY, AND CONSUMERISM

1. Cocaine is the clearest example of pharmacocurrency. Partly this is a result of its packaging and slim (dimelike) bulk. Marijuana is unmistakably an agricultural commodity *tout court,* and has little value in currency-sized denominations. Heroin, LSD, and other drugs of minute physical dosage are closer to cocaine in facility of exchange, concentration of value, and so on, but heroin is more about need than desire, and LSD entails only volition.

2. Conservative economist Milton Friedman goes even farther in this speculation, arguing that the effect of drug prohibition is to ensure the development of monopolies like the drug cartels: "In an ordinary free market business—let's take potatoes, beef, anything you want—there are thousands of importers and exporters. Anybody can go into the business. But it's

very hard for a small person to go into the drug importing business because our interdiction efforts essentially make it enormously costly. So, the only people who can survive in that business are these large Medellín cartel kind of people who have enough money so they can have fleets of airplanes, so they can have sophisticated methods, and so on. In addition to which, by keeping goods out and by arresting, let's say, local marijuana growers, the government keeps the price of these products high. What more could a monopolist want? He's got a government who makes it very hard for all his competitors and who keeps the price of his products high. It's absolutely heaven" (Milton Friedman and Thomas Szasz, *On Liberty and Drugs* [Washington, D.C.: Drug Policy Foundation Press, 199]), p. 72).

3. Arthur Schopenhauer, *The Essays of Arthur Schopenhauer,* trans. T. Bailey Saunders (New York: Willey Book Company, n.d.), p. 46.

15. SEX, DRUGS, TECHNOLOGY, AND THE BODY

1. For an extensive critique of allopathy from this point of view, see Andrew Weil, *The Natural Mind* (Boston: Houghton Mifflin, 1972).

2. "Thus, perhaps the most important function of our fashionable drug treatment rhetoric is to distract us from the fact that the drug user wants the drug of his choice, not the drug treatment the authorities choose for him. We are flooded with news stories about addicts robbing people to get money to pay for drugs. But who has ever heard of an addict robbing a person to get money to pay for drug treatment? Q.E.D." (Thomas Szasz, *Our Right to Drugs* [New York: Praeger, 1992], p. 20).

3. Alan Hollinghurst, *The Swimming-Pool Library* (New York: Vintage Books, 1988).

4. Erich Goode, *Drugs in American Society* (New York: Alfred A. Knopf, 1972), p. 6.

5. Nathan Adler, *The Underground Stream: New Life Styles and the Antinomian Personality* (New York: Harper and Row, 1972), p. 81.

6. See, for example, Gareth Branwyn, "Compu-Sex: Erotica for Cybernauts," in *Flame Wars,* ed. Mark Dery, special issue, *South Atlantic Quarterly* (fall 1993), pp. 779–91.

CONCLUSION:
TOWARD A DIVERSITY OF CONSCIOUSNESS

1. Dan Waldorf, Craig Reinarman, and Sheigla Murphy, *Cocaine Changes* (Philadelphia: Temple University Press, 1991), p. 280.

2. Thomas Szasz, *Our Right to Drugs* (New York: Praeger, 1992).

3. George Orwell, *1984* (New York: Harcourt Brace Jovanovich, 1949), p. 137.

4. Szasz, *Our Right to Drugs,* p. 37.

5. Ibid., p. 20.

6. William S. Burroughs, *Blade Runner, A Movie,* 2d ed. (Berkeley: Blue Wind Press, 1986). In a note, Burroughs credits *The Blade Runner* by Alan E. Nourse as the source of his treatment. In any case, this work should not be confused with the film *Blade Runner,* which was based on Philip K. Dick's novel *Do Androids Dream of Electric Sheep*.

7. Marijuana and tobacco require the same soil conditions and the same nutrients. A transition from tobacco to hemp farming would technically be an easy one, and might have great economic advantages for regions of the country now dependent on the more lethal drug.

8. What is the purpose of the interdiction of private marijuana cultivation? Ostensibly it is done in order to discourage people from getting high, and from participating in the outlawed pot trade. But in practice it accomplishes neither of these aims. A personal anecdote will illustrate this. Ten years ago I had six marijuana plants in my garden, concealed in the corn. They were discovered by a National Guard helicopter, which descended noisily and photographed the small crop. I expected to be arrested, but was not, presumably because the police had bigger fish to fry. Thereafter I never grew pot again, but returned to purchasing it from illegal dealers. Not only did the military fail to deter me from using the drug, they also forced me back into the illicit market.

9. Thomas B. Gilmore, *Equivocal Spirits* (Chapel Hill: University of North Carolina Press, 1987), p. 177n. Elsewhere Gilmore explains that "'spiritual' should certainly not be reduced in meaning to 'religious'; any good definition of the term would be capacious, including many elements of the irrational and emotional" (p. 11).

Abel, Ernest L., *Psychoactive Drugs and Sex*. New York and London: Plenum Press, 1985.

Adler, Nathan. *The Underground Stream: New Life Styles and the Antinomian Personality*. New York: Harper and Row, 1972.

Adler, Patricia A. *Wheeling and Dealing: An Ethnography of an Upper-Level Drug Dealing and Smuggling Community*. New York: Columbia University Press, 1985.

Ageyev, M. *Novel with Cocaine*. Trans. Michael Henry Heim. New York: E. P. Dutton, 1984.

"Ann M." "Listening to Heroin." *Village Voice*, August 23, 1994, pp. 25-30.

Baudelaire, Charles. *OEuvres complètes*. Paris: Bibliothèque de La Pléiade, 1961.

Benjamin, Walter. *Reflections*. Ed. Peter Demetz. Trans. Edmund Jephcott. New York: Harcourt Brace Jovanovich, 1978.

Brecher, Edward M. *Licit and Illicit Drugs*. Boston: Little, Brown, 1972.

Burroughs, William S. *Blade Runner, A Movie*. 2d ed. Berkeley: Blue Wind Press, 1986.

——. *Naked Lunch*. New York: Grove Press, 1959.

Cashman, Sean Dennis. *Prohibition: The Lie of the Land*. New York and London: Free Press, 1981.

Cocteau, Jean. *Opium*. Paris: Librairie Stock, 1930.

Creese, I., ed. *Stimulants: Neurochemical, Behavioral, and Clinical Perspectives*. New York: Raven Press, 1983.

Crowley, Aleister. *The Diary of a Drug Fiend*. New York: E. P. Dutton, 1923.

Dean, Ward, and John Morgenthaler. *Smart Drugs & Nutrients*. Santa Cruz, Calif.: B and J Publications, 1990.

De Quincey, Thomas. *Confessions of an English Opium-Eater*. London: Macdonald, 1956.

de Ropp, Robert S. *Drugs and the Mind*. New York: Grove Press, 1957.

———. *The Master Game*. New York: Delacorte Press, 1968.

Dery, Mark, ed. *Flame Wars*. Special issue, *South Atlantic Quarterly* 92, no. 4 (fall 1993).

Dick, Philip K. *A Scanner Darkly*. New York: Vintage Books, 1991.

Duster, Troy. *The Legislation of Morality*. New York: Free Press, 1970.

Eisner, Bruce. *Ecstasy: The MDMA Story*. Berkeley: Ronin Publishing, 1989.

Erickson, Patricia G., E. M. Adlaf, G. F. Murray, and Reginald G. Smart. *The Steel Drug: Cocaine in Perspective*. Lexington, Mass.: Lexington Books, 1987.

Fagles, Robert, trans. *The Odyssey*. New York: Viking/Penguin (1995).

Foucault, Michel. *The History of Sexuality*. Vol. I, *An Introduction*. Trans. Robert Hurley. New York: Vintage Books, 1980.

Freud, Sigmund. *Cocaine Papers*. New York: Stonehill, 1975.

Friedman, Milton, and Thomas Szasz. *On Liberty and Drugs*. Washington, D.C.: Drug Policy Foundation Press, 1992.

Frye, Northrop. *The Anatomy of Criticism*. Princeton, N.J.: Princeton University Press, 1957.

Gilmore, Thomas B. *Equivocal Spirits*. Chapel Hill: University of North Carolina Press, 1987.

Goldstein, Paul J. *Prostitution and Drugs*. Lexington, Mass.: D. C. Heath, 1979.

Goode, Erich. *Drugs in American Society*. New York: Alfred A. Knopf, 1972.

Goodwin, Donald W. *Alcohol and the Writer*. New York: Penguin Books, 1988.

Gould, Stephen Jay. "The War on (Some) Drugs." *Harper's*, April 1990, pp. 24-26. Excerpted from *Dissent* (winter 1990).

Grinspoon, Lester. *Marihuana Reconsidered*. Cambridge, Mass.: Harvard University Press, 1971.

Grinspoon, Lester, and Peter Hedbloom. *The Speed Culture*. Cambridge, Mass., and London: Harvard University Press, 1975.

Hayter, Alethea. *Opium and the Romantic Imagination*. London: Faber and Faber, 1968.

Hesse, Erich. *Narcotics and Drug Addiction*. Trans. Frank Gaynor. New York: Philosophical Library, 1946.

Himmelstein, Jerome. *The Strange Career of Marihuana*. Westport, Conn.: Greenwood Press, 1983.

Hofmann, Albert. *LSD: My Problem Child*. Trans. Jonathan Ott. New York: McGraw-Hill, 1980.

Hollinghurst, Alan. *The Swimming-Pool Library*. New York: Vintage Books, 1988.

Huxley, Aldous. *Brave New World*. New York: HarperCollins, 1992.

——. *The Doors of Perception* and *Heaven and Hell*. New York: Harper and Row, 1963.

——. *Island*. New York: Bantam Books, 1971.

Inglis, Brian. *The Forbidden Game*. London: Hodder and Stoughton, 1975.

Kalant, Oriana Josseau. *The Amphetamines: Toxicity and Addiction*. Toronto: University of Toronto Press, 1966.

Kirkland, Gelsey. *Dancing on My Grave*. New York: Jove Books, 1986.

Klein, Richard. *Cigarettes Are Sublime*. Durham, N.C.: Duke University Press, 1993.

Kolodny, R. C., W. H. Masters, R. M. Kolodner, and G. Toro. "Depresssion of Plasma Testosterone Levels after Chronic Intensive Marihuana Use." *New England Journal of Medicine* 290 (1974): 872-74.

Kramer, Peter D. *Listening to Prozac*. New York: Viking, 1993.

Leach, William. *Land of Desire*. New York: Pantheon, 1993.

Leary, Timothy. *Flashbacks*. Los Angeles: Jeremy P. Tarcher, 1990.

Leary, T., R. Metzner, and R. Alpert. *The Psychedelic Experience*. New Hyde Park, N.Y.: University Books, 1964.

Lee, Martin, and Bruce Shlain. *Acid Dreams*. New York: Grove Press, 1985.

Leiss, William, Stephen Kline, and Sut Jhally. *Social Communication in Advertising*. Toronto: Methuen, 1986.

Locke, John. *An Essay concerning Human Understanding*. Ed. Peter H. Nidditch. Oxford: Oxford University Press, 1975.

London, Jack. *John Barleycorn; or, Alcoholic Memoirs*. New York: Signet, 1990.

Ludlow, Fitz Hugh. *The Hasheesh Eater*. Upper Saddle River, N.J.: Literature House, 1970.

McInerney, Jay. *Bright Lights, Big City*. New York: Vintage Books, 1984.

McKenna, Terence. *The Archaic Revival*. San Francisco: HarperCollins, 1992.

——. *Food of the Gods*. New York: Bantam Books, 1992.

Michaux, Henri. *Light through Darkness*. Trans. Haakon Chevalier. New York: Orion Press, 1963.

——. *L'Infini turbulent*. Paris: Mercure de France, 1957.

——. *Miserable Miracle*. Trans. Louise Varèse. San Francisco: City Lights Books, 1963.

Musto, David F. *The American Disease: Origins of Narcotic Control*. Expanded ed. Oxford and New York: Oxford University Press, 1987.

Nabokov, Vladimir. *Ada*. New York: McGraw-Hill, 1969.

Ornstein, Robert. *The Psychology of Consciousness*. 2d rev. ed. New York: Viking/Penguin, 1986.

Orwell, George. *1984*. New York: Harcourt Brace Jovanovich, 1949.

Reeves, Jimmie L., and Richard Campbell. *Cracked Coverage*. Durham, N.C., and London: Duke University Press, 1994.

Ronell, Avital. *Crack Wars*. Lincoln: University of Nebraska Press, 1992.

Russo, J. Robert, ed. *Amphetamine Abuse*. Springfield, Ill.: Charles C. Thomas, 1968.

Sabbag, Robert. *Snowblind: A Brief Career in the Cocaine Trade*. New York: Avon Books, 1976.

Sandler, M., and G. L. Gessa. *Sexual Behavior: Pharmacology and Biochemistry*. New York: Raven Press, 1975.

Sankar, D. V. Siva, Harold Abramson, Ronald Bradley, Steven Eagle, Roland Fischer, Leonide Goldstein, Jack Peter Green, Albert Hofmann, Carl Johnson, Sungzong Kang, John R. Smythies, and Peter N. Witt. *LSD—A Total Study*. Westbury, N.Y.: PJD Publications, 1975.

Schopenhauer, Arthur. *The Essays of Arthur Schopenhauer*. Trans. T. Bailey Saunders. New York: Willey Book Company, n.d.

Siegel, Ronald K. *Fire in the Brain*. New York: E. P. Dutton, 1992.

Smart, Richard. *The Snow Papers: A Memoir of Illusion, Power-Lust, and Cocaine*. Boston and New York: Atlantic Monthly Press, 1985.

Smith, David E., ed. *Amphetamine Use, Misuse, and Abuse*. Proceedings of the National Amphetamine Conference, 1978. Boston: G. K. Hall, 1979.

Snyder, Solomon H. *Brainstorming*. Cambridge, Mass.: Harvard University Press, 1989.

————. *Drugs and the Brain*. New York: Scientific American Books, 1986.

Somers, Suzanne. *Keeping Secrets*. New York: Warner Books, 1988.

Stevens, Jay. *Storming Heaven*. New York: Harper and Row, 1987.

Stone, Robert. *Children of Light*. New York: Alfred A. Knopf, 1986.

Strausbaugh, John, and Donald Blaise, eds. *The Drug User: Documents 1840–1960*. New York: Blast Books, 1991.

Svevo, Italo. *La Conscienza di Zeno*. Pordenoma, Italy: Studio Tesi, 1985.

Szasz, Thomas. *Ceremonial Chemistry*. Holmes Beach, Fla.: Learning Publications, 1985.

————. *Our Right to Drugs*. New York: Praeger, 1992.

Tart, Charles T., ed. *Altered States of Consciousness*. New York: John Wiley and Sons, 1969.

Trimpey, Jack. *The Small Book*. New York: Delacorte Press, 1992.

Vaillant, George E. *The Natural History of Alcoholism*. Cambridge, Mass., and London: Harvard University Press, 1983.

Waldorf, Dan, Craig Reinarman, and Sheigla Murphy. *Cocaine Changes*. Philadelphia: Temple University Press, 1991.

Walton, R. P. *Marihuana, America's New Drug Problem*. Philadelphia: J. B. Lippincott, 1938.

Wasson, R. Gordon, Albert Hofmann, and Carl A. P. Ruck. *The Road to Eleusis*. New York: Harcourt Brace Jovanovich, 1978.

Wasson, R. Gordon, Stella Kramrisch, Jonathan Ott, and Carl A. P. Ruck. *Persephone's Quest: Entheogens and the Origins of Religion*. New Haven: Yale University Press, 1986.

Weil, Andrew. *The Natural Mind*. Boston: Houghton Mifflin, 1972.

Weil, Andrew, and Winifred Rosen. *From Chocolate to Morphine*. Rev. ed. Boston: Houghton Mifflin, 1993.

Weiss, Allen S. *The Aesthetics of Excess*. Albany: State University of New York Press, 1989.

Wilde, Oscar. *The Picture of Dorian Gray*. Harmondsworth, England: Penguin Books, 1949.

Williams, Terry. *The Cocaine Kids*. Reading, Mass.: Addison-Wesley, 1989.

——. *Crackhouse*. New York: Penguin Books, 1993.

Zinberg, Norman E. *Drug, Set, and Setting*. New Haven: Yale University Press, 1984.

Zweig, Paul. *The Heresy of Self Love: A Study of Subversive Individualism*. New York: Berkeley Medallion Books, 1969.

psychedelics, 152, 154–55; and
technology, 187; and thought, 80;
and truth, 80
Pot. *See* Cannabis
Pound, Ezra, 145
Prescription system, 4–5, 192–93
Prohibition (*see also* Alcohol; Criminalization; Interdiction of drugs),
5, 23, 25, 44, 135, 140, 207 n. 4
Protestantism, 172, 174
Prozac, 4, 115, 187–88, 193–94
Psilocybin. *See* Psychedelics
Psychedelics, 143–57; ayahuasca, 217
n. 1; bum trips, 57–59, 144, 156;
and the CIA, 58, 153–54, 191, 217 n.
3; and confession, 85; and Consumerism, 148, 153, 199, 219 n. 1;
and contemplation, 38, 71–73, 148,
152–53; and the counterculture, 10,
15, 65, 145–46, 149, 152–55, 179;
and death, 59; and desire, 71–72,
127; DMT, 151, 217 n. 1; Easternization of, xvi–xvii, 143–46,
152–53; ergot, 140, 151, 155, 217 n. 1;
flashbacks, 33; hangovers, 180–81;
interdiction of, 140, 149–50, 153,
194; and language, 147–52; and
logic, 78–79; LSD, xvi–xvii, 10,
16, 33–34, 57–59, 65–68, 71–74, 103,
132, 140, 143–57, 160, 170, 180–81,
191, 199, 217 n. 1, 217 n. 3, 218 n.
13, 219 n. 3, 219, chap. 14, n. 1;
medical use for, 179; and memory,
33–34, 59; mescaline, xvii, 74, 217
n. 1; morning glory, 151; and
music, 152; and mysticism, 143,
146–47, 149, 151–52, 154–55, 216–17
n. 3; and other drugs, 160, 217 n.
1, 219 n. 3; and perception, 65–68,
73–74, 88, 103, 132, 148–49,
180–81, 218 n. 13; peyote, xvii,
144, 146–47, 155, 198, 217 n. 1; and
pleasure, 70–74; and postmod-

ernism, 152, 154–55; psilocybin,
xvii, 3, 53, 144, 151–52, 154, 217 n. 1;
set and setting, 57–58, 70–71, 153,
156; and sex, 155; and space, 148;
STP, 217 n. 1; and time, 35–36,
73–74, 147–48, 152, 155–56; trypta-
mines, 151–52, 154, 217 n. 1; user
construction of, 57–59, 70, 147,
149, 153, 155–57; and violence, 156,
170–71; writing about, xi, xv;
withdrawal, 33; yagé, 217 n. 1
Psychiatry, xii–xiii, 54, 59, 136, 187,
214 n. 1
Psychoanalysis: and dreams, 133;
interpretation of stimulant high,
122; Jungian, 152; libido, 118, 126;
and memory, 212 n. 9; psychosis,
122, 126, 129; regression, 85–96;
rejection of drug consciousness,
xix–xx, 136, 197; repression, 113;
structural model of mind, 31–32;
superego, 81, 118; thanatos, 204–5
n. 2

Quantum mechanics, 32–33, 73,
104–5

Race, 23, 46, 91, 172, 190, 205 n. 3
Rastafarianism, 63, 108, 196, 198
Reagan, Ronald, x, xviii, 11, 13, 131,
173, 214 n. 2
Recovery: Alcoholics Anonymous,
35, 45–47, 135, 197–98, 219, chap.
13, n. 2; compulsory, 23; and contemplation, 34; and disease
model, 197–98; literature of, xi,
xvi; and memory, xvi, 33–34,
47–48, 94; and pleasure, 34; and
time, 33–34; twelve-step
programs, 34, 44–47, 140
Reeves, Jimmie L., 205 n. 7, 209 n.
10, 214 n. 2
Regression, 85–96, 137–38, 163

DAVID LENSON, professor of
comparative literature at the University of
Massachusetts, Amherst, is the author of *Achilles'*
Choice: Examples of Modern Tragedy and two books of
poetry. He is proudest of having played saxophone
with John Lee Hooker, Buddy Guy, and Junior Wells.